Bureaucracy and Public Economics

BUREAUCRACY AND PUBLIC ECONOMICS

William A. Niskanen, Jr.
Chairman, CATO INSTITUTE

EDWARD ELGAR

Published by
Edward Elgar Publishing Limited
Gower House
Croft Road
Aldershot
Hants GU11 3HR
England

Edward Elgar Publishing Company
Old Post Road
Brookfield
Vermont 05036
USA

British Library Cataloging-in-Publication Data
Niskanen, William A.
    Bureaucracy and Public Economics. –
    (John Locke Series)
    I. Title II. Series
    339.3

Library of Congress Cataloging-in-Publication Data
Niskanen, William A. 1933–
    Bureaucracy and public economics/William A. Niskanen, Jr. — 2nd
ed.
        p.   cm.
    Includes bibliographical references.
    1. Bureaucracy. 2. Representative government and representation.
    I. Title.
    JF1501.N55 1994
    350′.001—DC20   94–15926
                                                                 CIP

ISBN 1 85898 019 4 (cased)
     1 85898 041 0 (paperback)

Printed and Bound in Great Britain by
Hartnolls Limited, Bodmin, Cornwall.

Contents

Foreword
Charles K. Rowley

The early theories of bureaucracy emanated not from economics but from naive sociological scribblings by Max Weber (1947) that viewed senior bureaucrats as selfless purveyors and enforcers of the policies of elected governments. Economists imbued with insatiable appetites to perform as philosopher-kings, with research agendas dedicated to exposing the failure of capitalism and with an undisguised prejudice in favour of socialism, were only too happy to rely upon Weber's "neutered eunuchs" to implement the policies that they advanced. These would surely be enacted by the impartial and omniscient governments that majoritarian politics necessarily provides.

How far we have come during the second half of the 20th century from such ill-conceived notions and misplaced confidences was indelibly imprinted on history by the collapse in 1989 of the evil empire of the USSR—that dreadful nightmare of bureaucratic socialism as it really was. Much of our current more realistic understanding of bureaucracy stems from the seminal book by William A. Niskanen on *Bureaucracy and Representative Government* published in 1971, but long out of print, which is republished as part of this fine new book which also brings together twenty years of subsequent scholarship by an outstanding student of public choice.

An early challenge to the Weberian fallacy came in 1957 from Northcote Parkinson who chronicled the tendency for bureaucracies to expand at a fixed rate, irrespective of the conditions of demand. This was followed in 1965 (Tullock) and in 1967 (Downs) by public choice critiques that focused on the self-interested behavior of senior bureaucrats, on the chronic inefficiency of internal bureaucratic organizations and on the inevitable loss of information (control loss) associated with such command structure forms of economic organization. Each of these critiques of the public interest model centered attention on the internal organization of bureaucracy and ignored the external environment against which bureaucratic behavior occurs.

All this changed with Niskanen's 1971 publication which defined a bureau as a nonprofit organization, financed primarily by an appropriation or grant from a

vii

sponsor, in which no individual can legally appropriate any part of the difference between revenues and costs as direct personal income. In such circumstances, self-seeking senior bureaucrats will evidence an interest in any budget surplus only if such a surplus can be utilized in ways that augment their individual utilities and are not subject to mandatory confiscation by the sponsor. Since they supply output in markets predictably characterized by excess demand, bureaucrats normally will evidence little concern about satisfying the preferences of customers or about supplying output efficiently.

If bureaucrats are not the neutered eunuchs of Max Weber's vision, attention shifts to their personal motivations as an indispensable prerequisite for predicting their responses to the reward-cost structure that confronts them. Niskanen (1971) argued that the principal components of a senior bureaucrat's utility function—power, money income, security, perquisites of office and patronage—are all positive monotonic functions of budget size, and that an additional component—the easy life—is a positive monotonic function of the budget's rate of growth. In such circumstances, senior bureaucrats would coalesce in favor of large and rapidly growing budgets irrespective of ideological differences concerning the appropriate direction of the bureau's policies.

In 1975, responding to criticisms, Niskanen acknowledged that the budget-maximizing bureaucrat might be something of a special case and that the size of the discretionary budget would also be a matter of importance for the typical senior bureaucrat. At issue in this tension over budget policy is the precise balance struck among members of the top-level bureaucracy between those seeking money income, security and the easy life (which rest predominantly on budget size and rate of growth) and those seeking power, perquisites of office and patronage (which rest predominantly on the discretionary budget that remains once the total cost of the bureau's output has been accounted for).

Since all bureaucrats are rational, the balance between budget size and budget discretion ultimately pursued by a bureau will depend not only upon the distribution of preferences, but also upon the particular reward/cost environment within which the bureaucrats find themselves. Given their goals, budget-maximizing or discretionary budget-maximizing bureaucrats are seen as bargaining effectively with sponsors less well informed and less motivated than they are to secure the budget of their choice.

There is no doubt about the importance of Niskanen's book for understanding the relationship between bureaucracy and representative government. In his 1974 review, Mitchell refers to the book as "the most significant work yet produced by an economist on the role of bureaucracy". Mueller's (1989) survey of public choice commends the book as "the first systematic effort to study bureaucracies within a public choice framework". Following a rigorous theoretical and empirical reassessment of the book after 20 years, Blais and Dion (1991) conclude that "the great appeal of the Niskanen model lies, we believe, in its capacity to account for the well-established propensity of bureaucrats to seek larger budgets. It does make sense to assume that bureaucrats attempt to maximize their budgets and to make that assumption the central proposition of a theory of bureaucratic behavior".

I commend this book to all who are interested in the process of budget determination and bureaucratic behavior under conditions of representative government. Good wine does not need new labels and I leave to each reader the pleasure of uncorking the bottle and tasting this fine vintage in its full maturity.

References

Blais, André and Dion S. (eds) (1991), *The Budget-Maximizing Bureaucrat: Appraisals and Evidence*, Pittsburgh: University of Pittsburgh Press.

Downs, A. (1967), *Inside Bureaucracy*, Boston: Little Brown & Co.

Mitchell, W. C. (1974), "Book Review," *American Political Science Review*, 68 (4), 1775–1777.

Mueller, D. C. (1989), *Public Choice II*, Cambridge: Cambridge University Press.

Niskanen, W. A. (1971), *Bureaucracy and Representative Government*, Chicago: Aldine Press.

Niskanen, W. A. (1975), "Bureaucrats and Politicians," *Journal of Law and Economics*, XVIII (3), 617–644.

Parkinson, C. N. (1957), *Parkinson's Law and Other Studies in Administration*, New York: Ballantine Books.

Tullock, G. (1965), *The Politics of Bureaucracy*, Washington D.C.: Public Affairs Press.

Weber, M. (1947), *The Theory of Social and Economic Organization*, New York: The Free Press.

Preface

This book develops a theory of the behavior of bureaus, particularly in the setting of a representative government. The behavior of bureaus is also compared with that of other forms of organization facing similar conditions and with optimal behavior as defined by the normative theory of public goods. On the basis of these comparisons and other studies, I conclude with a set of suggestions for changing the bureaucracy and our political institutions to induce more nearly optimal behavior.

The approach of this book is that of "the new political economy" which applies the methods of economics to the study of the collective institutions of our society. Both my method and my conclusions should interest scholars in economics, political science, sociology, public administration, and the increasing number of other disciplines that are making contributions to understanding our collective institutions. This book should prove valuable as a supplementary text in college and graduate courses that are concerned with the behavior of collective institutions at more than the descriptive level. This book represents a new approach to the study of bureaus; only time and testing will prove whether the theory developed is valuable and merits further development and whether the conclusions merit some practical experiments.

Some parts of this book, particularly the middle chapters, may be rather difficult. My objectives, however, will be accomplished only if an occasional businessman, journalist, bureaucrat, or politician is induced to delve into these pages and understand the main argument. Our collective institutions, I believe, are not serving us very well, and this book is written to suggest those changes which would make them work better in the interests of the general population.

In several senses this book is the product of professional unease. In 1957 I packed my bag of recently acquired professional tools and flew off to the RAND Corporation, with the blessed optimism of youth, to solve the problems of the world. This was an exciting period at RAND, where there was a stimulating research environment and a superb community of professional colleagues. Most of us felt that we were beginning to understand how to analyze public policy problems and how to improve the management of the public sector. Some of the products of this period are the techniques that have become known as systems analysis and program budgeting. The then unrecognized assumption of this work and these techniques was that public officials, given the correct information and sufficient authority, would do the right thing.

Along with a few other RAND colleagues, I then joined the staff of Secretary of Defense Robert McNamara early in the Kennedy Administration. This staff should have provided the perfect testing-ground for these new techniques—a department that had a tradition of planning, a Secretary who was receptive to analysis and had the energy to translate the support of the President into effective command of the department, and the motivation of working on very important problems. Although I should have known better, I only slowly developed a sense of unease that something was seriously wrong with the premise of the information-analysis-directive approach to the management of the public sector. Briefly, this approach fails to account for the institutions of bureaucracy and representative government. By 1964 I came to recognize that there is nothing inherent in the nature of bureaus and our political institutions that leads public officials to know, seek out, or act in the public interest. Cynics and a few political scientists could have told me this earlier—but without effect, prior to my personal experience in the bureaucracy.

If not the public interest, then, to what do public officials respond? What is the best model for interpreting their behavior? How can the institutions be changed to make their behavior more nearly consistent with the public interest? To a large extent this book is an organization of my own perception of these problems, and to the extent that this organization represents a new approach, the book reflects the previous lack of any powerful tools to rationalize the many aspects of the behavior of collective organizations.

My views on these matters developed over the 1965–1969 period, when I was a research manager at the Institute for Defense Analyses, and are reflected in some of my writings in this period. The greatest stimulus to these views came from discussions with Gordon Tullock, who spent the summer of 1966 at IDA. At the end of the summer he left a paper with me, "The Parkinson–Niskanen Effect," which distilled the essence of these discussions. Tullock is always provocative and stimulating. I and many others owe him a great debt for stimulating our own thinking. At that stage it was difficult to sort out my ideas from those of Tullock. He later asked me to develop my ideas into a paper for the Washington meetings of the American Economic Association in December 1967. After some false starts and some valuable discussions at IDA and the University of Toronto, I prepared an early summary of my views in a paper, "The Peculiar Economics of Bureaucracy," reproduced in the May 1968 *American Economic Review*. The press of my regular duties prevented me from developing these ideas further until the summer of 1969. At that time IDA graciously agreed to relieve me of my duties as a research manager and to support me, under its central research program, to complete this book. I am most indebted to IDA for this support: it was ungrudging and generous in every regard. Neither IDA nor any of its contract sponsors, of course, necessarily endorse the views expressed in this book.

While I was writing the book, I benefited from frequent discussions with Jack Stockfisch, who was writing a book at IDA on the management of the military bureaucracy. At various stages of review I received valuable comments from Martin Bailey, Steve Brams, Louis DeAlessi, Roland McKean, Jack Stockfisch, Gordon Tullock, and Aaron Wildavsky. They do not, of course, share all of the views expressed in this book; it is only fair, however, that they share some responsibility for any errors that we all missed. I am also indebted to Leonard Bates for editing the final draft, to Morris Legum for preparing the graphics, and to Dorothy Mendonsa and Kay Wright for typing the several drafts.

As the fates would have it, at the time this book is published I am employed as a federal bureaucrat. It is too early to tell whether the behavior described in this book will also apply to me. If it doesn't I will consider it a personal success but a partial refutation of the theory of this book. If it does, of course, I have no excuses not to have known better. Maybe the reflections of an ex-bureaucrat will produce a different book than the reflections of an ex-systems analyst.

Contents

I

Introduction

Introduction

Context

Bureaucracy and representative government are at the center of a storm. A large part of our population wants to expand the role of government, particularly to alleviate poverty and improve the environment. A correspondingly large part of our population is exasperated by the methods of bureaucracy and dissatisfied by its performance. The world view of two smaller groups has been uprooted by both of these contrary attitudes: The "establishment liberals"—not understanding what went wrong—have withdrawn into academic specialization, the legends of a lost Camelot, and despair. The restless young—reacting to an experience limited to family paternalism, university bureaucracy, and military authority—are torn between collective expressions of rage and the mysticism of rock, sex, and drugs. Only the uninformed, unthinking, and unfeeling are complacent. Those who want to restrict the role of government are quick to use the poor performance of the bureaucracy to support their position. The "new social engineers" somehow maintain an optimism, in the face of the most devastating evidence, that systems analysis and program budgets will make bureaus more responsive and efficient. And the bureaucracy itself, like the eye of a meteorological storm, is calm and moving slowly, captured by the general direction of the storm but unaffected by its peripheral winds.

A condition of despair among the intellectuals and rage among the young is not unique to our time, and the precedents do not provide a basis for optimism.[1] Even if, as I believe, the most disturbing potential consequences will not be realized, we face two types of problems concerning our attitudes

---

1. The most direct precedent to this contemporary reaction to bureaucracy may be Germany during the first three decades of this century. For a lucid description and interpretation of the German reaction, see Ludwig von Mises, *Bureaucracy* (New Haven: Yale University Press, 1944), pp. 94–97.

3

toward government: We may unnecessarily accept undesirable methods and poor performance by the bureaucracy because of an overriding concern for the provision of certain public services. Such a reaction is characteristic of periods of system-threatening crises or wars, such as the Great Depression and World War II. Conversely, we may unnecessarily reject certain desirable public services because of a dissatisfaction with the methods and performance of the bureaucracy. Such a reaction dominates current attitudes toward some of the welfare and military programs initiated by the United States federal government during the 1960's. Can these problems be resolved? Can the responsiveness and efficiency of bureaus be significantly improved? Can some public services be efficiently supplied by other forms of organization? Can representative government better express our demands for public services? How?

Answers to these questions, even tentative answers, are not easily forthcoming. Our poor understanding of the behavior of bureaus, however, is not due to lack of experience. Bureaus are probably the oldest form of organization above the level of the communal tribe. Written language was first extensively used to record the directives and decisions of the ancient Sumerian bureaucracy. The earliest Egyptian literature was dominated by rules of conduct for young officials in the imperial bureaucracy, initiating a literary theme richly developed by Confucius, Plato, and Machiavelli. Bureaucracy has been the characteristic form of public administration for all governments with extensive territorial sovereignty from the ancient kingdoms of Sumer and Egypt to the modern nation-state. Around one-sixth of the national income of the United States, as of many other industrial nations, now originates in bureaus. The activities of bureaus dominate the front pages of the world's newspapers.

How can there exist such confusion concerning what behavior and performance should be expected of bureaus in the face of this historical and contemporary experience? The first television images from the moon provide a clue: They remind us how difficult it is to understand our sensory perceptions without a familiar frame of reference. Understanding of a new sensory stimulus by its nature involves relating this stimulus to a "model" which has proved successful in "explaining" other like stimuli. Our confusion about bureaucracy derives from the absence of a commonly accepted theory of the behavior of bureaus with which one might compare their behavior with that of other forms of organization. More accurately, I suspect, our contemporary confusion about bureaucracy derives from the absence of a theory of bureaus that is consistent with an instrumental concept of the state, that is, a concept of a state which is only an instrument of the preferences of its constituents. Most of the literature on bureaucracy, from Confucius to Weber, proceeds from an organic concept of the state, that is, a concept of a state for which the preferences of individuals are subordinate to certain organic goals of the state. Starting from the premise that the personal preferences of the general population are subordinate or irrelevant, this literature does not recognize the relevance of the personal preferences of the bureaucrats. Any theory of the behavior of bureaus that does not incorporate the personal preferences of bureaucrats, however, will be relevant only in the most rigidly authoritarian environments. In a fundamental sense, our contemporary confusion derives from a failure to bring bureaucracy to terms with representative government and free labor markets.

An Economic Approach

My method is that of economics, although the subject has been the almost exclusive domain of sociology.[2] In this book I develop a theory of "supply" by bureaus, based on a model of purposive behavior by the manager of a single bureau. In a similar way, economists have developed a theory of demand from a model of individual consumer choice and a theory of (market) supply from a model of a profit-seeking firm. The "compositive" method of economics, which develops hypotheses about social behavior from models of purposive behavior by individuals, contrasts with the "collectivist" method of sociology, which develops hypotheses about social behavior from models of role behavior by aggregative ideal types.[3] The individual consumer, entrepreneur, or, in this case, bureaucrat is the central figure of the characteristic method of economics. He is assumed to face a set of possible actions, to have personal preferences among the outcomes of the possible actions, and to choose the action within the possible set that he most prefers. He is a "chooser" and a "maximizer" and, in contrast to his part in the characteristic method of sociology, not just a "role player" in some larger social drama. The larger environment influences the behavior of the individual by constraining his set of possible actions, by changing the relations between actions and outcomes, and, to some extent, by influencing his personal preferences. The economist develops models based on purposive behavior by individuals, not to explain the behavior of

2. The article on "Bureaucracy" in the *International Encyclopedia of the Social Sciences*, edited by David Sills (New York: Macmillan, 1968), reflects the dominance of sociologists in the study of this subject. The article is written by the sociologist Richard Bendix. Around two-thirds of the 86 references are written by sociologists and one-third by political scientists. Not one study of the economics of bureaucracy is cited. This is not a criticism of Bendix, as there are only a few publications on bureaucracy by economists, but it indicates the dominance of the sociological scholarship on bureaucracy.

3. The terms "compositive" and "collectivist" are suggested by F. A. Hayek, *The Counter-Revolution of Science* (Glencoe, Ill.: Free Press, 1952), chapters 4 and 6. Other terms for the characteristic method of sociology might be "macroscopic" or "aggregative." As a substitute Hayek prefers "telescopic," since this method views social behavior as if from another planet or from an historical perspective. The characteristic method of economics has also been described as "methodological individualism." This term accurately describes the method of most positive economics, except for the Marxian tradition, and a small but growing part of normative economics.

individuals (that is necessarily the task of psychology), but to generate hypotheses concerning the aggregative consequences of the interaction among individuals. The economist and the sociologist thus bring characteristically different methods to bear on the same general level of social behavior. Neither profession, of course, has any claim to having the "right" method; but one method or another may be more useful in addressing certain questions.

Most of the modern scholarly literature on bureaucracy stems from the writings of the German sociologist, Max Weber (1864–1920).[4] Weber recognized bureaucracy as the characteristic form of public administration for a state with extended territorial sovereignty and developed what has become the standard definition of this form of organization. His writings focus primarily on the characteristics of bureaus and the behavior within bureaus.[5] He devotes little attention to the economic behavior of bureaus as it affects their performance in supplying public services. He writes rather favorably of the modern form of bureaucracy, reflecting a personal outlook strongly influenced by an organic concept of the state and the manifest superiority, from this viewpoint, of public administration in the Prussian-dominated German state relative to that in the provincial organization of the German nation prior to the middle of the nineteenth century. Until recently, the literature of public administration (which developed, primarily, as an offshoot of political science) was also strongly influenced by Weber's writings, with occasional infusions of Confucian and Platonist guidance on how a good bureaucrat, now "civil servant," ought to behave.

Although the scholarly literature usually represents bureaucracy as a desirable, or at least necessary, form of public administration, popular attitudes reflecting personal experience are often critical of the methods and performance of bureaucracy. These popular attitudes are probably best reflected in the irreverent and sometimes caustic form of literary satire, ranging from Balzac's observations on the mentality and behavior of minor bureaucrats to Parkinson's mock-scientific observations on the behavior and performance of bureaus. Joseph Heller's *Catch-22* will probably become the modern classic in this tradition.

Even the terms "bureaucracy," "bureaucrat," and "bureaucratic methods" are now charged and usually pejorative in popular usage. As a consequence both scholars and public officials have invented euphemisms like "public administration," "service" (in place of bureau), "civil servant," and "program management" to deflect the popular response to terms associated with bureaucracy. This is an unfortunate practice and will not

4. The best general sources for Weber's writings that are available in English translation are *From Max Weber: Essays in Sociology*, translated and edited by Hans Gerth and C. Wright Mills (New York: Oxford Univesity Press, 1946) and Max Weber, *The Theory of Social and Economic Organization*, translated by A. M. Henderson and Talcott Parsons (Glencoe, Ill.: Free Press, 1947).

5. A summary of Weber's characterization of bureaus is presented in Chapter 2.

be used in this book, as these euphemisms tend to gloss over the significant differences in the behavior and performance of bureaus as a distinct form of organization.

Economists, for the most part, have ignored the economic activity of bureaus. Most of economics deals with the behavior of profit-seeking firms, owners of productive factors, and consumers; this is appropriate, as most economic activity is organized through profit-seeking firms by the voluntary exchange of factors for money and money for consumer goods. Economists have also developed an elaborate structure of normative propositions about what goods and services ought to be supplied. Even the theory of public services (usually, but less accurately, termed public goods), however, implicitly assumes that public services, although financed by government, will be supplied by a competitive industry (or that the bureaus supplying the service will behave like a competitive industry). Economics has not, to date, provided a positive theory of supply by bureaus. This represents a significant gap in the body of positive economics. More importantly, the lack of a theory of supply by bureaus seriously reduces the relevance of the normative propositions about what services the government ought to finance, at least to the general extent that public services are supplied by bureaus.

Only a few venturesome economists have taken on the bureaucracy as a subject for scholarship. Ludwig von Mises's book, *Bureaucracy*, provides some of the earliest critical insights for a theory of bureaucracy:

> Bureaus specialize in the supply of those services the value of which cannot be exchanged for money at a per-unit rate.
> As a consequence of the above, bureaus cannot be managed by profit goals and "the economic calculus."
> In the absence of profit goals, bureaus must be centrally managed by the pervasive regulation and monitoring of the activities of subordinates.[6]

Mises's assertion of these characteristics of bureaus in their imperative form, however, prevented him from developing these insights into a theory of bureaucracy. He asserts that bureaucracy is the essential form of public administration for a territorially extensive state. The methods and performance of bureaus, he asserts, cannot be improved or meaningfully compared with that of profit-seeking organizations. He believes that the criticism of the methods and performance of bureaus is misdirected, and that the only way to reduce the undesirable characteristics of bureaucracy is to reduce the scope of government. Mises also provides some perceptive insights concerning the social, political, and psychological consequences of a pervasive bureaucracy, but his rigid interpretation of the character and role of bureaus limits the value of his book to that of a forcefully written polemic. Mises concludes with the hope, almost pathetic in retro-

6. Von Mises, *Bureaucracy*, pp. 47–49.

spect, that a broader education in economics will reduce the popular support for large government and the consequent pervasive bureaucracy.

One of Gordon Tullock's sorties into the poorly defended province of political science is recorded in his *The Politics of Bureaucracy*.[7] Tullock uses a model of a maximizing bureaucrat to examine the personal relations and advancement procedures within bureaus. In a less serious time this work could be titled, "How to Get Ahead in a Bureaucracy by Really Trying, or a Guide to the Maximizing Bureaucrat." This is a delightful book and full of scholarship; his method has more general applicability, but he does not use it to investigate the budget and output behavior of bureaus.

Similarly, Anthony Downs's book, *Inside Bureaucracy*, focuses primarily on the behavior within bureaus.[8] Downs develops a comprehensive theory of management processes within bureaus but stops short of developing the consequences of maximizing behavior on the budget and output performance of bureaus. Downs also accepts Mises's assertion that bureaucracy is the essential form of public administration. This leads him to temper his criticism of the methods and performance of bureaus because of a larger concern for the supply of public services.

All of these books are rich in insight and scholarship but do not address, for the bureaucratic form of organization, those questions for which the theory of the profit-seeking firm and the theory of market supply have proved valuable: For given demand and cost conditions, how much output is produced at what total cost? How do these output and cost levels change with changing conditions?

Two characteristics of the approach of my book should be understood: I develop a positive theory of the behavior of bureaus and representative government. A positive theory, of course, does not prove itself. Although I bring personal observations and casual evidence to bear in support of several of the behavioral hypotheses, this book does not present the set of critical tests that are ultimately necessary to confirm (or, more accurately, fail to disconfirm) this theory. The theory is developed primarily to interest others in taking it seriously enough to participate in the complex process of making the critical tests. As part of this process, at each stage of the development of this theory, I ask the reader to ask himself the following types of questions: Is this behavioral hypothesis consistent with my personal observation and understanding? Does this theory help organize my observations about related phenomena? This type of subjective empiricism is a relevant, but not complete, substitute for the more formal objective tests that are yet to be performed. My own incentive to write this book is largely based on affirmative answers to both of these types of questions.

7. Gordon Tullock, *The Politics of Bureaucracy* (Washington, D.C.: Public Affairs Press, 1965).

8. Anthony Downs, *Inside Bureaucracy* (Boston: Little, Brown & Co., 1967).

The development of this theory also involves the use of some simple mathematics, primarily because I do not know of any other way effectively to analyze and express what are, basically, maximization problems. The mathematics is used to improve the conceptual precision and, in some cases, to improve the exposition. The mathematics is simple because that is all that I am comfortable with and that is all that appears to be necessary. More complex mathematics may be *à la mode* and may even be necessary to extend this theory to more general conditions. At this stage, however, the use of simple mathematics appears both necessary and sufficient to express the main body of the theory. As an aid to understanding, the primary points are expressed in words, simple algebraic expressions, numerical examples, and graphics. I hope that the mathematically trained reader will tolerate this redundancy and that others will make an effort to understand some one or more of the forms in which the theory is expressed.

My book builds on the insights of Weber and von Mises concerning the characteristics of bureaucracy and the spirit and analytic method that Tullock and Downs bring to the study of bureaucracy to address a new set of questions: What budget and output behavior should be expected of bureaus under different conditions?

Objectives

The positive theory developed here focuses on the relations between a bureau and its environment, particularly the environment of representative government, and develops the consequences of these relations for the bureau's budget and output. Most bureaus supply public services and most public services are supplied by bureaus, so an alternative title for this book could be "The Supply of Public Services." The development of the modern state has been characterized by the parallel growth of government expenditures and the size and number of bureaucratic organizations. Although there are functional reasons for this parallel growth, one should not assume that public services necessarily need be supplied by bureaus. Some bureaus supply private goods and services, and some public services are supplied by other forms of organization.[9] One should be particularly careful to distinguish between the well-developed arguments for government financing of public services and the rather casual arguments for the bureaucratic supply of public services. Much of the debate about government expenditures derives from a failure to distinguish these arguments.

This book develops a theory of supply by bureaus, whatever the nature of their product. It bears on the supply of public services, primarily because most public services are supplied by bureaus, and political institutions are thus an important part of the environment in which bureaus operate.

9. This distinction between private and public services is based on the characteristics of the service, not the source of supply. See Chapter 13 for an elaboration of this distinction.

Observations about the behavior of bureaus do not necessarily bear one way or another on the desirability of the services supplied.

A comprehensive theory of bureaucracy should develop answers to three types of questions: constructual, behavioral, and normative.

Constructual questions are of the type: What are the structural characteristics of . . . ? Answers to such constructual questions can only be assumptions and, as such, are only the beginning of analysis. These assumptions should be judged only on the basis of their usefulness: Are these assumptions necessary to generate the behavioral hypotheses? Are the behavioral hypotheses confirmed by the available evidence? These assumptions should specifically *not* be evaluated by their "realism" or their consistency with some other author's characterization. The theory developed in this book builds on assumptions concerning the following types of constructual questions:

What are the critical elements of a theory of supply by bureaus?

What are the distinguishing characteristics of bureaus most useful for such a theory? Specifically, what do bureaucrats maximize?

What are the characteristics of the external conditions which constrain the behavior of bureaus? Specifically, what are the characteristics of the review process in representative government which most affect the supply of public services?

Behavioral questions are of the type: What would happen if . . . ? Hypotheses about such behavioral questions should be evaluated only by their consistency with observed behavior. The theory developed in this book provides a consistent analytic framework for generating testable hypotheses concerning the following types of behavioral questions:

What are the equilibrium budget and output of a bureau for given demand and cost conditions? How do these change in response to changes in demand and cost conditions?

How do these compare with the equilibrium conditions of other forms of organization faced by the same demand and cost conditions? What are the relative net benefits generated by bureaus and other forms of organizations faced by the same conditions?

What choice will be made by a bureau among two or more potential production processes for the same service?

What is the equilibrium price of a service provided by a bureau that receives only part of its financing from the per-unit sale of output?

What are the budget and the outputs of a single bureau that provides two or more services? How do these compare with the supply of each service by separate bureaus?

What are the effects of the time-distribution of costs on a bureau's choice among competitive processes or among two or more services?

What are the budgets and outputs of two or more bureaus supplying the same service? What are the equilibrium budget and output of a bureau supplying a service that is also supplied by a competitive industry?

What are the effects of different review processes, voting rules, and tax systems on the level of public services approved by a representative government?

Normative questions are of the type: What action should be taken concerning . . . ? Answers to such normative questions require an understanding of the behavioral consequences of alternative actions. This book is addressed primarily to the behavior of bureaus in supplying services financed through representative government, but some insight is developed concerning normative questions. If the demand for services faced by a bureau is "correct" and the net benefit from the supply of these services is accepted as the criterion for choice among alternative actions, the theory developed in this book, then, suggests answers to the following types of normative questions:

Should a given public service be supplied by one bureau, two or more bureaus, or by some other form of organization?

What changes in the bureaucracy and our political institutions should be made to increase the net benefits from the supply of public services?

Development of a theory of bureaucracy and representative government thus requires that these three types of questions be addressed in a logical sequence. Assumptions concerning the constructual questions are necessary conditions for developing consistent hypotheses concerning the behavioral questions. And answers to the behavioral questions are necessary conditions for addressing the normative questions. The structure of this book follows this logical sequence.

The first part (Chapters 2 through 12) develops a general theory of supply by bureaus. This part of the theory should be applicable to the behavior of bureaus supplying services financed through any form of private organization or government. Later (Chapters 13 through 15), an aggregative theory of the behavior of representative government is developed to describe the formulation of the demands for a bureau's output in this specific environment. Integrating these two theories, Chapter 16 then develops the consequences of the combination of bureaucratic supply of public services and representative government for conditions roughly approximating those in the United States. I conclude (Chapters 17 through 21) with a set of suggestions for changes in the bureaucracy, the sources of supply of public services, and our political institutions that would improve the performance of our system of supplying public services.

The theory developed here does not address the management processes internal to bureaus or the political processes internal to representative government, but does address the effects of the general characteristics of these institutions on the outcomes of these processes. As such, this is not a book on organization theory or political science, but rather, to use an old-fashioned term, one on the political economy of bureaucracy and representative government.

II

Critical Elements of a Theory of Supply by Bureaus

II

Characteristics of Bureaus

The three elements of a theory of supply by bureaus are the following: the distinguishing characteristics of bureaus, the nature of the relations between bureaus and their environment, and the maximand of bureaucrats. The *critical* elements are the smallest set of characteristics, types of relations, and elements in the maximand that are necessary to develop hypotheses concerning that part of the behavior of bureaus that is the subject of study.[1]

Definition of Bureaus

For this book, bureaus are defined as those organizations which have *both* of the following characteristics:

1. The owners and employees of these organizations do not appropriate any part of the difference between revenues and costs as personal income.
2. Some part of the recurring revenues of the organization derive from other than the sale of output at a per-unit rate.

In a single sentence: Bureaus are nonprofit organizations which are financed, at least in part, by a periodic appropriation or grant.

The first characteristic includes all nonprofit organizations, such as all government agencies and enterprises, most educational institutions and hospitals, and the many forms of social, charitable, and religious organizations. This characteristic clearly excludes corporate businesses, partner-

1. My nominalist preference for the smallest set of assumptions reflects an aesthetic preference for an economy of constructs. Some people may prefer a larger set of assumptions as being more "realistic," even though the additional assumptions are not necessary to address the subject of the book. I have no argument with these people if they recognize they have no argument with me. Our differences would be only in the specification of the subject of study or, possibly, in aesthetic preferences.

ships, and sole proprietorships. Some component units in profit-seeking organizations, however, may be bureaus. Any identifiable profit center such as a product division, cannot be considered to be a bureau, but some staff units providing such services as advertising, public relations, and research have both of the critical characteristics of bureaus. Thus, the more difficult it is to identify a component's contribution to corporate profits, the more likely that the component will behave like a bureau. This first characteristic also excludes mutual financial institutions, cooperatives, and families; although these organizations are normally classified as nonprofit organizations, the identity of owners and consumers permits the appropriation of residual revenues either in the form of personal income or in lower prices for certain goods and services.

The second characteristic includes all nonprofit organizations which receive a recurring appropriation or grant. These include most of the organizations with the first characteristic. Some government enterprises (such as public power, bridge, highway, and toll-road authorities) and private nonprofit organizations are excluded by this characteristic, as their recurrent operations are financed entirely by the sale of output at a per-unit rate, even though these organizations may have been established initially by an appropriation or grant.

The Contemporary Role of Bureaus

Given the above definition of bureaus, what is the role of bureaus in the economic activity of the United States, and how has it changed? No single indicator, unfortunately, adequately reflects the scope and scale of the activities of bureaus. The three indicators presented in Table 2.1, however,

Table 2.1 Relative size of economic activity by bureaus in the
United States (percent of Gross National Product)

	1929	1939	1949	1959	1969
Expenditures					
Total government	10.0	19.4	23.1	27.1	31.1
Goods and services					
Total government	8.2	14.7	14.8	20.1	22.8
Compensation of employees					
General government					
Government enterprises	7.7	11.9	10.9	12.7	15.3
Households and institutions					

SOURCES: 1929–1959—U.S. Office of Business Economics, *National Income and Product Accounts of the United States, 1929–1965 Statistical Tables* (Washington, D.C., 1966); 1969—
U.S. Office of Business Economics, *Survey of Current Business,* July 1970 (Washington, D.C., 1970).

provide rough estimates of the relative magnitude of the economic activities of bureaus.

The top row indicates the percent of the gross national product that passes through some government budget. The total expenditures of government are equal to the federal expenditures plus state and local expenditures minus federal grants to state and local governments; this total includes the compensation of government employees, purchases of goods and services from private organizations, and transfer payments to individuals and foreign governments. Total government expenditures have increased from around 10 percent of GNP in 1929 to around 31 percent in 1969. This somewhat underestimates the total expenditures by bureaus, as it excludes the expenditures and transfers by private bureaus other than those indirectly financed by government. On the other hand, this is a rather loose definition of the economic activities of bureaus, because it includes the government purchase of goods and services from private organizations and transfer payments; all of these funds pass through the bureaucracy, but in the first case private firms organize the production of intermediate goods and services, and, in the second, private individuals determine the expenditure of the transfer payments.

A somewhat more restrictive indicator of the relative size of the bureaucracy is the percent of GNP expended for goods and services supplied by all levels of government; this indicator is presented on the middle row of Table 2.1. The total expenditure for government goods and services (the gross government product in the GNP accounts) includes the compensation of government employees and the purchase of goods and services from private firms but excludes transfer payments; this total has increased from around 8 percent of GNP in 1929 to around 23 percent in 1969. This total represents the amount of resources which government bureaus control at the final stage of production. It is not clear whether this total over- or under-represents the activities of bureaus, as it includes the intermediate products produced by private firms but excludes the expenditures for services produced by private bureaus.

An even more restrictive indicator of the relative size of the bureaucracy is the percent of GNP expended as payments to the employees of bureaus. An estimate of the relative size of the payroll of the bureaucracy is presented on the third row of Table 2.1; this indicator is based on the total compensation of employees of general government, government enterprises, and households and institutions. This indicator is probably the best estimate of the income originating in bureaus in the United States. Some government enterprises and private nonprofit institutions are not strictly bureaus, as they receive no recurring appropriation or grant, but this is probably more than offset by the income originating in bureaucratic components of profit-seeking businesses. As shown in Table 2.1, the income originating in these nonprofit organizations increased from around 8 percent of GNP in 1929 to around 15 percent in 1969, with around one-half of the relative increase occurring in the 1930's.

The first and last of these three indicators roughly bracket the range of control by bureaus over the allocation of resources in the United States. Around 30 percent, roughly triple the percent in 1929, of the GNP now passes through some government budget. Around 15 percent of the GNP is now paid to the employees of bureaus—roughly double the percent in 1929. Since 1939, however, most of the increase in the relative size of the bureaucracy has been due to relative increases in transfer payments and government purchases from private firms, with a smaller relative increase in the payroll of the bureaucracy. Bureaus, then, can be represented as organizing a significant and growing, but not yet dominant, proportion of the economic activity of the United States.

The public concern about bureaucracy, however, is probably disproportionate to the role indicated by these percentages of GNP, testifying to its irritating methods and unsatisfactory performance. The full role of bureaus in the economic activities of the United States, of course, is larger than these indicators suggest. Government bureaus also regulate the activities of profit-seeking firms both through direct controls on profits, prices, business practices, and entry, and through the more pervasive indirect forms of subsidy and taxation. My focus here, however, is on the supply of services by bureaus and not on their regulatory practices, so these three indicators roughly represent the magnitude of the behavior under study.

Functional Specialization of Bureaus

What goods and services do bureaus specialize in providing? A clue to the answer is the second characteristic of bureaus: Bureaus specialize in providing those goods and services that some people prefer be supplied in larger amounts than would be supplied by their sale at a per-unit rate. People with such preferences form or join collective organizations and contribute resources to these organizations. In various ways, either through political processes or by moving, people choose their government and thus agree to be taxed to provide resources to augment the supply of certain goods and services. In a similar way and for similar purposes, people form or join private collective organizations. Both churches and country clubs, in effect, tax their regular members. Charitable organizations and alumni associations in similar ways tax those people who most strongly identify with a community, activity, or university.

The most important difference among levels of government and private collective organizations is not the degree or nature of an individual's influence on the activities of the organization or the degree of coercion in collecting revenues, but the cost of transferring membership from one

such organization to another. It is inappropriate to characterize governments as coercive organizations and private collective organizations as
cooperative. Both public and private collective organizations are cooperative
in that one chooses to be a member of the organization. Both types are
also coercive in that a contribution of resources and adherence to certain
rules are a requisite of membership. Governments differ from private
collective organizations primarily in that one can transfer membership
among governments only by moving.[2] The resources collected by these
organizations are then expended primarily, but not exclusively, by bureaus.
The primary characteristic of the goods and services supplied by bureaus
is thus that some group of people contributes resources to augment their
supply beyond that which would be supplied by market transactions.

Some other characteristics of the goods and services supplied by bureaus
can be derived from the primary characteristic. Many goods and services
supplied by bureaus are characterized by high fixed costs of production
or by difficulties in collecting fees, caused either by the definition of property
rights or by the technology of marketing. It is incorrect, however, to interpret these secondary characteristics as rigidly defining the role of bureaus.
Contrary to von Mises's assertion, bureaus provide many goods and services
that can be quite adequately marketed. For centuries bureaus have provided both bread and circuses in various forms, although these products
are quite efficiently supplied by profit-seeking organizations—though,
possibly, not in adequate amounts. The larger list of such "private"
services supplied by bureaus includes postal, educational, hospital, and
recreational services. Many "public" services are also provided by profit-
seeking firms, under subsidy from some collective organization. Prior to
the nineteenth century even such essential activities of government as the
collection of taxes and the organization of military units were often performed by profit-seeking organizations.

2. This book is not primarily addressed to political behavior. However, most of the political science literature seems to have missed this important point. The most important differences among all types of organizations probably involve the cost and procedures for the
transfer of an individual's property rights among organizations. The sustained growth of the
corporate form of business is undoubtedly due, in part, to the low cost of transferring property
rights in and out of each such organization. Even the most autocratic government would have
to be approved by *every* resident if the costs of moving were zero. Effective popular control of
government is more important, the greater the continuous territorial sovereignty of the government and the greater the restrictions on moving across the borders of the state, both of which
increase the economic and psychic costs of moving. Unfortunately, the difficulties of popular
control of government also increase with the size of the state.

The superiority of private collective organizations and local governments in providing certain
services is due more to the lower cost of transferring membership or moving than to greater
individual control—which, except in the smallest organizations, is still negligible. A purely
autocratic government of a small area must be more responsive to each resident, if there are
no coercive controls on moving, than the best conceivable democratic government of a large
state.

In the contemporary environment, when most goods and services that are augmented by collective action are supplied by bureaus, it is often difficult to understand the functional and historical bases for choosing bureaus, rather than profit-seeking organizations, to supply these services. The primary functional reason for choosing bureaus to supply these services, I suspect, is the difficulty of defining the characteristics of the services sufficiently to contract for their supply. This difficulty leads collective organizations directly to organize the supply of these services, hoping to substitute incentives associated with loyalty to the collective organization for the motivation of profits. The early bureaucracies were largely staffed by slaves, clerics, and sons of the nobility—individuals with a relatively low pecuniary motivation or those whose loyalty was more fully assured; the civil servant and the professional military officer are their modern counterparts. Around this functional basis there has developed a surprisingly pervasive ethical attitude (usually reinforced by the bureaucracy) that it is somehow wrong for an individual to profit by the supply of educational services, hospital services, and military forces.

The very problem which leads to the supply of some services by bureaus (the difficulty of defining output), however, creates one of the more important problems of controlling bureaus in any condition for which the objectives of the employees of bureaus are not completely consistent with those of the collective organization. The difficulty of defining the desired characteristics of a service also makes it difficult to give appropriate instructions to the bureaucrat. When the objectives of the collective organization and the bureaucrat are consistent, the difficulty of instructing the bureaucrat can lead to a substantial variance of the actual output around the desired output. When the objectives are not consistent, the difficulty of defining output and the consequent difficulty of instructing the bureaucrat can lead to an actual output that is systematically different from that desired. Bureaus are thus likely to have a comparative advantage in the supply of those services for which it is difficult to define (and contract for) output and during periods, such as a system-threatening crisis or war, when objectives are more nearly consistent. An improvement in contracting and monitoring procedures would increase the opportunity to use profit-seeking organizations for the supply of these services, and the normalization of activities between generally perceived crises may make it more important to explore non-bureaucratic sources of supply.

A more complete definition of the role of bureaus would be the following: Bureaus specialize in the supply of those services that some collective organization wishes to augment beyond that supplied by the market and for which it is not prepared to contract with a profit-seeking organization. This is the most general possible definition, consistent with the recognition that the role of bureaus differs among environments, depending on the preferences of individuals and specific institutional conditions.

Comparison with Other Definitions of Bureaus

It is probably valuable to compare the definition of bureaus used in this book with that of the more important earlier authors. Max Weber's writings provide the standard definition of bureaus as an "ideal type" that has been the basis for most scholarly literature on bureaucracy. Weber distinguishes three types of legitimate authority: rational-legal, traditional, and charismatic; he used the term "bureaucracy" largely as a synonym for a system of relations based on rational-legal authority.[3] Modern bureaus, according to Weber, manifest the following characteristics:

1. Bureaus are large organizations.
2. Most employees of bureaus work full time, most of their working lives, for bureaus and receive most of their income from bureaus.
3. Employees are appointed, retained, and promoted primarily on the basis of expected role performance within the bureau (rather than by election or on the basis of *a priori* characteristics).
4. Bureaus are managed by hierarchically structured authority relations between superior and subordinate, with the rights and duties of the subordinate prescribed in written regulations.
5. Office and incumbent are strictly separated. Superiors do not own their position or the means of production. The subordinate is subject to the authority of the bureau only in his role as an employee.
6. Bureaucratic activity is characterized by the complexity of administration, functional specialization of tasks, and secrecy of operations. The specialization of tasks increases the importance of a bureaucrat's prior formal training and his initial appointment as a result of qualifying in an examination.

Weber fully intended this definition to apply to all large modern organizations including profit-seeking organizations. His purpose was to describe those common characteristics of the structure of these organizations and behavior within these organizations. By its nature, his definition does not provide a basis for explaining the differences in the cost and output behavior of organizations that have the above characteristics in common but differ on other characteristics, such as legal form or method of financing.

Anthony Downs developed a theory of behavior within bureaus from a similar, but somewhat shorter, list of characteristics.[4] Downs starts with the first three of the above characteristics and adds a fourth, "The major portion of [a bureau's] output is not directly or indirectly evaluated in any markets external to the organization by means of voluntary *quid pro pro*

3. Weber, *From Max Weber*, pp. 196–244, and *The Theory of Social and Economic Organization*, pp. 328–341.
4. Downs, *Inside Bureaucracy*, pp. 24–31.

transactions."[5] Downs then derives the other characteristics identified by Weber, and a remarkably rich set of propositions about bureaucratic behavior, from these four primary characteristics. Downs's fourth characteristic of bureaus (basically identical to my second characteristic) is necessary to distinguish bureaus from other types of large modern organizations. Bureaus, according to Downs, are large organizations which receive some recurrent block appropriation or grant. Downs is not explicit about whether he would include both profit-seeking and nonprofit organizations in this definition. In a sense, however, Downs's definition is too restrictive. His first three characteristics (in common with Weber's) may be necessary to explain the structure of bureaus and the behavior within bureaus, but seem unduly restrictive in explaining the budget and output behavior of bureaus. Some small organizations with personnel conditions and selection procedures different from those defined by the second and third characteristics may exhibit similar budget and output behavior.

To the extent that most bureaus (by my definition) exhibit the other characteristics identified by Weber and Downs, they should be considered derivative characteristics. I have no argument with these more standard definitions if it is recognized that the earlier literature on bureaus addressed a somewhat different aspect of their behavior.

Definition of "Bureaucrat" and "Bureaucracy"

It is also useful to define the terms "bureaucrat" and "bureaucracy" as they are used here. The term "bureaucrat" will sometimes be used in the more general sense to define any full-time employee of a bureau; in this sense the term is nearly synonymous with "civil servant," although the latter term also often implies a full-time career employee. For the most part, however, the term will be used to define the senior official of any bureau with a separate identifiable budget. (Most large bureaus will include component bureaus, so there will usually be more than one bureaucrat, in this sense, in large bureaus.) These bureaucrats may be either career officials or directly appointed by the elected executive. The position of those directly appointed by the elected executive is necessarily somewhat ambiguous. Conceptually, they are representatives of the elected executive and may even begin their tenure in office with this outlook. These temporarily appointed officials, however, very quickly become representatives of the bureaus they head (for reasons that will be discussed later). For most purposes it is thus not necessary to distinguish the behavior of a career bureaucrat from that of a temporarily appointed bureaucrat.

The term "bureaucrat" is used in this descriptive sense and has no inherently pejorative connotations. It is inaccurate, however, to believe

5. *Ibid.*, p. 25.

that "Bureaucrats as individuals are neither more nor less efficient, honest, hard-working, thorough, public-spirited, and generally worthy of admiration than non-bureaucrats "[6] Any form of organization, including bureaus, will differentially reward those whose capabilities and attitudes best serve the organization, and people will sort themselves out among forms of organization depending on their perceived reward. Bureaus reward a different type of personal behavior than do other forms and, as a group, bureaucrats will be those individuals who are most adept at this type of behavior. If bureaus differentially reward behavior that other people consider undesirable, the pejorative connotation of the term "bureaucrat" is neither surprising nor inaccurate. Bureaucrats are not "just folks" any more than ball players, businessmen, and bishops are "just folks." They have different latent or developed characteristics, just as individuals in other professions have different characteristics. As individuals, bureaucrats are neither inherently superior nor inferior, but it is unwise not to recognize that they have some differentiating characteristics.[7]

For this book, a precise and consistent definition of the term "bureaucracy" is not important. The term will generally be used in reference to a set of bureaus and their relations with their external environment; this is the sense of terms such as the "welfare bureaucracy" and the "federal bureaucracy." Sometimes the term is used in reference to a set of bureaucrats. Sometimes it is used in a more general sense in reference to the organizational structure, methods, and behavioral characteristic of bureaus. In all cases, however, the term will be used in ways consistent with the more precise definitions of bureaus, and the reader should have no difficulty in distinguishing the specific meaning in context.

As I use it here, "bureaucracy" is not always identical with what is meant by "bureaucracy" when used by political scientists and sociologists. The original use of the term, I understand, referred to a cloth covering the desk (*bureau*) of eighteenth-century French officials, and the term soon became used to identify a form of government ruled by officials; this use by political scientists is a precise and valuable definition of an important phenomenon. From Weber to Galbraith, however, "bureaucracy" has been used by many scholars in reference to all large modern organizations, and this usage impresses me as being too broad to be valuable, given the significant differences in behavior among such organizations. A more limited definition is used in this book, always in reference to bureaus as a conceptually distinct and functionally specialized form of organizing economic activity.

6. *Ibid.*, p. 26.
7. It is only fair to Downs to point out that he recognized this effect of the selection process for bureaucrats. His taxonomy of bureaucrats, in fact, is largely based on the distinguishing characteristics of bureaucrats.

3

Bureaus and Their
Environment

A bureau's environment is defined by its relations with three groups: the collective organization which provides the bureau's recurring appropriation or grant, the suppliers of labor and material factors of production, and, in some cases, the customers for those services that are sold at a per-unit rate. Among the three, a bureau's relations with its sponsor most strongly distinguish its environment from that of other forms of organization.

Relations with the Sponsor Organization

Most bureaus are financed by a single or dominant collective organization which, in turn, is financed by tax revenues or by more or less compulsory contributions. The officers of the collective organization are usually elected by a larger constituency but are often effectively self-perpetuating. These officers review the bureau's proposed activities and budget, approve the budget, monitor the methods and performance of the bureau, and, usually, approve the appointment of the bureau head. As a consequence, the activities of the bureau head are largely dominated by his relations with the officers of the sponsoring organization. The sponsoring organization is usually dependent on a specific bureau to supply a given service, and the bureau usually does not have a comparable alternative source of financing. In the jargon of economics, the relation between the bureau and its sponsor is that of a "bilateral monopoly." As with all such relations (including conventional marriage), this relation is awkward and personal—characterized by both threats and deference, by both gaming and appeals to a common objective. No other type of relation combines threat, exchange, and integrative relations (in Boulding's terminology) in such equal proportions.[1] Such is the nature of the relation between a federal bureaucrat

1. This valuable taxonomy of social behavior is developed in Kenneth E. Boulding, *Beyond Economics* (Ann Arbor: University of Michigan Press, 1968).

24

and Congress, between a university president and the state legislature (or the trustees of the university endowment), between a hospital director and the community fund, and between a research manager and the sponsoring agency. These relations could hardly be more unlike the rational-legal, impersonal relations which Weber finds characteristic of bureaucracy.

What does a bureau exchange with its sponsor? *A bureau offers a promised set of activities and the expected output(s) of these activities for a budget.* The primary difference between the exchange relation of a bureau and that of a market organization is that a bureau offers a total output in exchange for a budget, whereas a market organization offers units of output at a price. The bureau's characteristic "package" offer of a promised output for a budget has important implications for the behavior of bureaus: Under many conditions it gives a bureau the same type of bargaining power as a profit-seeking monopoly that discriminates among customers or that presents the market with an all-or-nothing choice.[2] The primary reason for the differential bargaining power of a monopoly bureau is the sponsor's lack of a significant alternative and its unwillingness to forego the services supplied by the bureau. Also, as demonstrated in Chapter 14, the interests of those officers of the collective organization responsible for reviewing the bureau are often best served by allowing the bureau to exploit this monopoly power.

From the viewpoint of a bureau, the preferences of a sponsor are summarized by what will be termed a "budget-output function." Any point on this function represents the maximum budget the sponsor is willing to grant to the bureau for a specific expected level of output; the budget-output function represents the relation among these points. This function has the following properties: Over some range of expected output, the sponsor is willing to grant a higher budget for a higher expected output. In mathematical terms, the first derivative of this function is positive over the relevant range. Also, over some range, the sponsor is willing to grant a higher budget per unit of output for a smaller expected output than for a larger expected output. The second derivative of this function, thus, is negative over the relevant range. Several types of functions share these two properties, but a function of the following form is used to represent the budget-output function in this book (see Figure 3.1):

$$B = aQ - bQ^2, \quad 0 \le Q < \frac{a}{2b}, \tag{3.1}$$

where $B \equiv$ maximum budget sponsor is willing to grant to bureau during a specific time period, and

2. I am indebted to Gordon Tullock for this important insight. A discussant of an article summarizing an earlier version of this theory misinterpreted this point: Bureaus do not, in fact, present their sponsors with an all-or-nothing choice. But the offer of a total output for a budget, under many conditions, gives them the same type of bargaining power.

$Q \equiv$ expected level of output by bureau
during a specific time period.

A total budget-output function is a necessary building-block of a theory of supply by bureaus, because the exchange of promised activities and expected output for a budget is conducted entirely in total rather than in unit terms.

Bureaucrats and their sponsors do not, in fact, talk much about output—in terms of military capability, the value of educational services, the number and condition of the poor, etc. Most of the review process consists of a discussion of the relation between budgets and activity levels, such as the number of infantry divisions, the number of students served, the number of the poor served by a program, etc. The relation between activity level and output is usually left obscure and is sometimes consciously obscured. Unless a bureau's activities are being continuously tested—by war, air traffic congestion, etc.—neither the bureau nor the sponsor may have a good understanding of the relation between activity level and output. My guess is that the Post Office, for example, performs rather better than most national bureaus, and that the prevalent dissatisfaction with this bureau is primarily due to its being tested continuously by many people. The budget-output function thus should be considered to be the product of two relations—the relation between budget and activity level, and the relation between activity level and output. Unless the activity is continuously tested, there is likely to be less variance in the first relation than in the second. For those readers who have trouble with the concept of the output of a bureau, the theory developed in this book may be better understood in terms of the relations between budget or cost and the activity level, rather

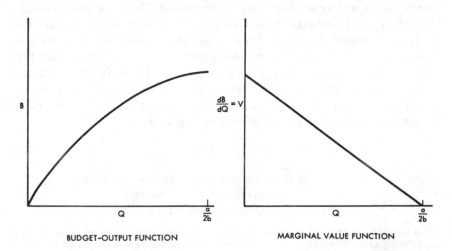

BUDGET-OUTPUT FUNCTION　　　　　MARGINAL VALUE FUNCTION

Figure 3.1　Graphic Representations of Budget-Output Function

than the output of a bureau. The activities of a bureau, however, should be recognized as intermediate services which are valuable only as a function of their effectiveness.

It is important to recognize that the relevant budget-output function for developing a positive theory of bureaucracy is that of the collective organization and *not* that of the organization's larger group of constituents. The budget-output function of the sponsor as revealed to the bureau will be related to that of the constituents through the processes by which the officers of the collective organization are selected and by its internal decision processes, but will not necessarily be identical with that of the constituents. The demand for services expressed by the collective organization and revealed to the bureau may be either more or less than the demand by the larger population. The relation between the population's demands and the collective organization's expressed demands in a particular institutional setting is one of the more important problems of political science—and one, incidentally, that is not well understood.[3] In any case, the population demands for services are never directly revealed to a bureau. A bureau may appeal to the constituents of its sponsor organization in an attempt to increase the sponsor's demand for the bureau's services, but it is not the preferences of the constituents that are important to the bureau, but rather their influence on the revealed preferences of the bureau's sponsor.

Until recently, economists' discussions of public services have been conducted, so to speak, in a vacuum, disregarding both the political institutions which express the preferences for public services and the bureaucratic organizations which supply these services. The theory developed here starts with the demands for services as expressed by the collective organization (and thus avoids the first problem) in order to address the supply of services by bureaus. Only when the first problem is better understood, however, will economics provide a positive theory of both the demand and the supply of public services.

Most private bureaus and many local government bureaus are subject to only a single-stage budget review and approval process. This happens where the executive and the other officers of the collective organization are either identical or represent the same constituency and, usually, where the budgets and bureaus are relatively small. Private universities and hospitals, and bureaus financed by city councils, churches, and country clubs, are usually in this situation. In these cases, a board of trustees or a council exercise both the first and the final review.

Most bureaus financed by state or national governments, however, are

3. The most important contributions to understanding this problem have been made by economists. See James M. Buchanan and Gordon Tullock, *The Calculus of Consent* (Ann Arbor: University of Michigan Press, 1962). Also, see Anthony Downs, "Why the Government Budget Is Too Small in a Democracy," *World Politics* XII (July 1960).

now subject to a multi-stage review, first by the executive and subsequently by the legislature, and, in effect, they have a composite sponsor.[4] Because the executive and the legislature represent different constituencies, are selected by different processes, and use different internal decision processes, the demands for services expressed by the legislature will usually be different from those initially expressed by the executive. These differences will finally be resolved into a single budget-output function as revealed to the bureau by the legislatively approved budget through a process of bargaining, initially within the executive branch and then between the executive and the legislature.[5] Most bureaucrats (even those directly appointed by the executive) are cognizant of the differences in the demands for their bureau's services between the executive and the legislature and will use this difference to bargin either with the executive or with the legislature to obtain a higher budget than the other would approve. Where the executive has a higher demand for a specific program, the bureau will bargain with the legislature to sponsor a larger program of services for which the legislature has a higher demand in exchange for legislative approval of the executive's preferred program.[6] This process works very well for the several parties involved—as demonstrated by the relatively few times that Congress adds to the executive budget. The effect of all this bargaining is that a state or federal bureau finally faces only one budget-output function, directly revealed by the legislature but reflecting the composite demands of both the executive and the legislature as worked out in the bargaining process.

A derivative function of the sponsor's budget-output function corresponds to the standard concept of a "demand" or "marginal valuation" function. For the budget-output function (3.1) the marginal valuation function (see Figure 3.1) would be

$$V = a - 2bQ, 0 \leq Q < \frac{a}{2b} \tag{3.2}$$

where $V \equiv$ maximum price per unit of output
that sponsor is willing to pay.

4. Many people will be surprised to learn that this is a comparatively recent development. The first executive budget of a U.S. state was prepared in 1911 and the first executive budget for the U.S. federal government in 1921!

5. This process is best described by Aaron Wildavsky, *The Politics of the Budgetary Process* (Boston: Little, Brown & Co., 1964).

6. Charles Zwick, a Director of the Bureau of the Budget during the Johnson Administration, relates one example of this process. He describes how the Bureau purposefully endorsed a program which the Bureau examiners had strongly criticized but which Congress favored, in exchange for approval by Congress of the Model Cities program which the President wanted and knew was not a favorite program of Congress. Both programs were approved by Congress, largely in the form proposed in the executive budget. Alan Schmidt relates a similar example during this same period, of Johnson's supporting a dubious agricultural bill in exchange for Congressional support of a civil rights bill.

This function has no operational relevance for a bureau, as it does not offer its services at a price. This function is relevant to the sponsor, however, if the services demanded by the sponsor are also supplied by a competitive industry, when this function indicates how much of the services the sponsor would purchase from a competitive industry at various offer prices. Since much of the verbal and graphical exposition of economics is expressed in such marginal functions, it is helpful to use this marginal valuation function in comparing the budget-output behavior of bureaus with that of profit-seeking forms of organization.

The incentives, knowledge, and behavior of the officers of collective organizations are probably more heterogeneous than those of the bureau. Nevertheless, some generalizations appear valid. Most important, the collective organizations are not profit-seeking. There is seldom any way for the officers of these organizations to appropriate as personal income part of the difference between the budget they would be willing to grant and the budget they in fact do grant to the bureau. On the contrary, some officers are more likely to be able to appropriate some part of the bureau's expenditures as personal income or as a contribution to campaign expenses. The behavior of elected officers of the collective organizations can probably be best explained by the assumption that they wish to be reelected or, at least, to be well regarded for the period of their elected service, and these incentives are only weakly related to the total net benefits generated by the services financed by the organization. The sponsors of many private bureaus are either other private bureaus (for example, foundations) or government bureaus.

Also—possibly as important—there is usually a great disparity in the relative information available to the sponsor and to the bureau. A bureaucrat can usually estimate his sponsor's budget-output function quite accurately from previous budget reviews, recent changes in the composition of the sponsor organization, and recent constituent influences on these officers. As a rule, however, a bureaucrat will know a great deal more about the factor costs and production processes for the bureau's services than will the officers of the sponsor organization. Previous budget-output offers by the bureau sometimes reveal little to the sponsor about the minimum budget that would be sufficient to supply a given output. A bureaucrat needs relatively little information, most of which can be estimated by revealed behavior, to exploit his position as a monopoly supplier of a given service. The officers of the collective organization, in contrast, need a great deal of information, little of which can be estimated from revealed behavior, to exploit their position as a monopoly buyer of this service.

Moreover, a bureaucrat has a stronger relative incentive and can work full time to obtain the information relevant to his position (and to obscure information relevant to the sponsor). Most officers of private collective organizations and of state and local governments, however, serve only part time in these positions. Even when the position is nominally a full-time obligation, the officer usually has little incentive or finds little time to review the activities of the sponsored bureaus in competition with personal services for his constituents and other activities to assure his reelection.[7] Although the nominal relation of a bureau and its sponsor is that of a bilateral monopoly, the relative incentives and available information, under most conditions, give the bureau the overwhelmingly dominant monopoly power.

For this reason, the theory developed here initially assumes a passive sponsor which knows the budget it is prepared to grant for a given level of services but does not have the incentive or the opportunity to obtain information on the minimum budget necessary to supply this service. This assumption most accurately describes larger collective organizations which finance a number of services and are faced by monopoly suppliers. It is less accurate for small functionally specialized collective organizations, where the officers have a personal relation with the constituents, where the production processes are simple, and where there are potential alternative sources of supply. The assumption of a passive sponsor and monopoly bureaus is probably most applicable to national and state governments, less applicable to local governments, and least applicable to private collective organizations like churches and country clubs. In Chapter 15, the influences of alternative sources of supply and improved information available to the sponsor on the relations between the bureau and sponsor and, in turn, on the behavior of the bureau, are developed, in order to provide a more comprehensive theory of the behavior of bureaus and representative government and to suggest methods to improve the efficiency of the supply of those services.

Relations with Suppliers of Factors

Most bureaus hire most labor and material factors of production on competitive markets. Although the supply price of a factor to a single bureau or a set of bureaus may increase with the quantity hired, most bureaus must pay the same price for all like factors. Under these conditions, a bureau's employment and procurement practices will be similar to those of a comparably sized profit-seeking firm.

Labor legislation, the automobile, and unions have destroyed most wage

---

7. For an effective description of the attitudes and activities of a congressman, his problems of eliciting information from bureaus, and some of his techniques, see Charles L. Clapp, *The Congressman: His Work as He Sees It* (Washington, D.C.: Brookings Institution, 1963). One of Clapp's more disturbing findings is that most Congressmen believe their constituents don't know and are little interested in what he does in his committee activity (where most of the review process is conducted). Also, see the section by L. A. Dexter in R. A. Bauer, I. deS. Pool, and L. A. Dexter, *American Business and Public Policy* (New York: Atherton Press, 1964), pp. 403–461.

discrimination (among those employees with comparable skills in a given firm) in the private labor market, and most like material factors are traded at a common price. For several reasons, however, the bureaucracy is the last stronghold of wage and factor price discrimination. Such discrimination is not general among bureaus, but it is more widely practiced than among profit-seeking firms. The first basis for wage and factor price discrimination is that bureaus are often monopoly suppliers of some services. These bureaus are thus also monopoly buyers of those labor skills and material factors that are specialized in the production of these monopolized services. Infantry officers are paid less than pilots in the same staff or management position, for example, because infantry officers have few alternative employments where they can market their specialized skills. The Navy pays shipyards different prices for the same type of ship, because these ships cannot be sold to any other buyer. Hospitals discriminate in their recruitment of nurses, and local governments discriminate in hiring several types of personnel.[8]

The second basis for such monopsony discrimination is that bureaus often have a prior claim on certain resources considered to be in the public domain. These resources include healthy and intelligent young men, nuclear materials, land, the electronic frequency spectrum, the air space, etc. First-term soldiers are paid less than career soldiers in the same position because the military can draft more first-term manpower. The military pays less (in fact, zero) for nuclear materials and public-domain land than for non-nuclear weapons and other land performing the same function, because it can usually command more of these resources from another bureau. Federal bureaus pay less (again, zero) for use of the frequency spectrum and congested air space than for equipment and operating practices that would use these resources more efficiently, because they can often command more of these resources on the approval of another bureau.

Such opportunities for monopsonistic discrimination are exploited by bureaus because, as I shall demonstrate later, this increases both the bureau's budget and output. Not incidentally, the transfer of resources from another bureau or regulatory commission at less than their opportunity cost also increases their budget or regulatory power. The exercise of wage and factor price discrimination is primarily limited to national bureaus (particularly the military) because of their greater monopoly power, use of specialized resources, and command of the public domain. It should not be considered a general characteristic of bureaus.

The wages and factor prices paid by bureaus are reflected in a second type of function which will be termed the "cost-output function." Any point on this function represents the minimum total payment to factors necessary

---

8. The wage discrimination by hospitals and local governments is well documented by Eugene Devine, *Analysis of Manpower Shortages in Local Government* (New York: Praeger, 1970).

to produce a given output, given the factor prices and available production processes; the cost-output function represents the relation among these points. This function has the following properties: Over some range of expected output, a larger output can be achieved only by a larger payment to factors. The first derivative of this function is always positive. Also, a larger output can generally be achieved only with higher costs per unit of output but sometimes can be achieved at lower unit costs. The second derivative is thus generally positive but can be negative. Again, there are several types of functions that share these properties, but in this book a function of the following form is used to represent the cost-output function:

$$TC = cQ + dQ^2, 0 \leq Q, \tag{3.3}$$

where TC = minimum total payment to factors
during a specific period.

For a competitive industry, the average cost function (determined by dividing [3.3] by Q) would represent the output that would be offered at various price levels and is thus a long-run "supply function." Both profit-seeking and bureaucratic monopolies, however, do not offer a specified amount of output at a given price, and thus do not directly reveal their minimum cost conditions. The profit-seeking monopolist makes a joint price-output decision, and the bureau makes a joint budget-output decision. The minimum total cost function will thus usually be known within the bureau but will not be directly revealed by its behavior. For the cost-output function (3.3) the respective minimum marginal cost function would be

$$C = c + 2dQ, 0 \leq Q, \tag{3.4}$$

where $C \equiv$ minimum marginal payment to factors
during a specific period.

For the identical underlying conditions (concerning the value of alternative use of factors and the available production processes) reflected in the above minimum total and marginal cost functions, a bureau that is a discriminating monopsonist will have lower minimum total and marginal costs for all levels of output. If the minimum marginal costs increase with output *only* because of an increased price of specialized factors used by the bureau (and not because of an increased price of nonspecific factors or reduced marginal factor productivity), and the bureau pays different units of those specialized factors only that sufficient to maintain their employment in the bureau, then the cost-output function for the discriminating monopsony for conditions corresponding to (3.3) would be (see Figure 3.2):

$$TC = cQ + \frac{d}{2}Q^2, 0 \leq Q. \tag{3.5}$$

For the cost-output function of a discriminating monopsony (3.5), the respective minimum marginal cost function would be

$$C = \iota + dQ, 0 \leq Q. \tag{3.6}$$

In most cases, only a part of the higher minimum marginal costs at higher output levels is attributable to the increased price of specialized factors, so even those bureaus which discriminate in their payment to specialized factors will face a cost-output function somewhere between that represented by (3.3) and (3.5). Because the officers of the sponsor organization often represent the interests of the specialized factors, bureaus often do not exploit even this advantage. Wage and factor price discrimination should thus be considered a significant but not general characteristic of the behavior of bureaus.

Relations with Market Customers

Some bureaus, in addition to a recurrent grant from a collective organization, receive revenues from the sale of output to individuals at a per-unit rate. This condition is characteristic of universities, hospitals, country clubs, cultural organizations, government printing offices, and postal services. These bureaus, in effect, face two groups of customers with different demands for the same service—one group is represented by a collective organization financing the supply of services by a grant, and the other group directly purchases the services at a price. In most cases the group of customers includes, but is not limited to, the constituents of the collective organization.

When a bureau is strongly dependent on the revenues from the per-unit sale of services, its relations with customers will be similar to those of a

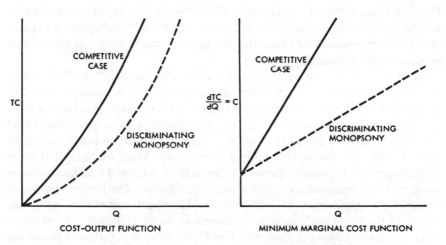

Figure 3.2 Comparison of Cost-Output Functions

profit-seeking business. It is interesting to contrast the general connotations of the terms "bureaucratic methods" and "businesslike methods." In bureaus, the attention to customer interests depends on the addition to the total financing that originates in the sale of a specific service; in profit-seeking firms, this attention depends on the addition to total profits. A bureau whose sponsor is willing to compensate for any loss of revenues from sales, or that is a monopoly supplier of a service with a nearly invariant demand, will usually be quite indifferent to the interests of its customers, even if a large proportion of the total financing is from the sale of services. (The U.S. Post Office, unfortunately, appears to have all of these characteristics.)

For those services which a bureau sells at a per-unit rate, the customer demands are represented by a price-output relation, that is, a "demand function," of the following form:

$$P = a - 2bQ, 0 \leq Q < \frac{a}{2b}, \tag{3.7}$$

where $P \equiv$ price at which marginal unit
of service is sold.

If all units of service are sold at the same price, the revenue–output function corresponding to the demand function (3.7) is the following:

$$PQ = R = aQ - 2bQ^2, \quad 0 \leq Q < \frac{a}{2b}, \tag{3.8}$$

where $R \equiv$ total revenues during a specific
period from per-unit sale of
output.

The total financing of a bureau attributable to the supply of a specific service will thus be the sum of the budget approved by the sponsor organization, as represented by (3.1), and the total revenues from the sale of this service, as represented by (3.8).

Some bureaus, by the nature of the services they supply, can sell the same service at a different price to different customers. The necessary conditions for price discrimination among customers (for both profit-seeking organizations and bureaus) are that there is some degree of monopoly power (the coefficient b in [3.7] and [3.8] must be greater than zero) and that customers cannot exchange the service among themselves. Most bureaus that have some degree of monopoly power in the sale of service do in fact exercise some price discrimination. Universities set different (net) prices by a discriminating distribution of scholarships. Hospitals sometimes set prices based on the customer's income or insurance level. Cultural organizations often set lower prices for students. The Post Office sets different prices for different classes of mail that receive the same service. Such opportunities for price discrimination are generally exploited by bureaus, as the discrimination increases both total revenues and output.

For the identical demand conditions represented in (3.7) and where the opportunities for price discrimination are fully exploited, the total revenue-output function of a bureau will be:

$$R = aQ - bQ^2, 0 \leq Q < \frac{a}{2b}. \tag{3.9}$$

In this case, the total financing of a bureau attributable to the supply of a specific service will be the sum of the budget approved by the sponsor, as represented by (3.1), and the total revenues from the sale of this service, as represented by (3.9). Some price discrimination is not a uniform characteristic of bureaus which sell services, but it is a fairly general characteristic, as most bureaus have some monopoly power and many services are inherently difficult to exchange among customers.

4

The Bureaucrat's Maximand

What, if anything, do bureaucrats maximize? Some assumption about the objectives of individuals is a necessary element in any theory of social behavior. Although natural science made its greatest advances only when freed from its anthropomorphic and teleological chains, theories of social behavior that represent individuals as automatons in some social mass, although they have fascinated many people, have rarely proved valuable.[1] Purposive behavior by individuals is the essence of social behavior. Most of the literature on bureaucracy, however, has represented the bureaucrat either as an automaton or as maximizing some concept of general welfare, the latter usually considered to be identical with the objectives of the state.[2] For a positive theory of bureaucracy, though, the beginning of wisdom is the recognition that bureaucrats are people who are, at least, not entirely motivated by the general welfare or the interests of the state.

The Theory of the Firm, as an Analogy

Again, what, if anything, do bureaucrats maximize? An economist's initial response will be that a bureaucrat, like anyone else, maximizes his

1. The problems and consequences of applying the models and methods of natural science to social behavior are probably best described in Hayek, *The Counter-Revolution of Science.*
2. The following description by von Mises may seem unduly harsh, but it accurately represents the image of the bureaucrat in most of the literature on bureaucracy: "It was a purposeful confusion on the part of the German metaphysicians of statolatry that they clothed all men in the government service with the gloriole of altruistic self-sacrifice. From the writings of the German estatists the civil servant emerges as a saintly being, a sort of monk who forsook all earthly pleasures and all personal happiness in order to serve, to the best of his abilities, God's lieutenant, once the Hohenzollern king and today the Führer. The *Staatsbeamte* does not work for pay because no salary however large could be considered an adequate reward for the invaluable and priceless benefits that society derives from his self-denying sacrifice. Society owes him not pay but a maintenance adequate to his rank in the official hierarchy" (von Mises, *Bureaucracy*, p. 78).

personal utility. By itself this is not very helpful, but it does suggest that a bureaucrat will engage in purposive behavior and that there are probably some elements in his utility other than the general welfare and the interests of the state.

The economist's theory of the firm provides some suggestions concerning how to look for some less abstract proxy for a bureaucrat's utility. The businessman in this role is represented as being unambiguously selfish. There may be elements in his utility other than personal income, but there are no prior assumptions that he has any personal interest in either efficiency or the general welfare; for some conditions these may be *consequences* of his purposive behavior, but they are not the *objectives* of his behavior. The central motivational assumption of this theory is that a businessman maximizes the profits (more precisely, the present value) of the firm.

Two types of arguments are advanced to support the plausibility of this assumption (not to prove it, but to argue that the theory should be seriously considered and tested). First, profit maximization by a competitive firm is demonstrated by Scitovsky to be a property of rational behavior (that is, consistent with utility maximization) if the labor which the business-man contributes to the firm is independent of his income.[3] This latter condition is culturally determined, but appears to be a more or less accurate representation of actual conditions. Second, profit maximization by a competitive firm is demonstrated by Alchian to be a property of organiza-tional survival; some businessmen, for a time, may choose to maximize something other than profits, but, if entry costs are low, are likely to be replaced by profit-maximizing businessmen.[4]

An assumption of profit maximization is also central to the classic model of monopolies. Economists are increasingly concerned, however, that the rationality and survival arguments for profit maximization may not strictly apply to managers of private monopolies which have a higher potential profit than that of other investments available to the stockholders or for which there are significant costs of transferring stock from the firm (primarily because of the present taxation of capital gains only at transfer). In part this reflects a concern for the "descriptive realism" of the theory of the firm; more importantly, this reflects a concern that the profit-maximizing model may not lead to unbiased estimates of the behavior of large corporations. Managers of these firms, as demonstrated by Williamson, have a range of discretionary behavior within the necessary profit con-straint.[5] The exercise of discretionary behavior, however, may actually reduce the adverse social consequencies of private monopolies, as it may

3. Tibor Scitovsky, "A Note on Profit Maximization and its Implications," *Review of Economic Studies* XI (1943), 57–60.

4. Armen A. Alchian, "Uncertainty, Evolution, and Economic Theory," *Journal of Political Economy*, June 1950, pp. 211–221.

5. Oliver E. Williamson, *The Economics of Discretionary Behavior: Managerial Objectives in a Theory of the Firm* (Englewood Cliffs. N.J.: Prentice-Hall, 1964).

lead to the expansion of the monopoly's output beyond the profit-maximizing level.

Criteria for Choice of the Bureaucrat's Maximand

What objective proxy for a bureaucrat's utility is suggested by corresponding rationality and survival arguments? Although I accept the positivist view that a theory is not proved by proving its assumptions, I believe that these arguments are necessary to establish the plausibility of the central motivational assumption sufficiently for the theory to be seriously considered and tested. The "proof" of the theory, of course, will depend on whether the hypotheses developed are generally consistent with observed behavior.

First, the rationality argument. Among the several variables that may enter the bureaucrat's utility function are the following: salary, perquisites of the office, public reputation, power, patronage, output of the bureau, ease of making changes, and ease of managing the bureau. All of these variables except the last two, I contend, are a positive monotonic function of the total *budget* of the bureau during the bureaucrat's tenure in office.[6]

The problems of making changes and the personal burdens of managing a bureau are often higher at higher budget levels, but both are reduced by *increases* in the total budget. This effect creates a treadmill phenomenon, inducing bureaucrats to strive for increased budgets until they can turn over the management burdens of a stable higher budget to a new bureaucrat. This suggests an interesting cyclical pattern, with those bureaucrats who are interested in making changes resigning when budgets are stabilized; their replacements will be satisfied with the other rewards of high budgets, or strive for further increases, or, possibly, cut the budget in order to provide a basis for further increases.

It is not necessary that a bureaucrat's utility be strongly dependent on every one of the variables which increase with the budget, but only that it is positively and continuously associated with the level of the budget.[7] For these reasons, budget maximization should be an adequate proxy even for those bureaucrats with a relatively low pecuniary motivation and a relatively high motivation for making changes in the public interest. This

6. Here the word "budget" is used in the more general sense to include both the budget approved by the collective organization and any revenues from the direct sale of services.

7. The rationality of budget maximization by bureaucrats may best be illustrated by considering the consequences of contrary behavior. Consider the probable consequences for a subordinate manager who proves without question that the same output could be produced at, say, one-half the present expenditures. In a profit-seeking firm this manager would probably receive a bonus, a promotion, and an opportunity to find another such economy; if such rewards are not forthcoming in a specific firm, this manager usually has the opportunity to market his skills in another firm. In a bureau, at best, this manager might receive a citation and a savings bond, a lateral transfer, the enmity of his former colleagues, and the suspicion of his new colleagues. Those bureaucrats who doubt this proposition and who have good private employment alternatives should test it . . . once.

is supported by the observation that the most distinguished public servants of recent years substantially increased the budgets of the bureaus for which they were responsible.

The budget maximization assumption is not necessarily based on a cynical interpretation of the personal motivations of bureaucrats. Some bureaucrats, by either predisposition or indoctrination, undoubtedly try to serve (their perception of) the public interest. A bureaucrat, however, is neither omniscient nor sovereign. He cannot acquire all of the information on individual preferences and production opportunities that would be necessary to divine the public interest, and he does not have the authority to order an action that is contrary to either the personal interests or the different perceptions of the public interest by some other bureaucrats or officers of the collective organization. In a competitive industry one profit-maximizer is often sufficient to induce all other firms to be profit-maximizers. In contrast, in a bureaucratic environment, one person who serves his personal interests or a different perception of public interest is often sufficient to prevent others from serving their perception of the public interest. It is *impossible* for any one bureaucrat to act in the public interest, because of the limits on his information and the conflicting interests of others, regardless of his personal motivations. This leads even the most selfless bureaucrats to choose some feasible, lower-level goal, and this usually leads to developing expertise in some narrow field. The development of expertise usually generates a sense of dedication, and it is understandable that many bureaucrats identify this dedication with the public interest. Moreover, as discussed in the following paragraphs, a bureaucrat who may not be personally motivated to maximize the budget of his bureau is usually driven by conditions both internal and external to the bureau to do just that. One should not be surprised, therefore (as I was initially), to hear the most dedicated bureaucrats describe their objective as maximizing the budget for the particulars service(s) for which they are responsible.

Some people resist accepting this rationality argument for budget maximization by bureaucrats because this behavioral assumption is not clearly consistent with higher-level goals. It should be sufficient to remember that profit maximization is also not inherently consistent with higher-level goals; in some conditions, profit-maximizing behavior leads to exploiting either consumers, owners of factors, or both. Budget maximization, also, may or may not be consistent with higher-level goals; in different conditions it can lead to the supply of a valued service or to exploitation. The public policy analyst's responsibility is to explore those conditions for which the behavior of bureaus is consistent with the goals of collective organizations and *not* to reject out of hand a motivational assumption that does not include these goals.

The survival argument reinforces the budget maximization assumption. Two groups of people significantly influence a bureaucrat's tenure in office:

the employees of the bureau and the officers of the collective organization. The reasons for their interest in budget maximization by the bureaucrat are different but reinforcing.

A bureau's employees (the suppliers of other factors should also be included in this group) indirectly influence a bureaucrat's tenure both through the bureaucrat's personal rewards and through the real and perceived performance of the bureau. They can be cooperative, responsive, and efficient, or they can deny information to the bureaucrat, undermine his directives, and embarass him before the constituency and officers of the collective organization—all depending on their perceived rewards of employment in the bureau. The employees' interests in larger budgets are obvious and similar to that of the bureaucrat: greater opportunities for promotion, more job security, etc., and more profits to the contract suppliers of factors. A bureaucrat's life is not a happy one (tra la) unless he can provide increasing budgets for his subordinate bureaucrats, in turn, to disburse in salaries and contracts.

The powers of the collective organization's over the bureaucrat's tenure are more obvious, but their interests in his budget maximization are not. These officers nominate and confirm the appointment of the bureaucrat and can force him to resign (few bureaucrats are openly fired), so they have direct control of his tenure. A point made forcefully by Wildavsky, however, is not generally understood: Both the executive and the legislative officers reviewing the bureau fully expect the bureaucrat aggressively to propose more activities and higher budgets. In fact, these officers would not otherwise know how to perform their review role.[8] They lack the time, the information, and the staff necessary to formulate new programs. They depend on the bureau to seek out and propose new programs and to make a case for larger expenditures in old programs. The total activities and budget of most bureaus are beyond comprehensive understanding, so the executive and legislative officers focus most of their review on the proposed *increments* and reveal their priorities by approving different proportions of these. At every stage of a multi-stage review process, the review officers are dependent on the bureaucrat's making a forceful case for his proposed budget, in part to determine whether a previous review has made too large a reduction. Any other behavior by the bureaucrat would reduce the information on which such reviews are made. In Wildavsky's words: 'If the agencies suddenly reversed roles and sold themselves short, the entire pattern of mutual expectations would be upset, leaving the participants without an anchor in a sea of complexity. For if agencies refuse to be advocates, congressmen would not only have to choose among the margins of the best programs placed before them, they would also have to discover what these good programs might be."[9]

8. Wildavsky, *The Politics of the Budgetary Process,* pp. 160–165.
9. Aaron Wildavsky, "Budgeting," *International Encyclopedia of the Social Sciences,* Vol. 2, p. 192.

From the viewpoint of Congress, one of the least popular bureaucrats in recent years was Secretary of Defense Robert McNamara who, for several years, proposed a stable budget and forcefully and effectively defended it against either reductions or increases. The major disagreement did not concern the decisions that were made, but that decisions were made within his department that Congressmen believed were their responsibility; some Congressmen purposefully attempted to discredit McNamara, usually by attacking his review staff. One gains the impression that "playing the game" is often more important in a bureaucratic environment than the value of the game. Also, as is demonstrated in Chapter 14, the secretary of any department is more likely to be in conflict with the legislative review committees the better he serves the interests of the President.

For some bureaucrats, for some time, budget maximization may not be a property of rational behavior (that is, consistent with the maximization of their utility), but the nature of a bureaucrat's relations with both the bureau's employees and sponsor are such that bureaucrats who do not maximize their budget will have an unusually short tenure. I do not, of course, claim paternity for the idea that bureaucrats act to maximize their bureau's budget. Indeed, the plausibility of "Parkinson's Law" is based on a popular belief that bureaus have an inherent tendency to grow.[10] This tendency is also central to Downs's study of bureaucracy. The personal rewards to a bureaucrat of a higher budget are recognized in a seminal article, by McKean, that also suggests that this motivation probably leads to the gradual expansion of central government.[11] Here, however, I place the assumption of budget maximization by bureaucrats in a rather simple formal model in order to develop the consequences of this assumption for the budget and output behavior of bureaus.

The Constraint on Budget Maximization

Budget maximization is a necessary but not sufficient statement of the central motivational assumption of this theory of supply by bureaus. What limits the size of bureaus? More specifically, what ultimately relates the available budget to the necessary costs?

In the classic theory of the firm, profit maximization is a sufficient motivational assumption, as this, by itself, leads to equating marginal revenues with marginal costs. Those models of the private firm that postulate some other maximand—like maximization of revenues, sales, or the manager's utility—necessarily include some constraint (usually, the

10. C. Northcote Parkinson, *Parkinson's Law and Other Studies in Administration* (Boston: Houghton Mifflin Co., 1962).

11. Roland N. McKean, "Divergencies between Individual and Total Costs within Government," *American Economic Review*, May 1964, pp. 243–249.

minimum necessary profits) to limit the size of the firm.[12] Although those models that assume that businessmen maximize something other than profits have not (yet) proved very valuable in explaining the behavior of private firms, the *form* of these models (maximizing some total variable subject to a constraint) is essential for any theory based on other than the maximization of some residual (like profits).[13]

The constraint that ultimately limits the size of bureaus is that a bureau, on the average, must supply that output expected by the sponsor on its approval of the bureau's budget. A bureau that consistently promises more than it can deliver will be penalized by the discounting of future promises and lower budgets. Conversely, a bureau that performs better than expected is likely to be rewarded by higher future budgets. As the output of most bureaus (even, sometimes, the *concept* of output) cannot be precisely determined, there will be substantial variance around the expected output. Also, a short-term bureaucrat who is an effective salesman (liar?) can often obtain a larger budget during his tenure by promising (usually, only implicitly) more output than the bureau can supply. Any bureau, in any budget period, may supply more or less than the expected output. Every bureau, over time, however, will be constrained to supply the output expected by the sponsor.

As there are no apparent reasons why the rewards and punishments to the bureaucrat of higher and lower output are asymmetric, this constraint will be expressed in terms of the expected output. If, in fact, the rewards and punishments are asymmetric, the constraint should be expressed in terms of some other level of confidence in achieving the output expected by the sponsor. The necessary condition for achieving the expected output is that the budget must be equal to or greater than the minimum total expected costs of supplying this level of output.

A complete statement of the central motivational assumption of this theory is the following: Bureaucrats maximize the total budget of their bureau during their tenure, subject to the constraint that the budget must be equal to or greater than the minimum total costs of supplying the output expected by the bureau's sponsor. Added to the earlier definition of bureaus and a description of their environment, this motivational assumption is the third critical element from which a theory of supply by bureaus is developed in the following eleven chapters.

---

12. A summary and interpretation of these models of the private firm is presented in Armen A. Alchian, "The Basis for Some Recent Advances in the Theory of Management of the Firm," *Journal of Industrial Economics* XIV (November 1965), 30–41.

13. Some recent statistical tests of the profit-maximizing and sales-maximizing assumptions concerning the motivations of corporate managers strongly support the view that profit-maximizing is still the best motivational assumption, even in large corporations. See Wilbur Lewellen and Blaine Huntsman, "Managerial Pay and Corporate Performance" *Economic Review*, September, 1970, pp. 710–720.

III

The Basic Model

5

Budget and Output Behavior

The Elementary Bureau

We first explore the behavior of a bureau, building on the instrumental constructs described in Chapters 2 through 4, for an elementary bureau. This bureau supplies one service, which is exchanged with a single sponsor for one budget. The bureau does not sell this service to market customers at a per-unit rate, so the budget approved by the sponsor constitutes the bureau's entire financing. In the general case the bureau purchases all factors at a competitive price. All necessary expenditures to supply this service are made during a single budget period.

The basic model is thus a one-period model of a "pure," single-service bureau which is a competitive purchaser of factors. We shall also explore the consequences of price discrimination in the factor market in this chapter. The consequences of changes in the other conditions will be explored in later chapters. At this stage, the bureau is considered to be a monopoly supplier of the service, but the sponsor is assumed not to exercise its potential monopoly power as a single buyer of the service, for either lack of incentive or opportunity; the consequences of relaxing this assumption will be explored in Chapter 14.

The total potential budget available to the bureau during the budget period is represented by the following budget-output function:

$$B = aQ - bQ^2, \quad 0 \leq Q < \frac{a}{2b}. \tag{5.1}$$

The minimum total cost during the budget period, given the competitive purchase of factors, is represented by the following cost-output function:

$$TC = cQ + dQ^2, \quad 0 \leq Q. \tag{5.2}$$

The constraint that the budget must be equal to or greater than the minimum

45

total cost is represented as follows:

$$B \geq TC \tag{5.3}$$

These two functions and the budget constraint constitute the complete model of the elementary bureau.

For these demand and cost conditions, the first task is to find the maximum level of budget that the sponsor will approve and the expected output of services that will be supplied by the bureau at the approved budget level.[1] With full consideration for the probable reductions made by the sponsor's review process, the bureaucrat will submit a budget-output proposal which maximizes the expected approved budget subject to the constraint that the approved budget must be sufficient to cover the costs of the output expected by the sponsor at that budget level.

The equilibrium level of the expected output of services at the approved budget level, for these conditions, is determined as follows: Maximization of B (by setting the first derivative of [5.1] equal to zero) leads to an upper level of $Q = \left[\dfrac{a}{2b} \right]$. The constraint (5.3) that B must be equal to or greater than TC leads to a lower level (by solving for the equality of [5.1] and [5.2] of $Q = \left[\dfrac{a-c}{b+d} \right]$. These two levels of Q are equal where $a = \left[\dfrac{2bc}{b-d} \right]$. For an elementary bureau which buys factors in a competitive market the equilibrium level of Q is where

$$Q \begin{cases} = \dfrac{a-c}{b+d} \text{ for a} < \dfrac{2bc}{b-d} \\[3ex] = \dfrac{a}{2b} \text{ for a} \geq \dfrac{2bc}{b-d} \end{cases} \tag{5.4}$$

Figure 5.1 illustrates these equilibrium levels of the output of a bureau for representative demand and cost conditions.

For the lower-demand conditions represented by the marginal valuation function V_1, the equilibrium output of a bureau will be in the "budget-

1. The budget and output proposed by the bureau will generally be higher than the approved levels. Under most conditions the bureau will propose a higher budget and output, consciously expecting the sponsor to reduce the proposed budget by a proportionate amount. The proportionate reductions made by the several review levels in the sponsor organizations are usually quite predictable. See Otto Davis, M. A. H. Dempster, and Aaron Wildavsky, "Theory of the Budgetary Process," *American Political Science Review* LX (1966). The stability of these proportionate reductions in the proposed budget allows a bureaucrat to plan a bureau's activities on the basis of an anticipated budget which is some proportion of the proposed budget. A bureau's proposed budget will be based on what the bureaucrat expects will be approved plus the normal reductions made by the sponsor's review. This book focuses on the approved budget and the output that will be supplied at that budget. The politics of the budgetary process, which generally reduce the proposed budgets, are fascinating and are richly documented by Wildavsky and others.

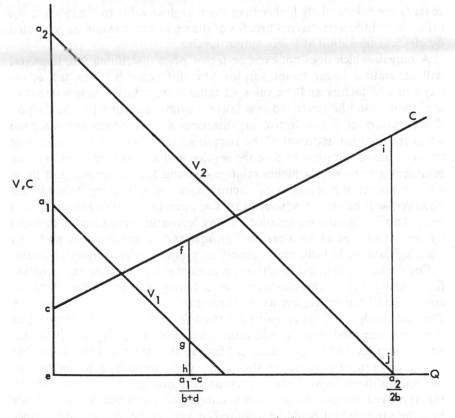

Figure 5.1   Equilibrium Output of a Bureau

constrained" region where the area of the polygon ea_1gh is equal to the
area of the polygon $ecfh$. At the equilibrium level of output, there is no
"fat" in this bureau; the total budget just covers the minimum total costs,
and no cost-effectiveness analysis would reveal any inefficiency. The output
of this bureau, however, is higher than the optimal level.[2] The equilibrium
level of output is in a region where the minimum achievable marginal

2. Some elaboration on my use of the terms "efficient" and "optimal" is necessary at this
point. A bureau's production behavior is efficient if it produces a given output at the minimum
possible cost; economists sometimes use the term "productive efficiency" to describe this
condition. A bureau's output behavior is optimal if the level of output generates the largest net
benefits; economists sometimes use the term "allocative efficiency" to describe this condition.
   In the budget-constrained equilibrium a bureau's behavior is efficient but not optimal. A cost-
effectiveness analysis, which addresses only the efficiency of the bureau's production behavior,
would not reveal any inefficiency. A (correct) cost-benefit study, which addresses only the
optimality of the bureau's output behavior, would indicate that the bureau's output is too large,
as the *marginal* benefit-cost ratio is less than unity, although, in this region, the total benefit-
cost ratio is just unity. For most public services, however, cost-benefit analysis is inherently
limited by the subjective nature of the benefits and because the marginal costs are not revealed
by the bureau's behavior.

costs *hf* are substantially higher than the marginal value to the sponsor *hg*, offsetting all the potential net benefits of the service that would be generated by efficient operation at lower output levels.

A bureau which does not exercise factor price discrimination, however, will generate a larger factor surplus (the difference between the actual payments to factors and the value of these factors in the best alternative use) than would be generated at a lower, optimal output.[3] In equilibrium, those officers of the collective organization who represent the marginal votes required for approval of the bureau's budget will be just indifferent between the equilibrium level of the service and a zero level. Officers who represent groups with a higher relative demand for the service and those who represent the interests of factors used in producing this service, however, will be strong advocates of the operation of the bureau at this level. This is a partial explanation of why legislatures are often dominated by representatives of high-demand groups and factor interests and why such legislatures, in turn, prefer supplying public services through bureaus.

For the higher-demand conditions represented by the marginal valuation function V_2, the equilibrium output of a bureau will be in the "demand-constrained" output region where the marginal value of output is zero. The total budget will be equal to the triangle ea_2j and will be larger than the minimum total costs of that output equal to the polygon *ecij*. At the equilibrium level of output, there is "fat" in this bureau. This bureau has no incentive to be efficient; on the contrary, it should be expected to seek out expenditures beyond those minimally required in order to exhaust the approved budget. A careful cost-effectiveness analysis would indicate that the same output could be achieved at a lower budget, but the analyst should expect no cooperation from the bureau, as it has no incentive either to know or to reveal its minimum cost function. In this region, the equilibrium output is constrained only by demand conditions, and no (small) change in cost conditions will change the budget. The output of this bureau is also higher than the optimal level, operating at an output level where the minimum marginal costs are equal to *ji* and the marginal value of the service is zero, again offsetting the potential net value of the service at lower output levels. The factor surplus generated by this bureau is also higher than would be generated at a lower, optimal output level.

A numerical example will be helpful at this point. Consider two elementary bureaus with different demand conditions but identical cost conditions. The functions and constraints for the two bureaus are as follows:

Bureau A

$$B_A = 100Q - .5Q^2, \, 0 \leq Q < 100 \qquad (5.5)$$

---

3. This factor surplus accrues to the specific factors used by the bureau. This is not a net surplus to the economy, however, as the additional expenditures for this service represent a diversion of resources from other services and, consequently, a lower factor surplus for factors specific to these services.

$$TC_A = 40Q + .25Q^2, 0 \le Q \tag{5.6}$$

$$B_A \ge TC_A \tag{5.7}$$

Bureau B

$$B_B = 200Q - .5Q^2, 0 \le Q < 200 \tag{5.8}$$

$$TC_B = 40Q + .25Q^2, 0 \le Q \tag{5.9}$$

$$B_B \ge TC_B \tag{5.10}$$

For both bureaus, the output threshold between the budget-constrained and demand-constrained output regions is $\left[\dfrac{2 \cdot (.5) \cdot 40}{.5 - .25} \right] = 160.$

For Bureau A, since $100 < 160$, the equilibrium output is in the budget-constrained region at a level of $\left[\dfrac{100 - 40}{.5 + .25} \right] = 80.$ The budget of Bureau A is $[100 \cdot 80 - .5 \cdot (80)^2] = 4800.$ The total minimum cost of the equilibrium output is $[40 \cdot 80 + .25(80)^2] = 4800$, just equal to the available budget. The average budget and costs per unit of service supplied are $\left[\dfrac{4800}{80} \right] = 60.$ The total factor surplus generated by Bureau A is $\left[\dfrac{.25}{2} (80)^2 \right] = 800.$

For Bureau B, since $200 > 160$, the equilibrium output is in the demand-constrained region at a level of $\left[\dfrac{200}{2 \cdot (.5)} \right] = 200.$ The total budget of Bureau B is $\left[\dfrac{(200)^2}{4 \cdot (.5)} \right] = 20,000.$ The total minimum cost of the equilibrium output level is $[40 \cdot 200 + .25(200)^2] = 18,000$, less than the available budget. The average budget per unit of service supplied is $\left[\dfrac{20,000}{200} \right] = 100$, although the minimum average cost is only $\left[\dfrac{18,000}{200} \right] = 90.$ The total factor surplus generated by Bureau B is $\left[\dfrac{.25}{2}(200)^2 \right] = 5,000.$ Bureau B, with a demand just twice that of Bureau A, has an output, budget, and factor surplus several times larger than Bureau A.

This initial analysis has produced several important hypotheses concerning the budget and output behavior of bureaus:

1. Given the demand for service represented by the collective organization, all bureaus are too large, that is, both the budget and output

of all bureaus will be larger than that which maximizes the net value to the sponsor.[4]

2. As a consequence of the overly large equilibrium output, all bureaus which purchase factors on a competitive market with rising supply prices generate a larger net value to the owners of specific factors used in the production of the bureau's services than would be the case at a lower, optimal output level.

3. Some bureaus, particularly new ones (for which the demand has only recently become higher than the minimum cost) and bureaus that are faced by a substantial exogenous increase in costs, supply the equilibrium level of services at the minimum possible budget. In contrast, other bureaus, particularly older ones (for which the demand has continuously increased relative to costs) and bureaus that are faced by a substantial exogenous reduction in costs, supply the equilibrium level of services at a budget higher than the minimum necessary costs.

The relative magnitude of these effects will be made more clear by comparison with other forms of organization and analysis of the consequences of changes in demand and cost conditions in Chapters 7 and 8.

The Bureau as a Discriminating Monopsonist

Bureaus which have the opportunity for factor price discrimination will have lower minimum costs for any output. For the same opportunity cost and production conditions reflected in (5.2), a bureau which is a discriminating monopsonist has the following cost-output function:

$$TC = cQ + -\frac{d}{2}Q^2, 0 \le Q. \qquad (5.11)$$

The complete model of an elementary bureau which is a discriminating monopsonist thus consists of budget-output function (5.1), the cost-output function (5.11), and the budget constraint (5.3).

For the same budget-output function (5.1), the demand-constrained output level will be the same, with or without factor price discrimination. In this region a bureau will probably not exploit the opportunity for factor price discrimination, both because it cannot increase either its budget or output by this practice, and so that it will avoid losing the support of those sponsor officers who represent factor interests. In the budget-constrained region, however, the equilibrium output (by solving the equality of [5.1] and [5.11])

---

4. The observed characteristic that bureaus are large organizations turns out to be a derivative characteristic of the bureaucratic form of organization. This is just the opposite from the inference drawn by sociologists that the bureaucratic form of organization is a derivative characteristic of large organizations.

will be higher with factor price discrimination at a level of $Q = \left[\dfrac{2(a-c)}{2b+d}\right]$.

In this case, the two levels of Q are equal where $a = \left[\dfrac{4bc}{2b-d}\right]$. For an elementary bureau that is a discriminating monopsonist, thus, the equilibrium level of Q is where

$$Q \begin{cases} = \dfrac{2(a-c)}{2b+d} & \text{for } a < \dfrac{4bc}{2b-d} \\[4mm] = \dfrac{a}{2b} & \text{for } a \geq \dfrac{4bc}{2b-d} \end{cases} \tag{5.12}$$

In the budget-constrained region, the difference between the equilibrium output and budget with and without factor price discrimination depends on how much factor prices increase with increasing output (indicated by the parameter d); the difference will be larger the more factor prices increase with output.

A numerical example will help illustrate these points. Consider two elementary bureaus with the same demand conditions, cost conditions, and constraints represented in (5.5) through (5.10), except that both bureaus have the opportunity for factor price discrimination. The new total cost function for both bureaus is

$$TC_C = TC_D = 40Q + \frac{.25}{2}Q^2, 0 \leq Q. \tag{5.13}$$

Bureau C, thus, is represented by (5.5), (5.13), and (5.7), and Bureau D is represented by (5.8), (5.13), and (5.9). For both bureaus, the threshold between the budget-constrained and demand-constrained output region is $\left[\dfrac{4(.5)40}{2(.5)-.25}\right] = 106.7$.

For Bureau C, since $100 < 106.7$, the equilibrium output is in the budget-constrained region at a level of $\left[\dfrac{2(100-40)}{2(.5)+.25}\right] = 96$. The budget of Bureau C is $[100 \cdot 96 - .5(96)^2] = 4992$, and the total minimum costs for this output are the same. The average budget and cost per unit of service supplied is 52. No factor surplus is generated by Bureau C. Notice that the output and budget of Bureau C are higher than Bureau A's, with the same demand conditions and the same opportunity cost of factors, although the average budget per unit of output is lower.

For Bureau D, since $200 > 106.7$, the equilibrium output is in the demand-constrained region. The output and budget of Bureau D is the same as Bureau B, unaffected by the opportunity for factor price discrimination. The minimum total costs are $\left[40 \cdot 200 + \dfrac{.25}{2}(200)^2\right] = 13,000$, lower than those for Bureau B by the amount of the factor surplus. Bureau D, however, will probably not exploit the opportunity for factor price discrimination; no one would be better off—the owners of factors would have less income, and the bureau would just have to find another way to spend the available budget.

It may initially seem paradoxical that budget-maximizing bureaus would exploit the opportunities for factor price discrimination. Such discrimination, however, permits a bureau to increase both output and budget. This is a risky practice for a bureau when the factor interests are strongly represented in the sponsor organization, as the bureau would then appropriate more of the potential net value to the sponsor of the bureau's activities; in this condition a bureau may not fully exploit the opportunities for factor price discrimination, in order to maintain the support of those sponsor officers who represent factor interests. When the owners of some factors subject to potential discrimination, such as draft-eligible young men and public-domain land, however, are not adequately represented in the collective organization, a bureau should be expected to exploit the opportunities for price discrimination among different units of these resources. This discrimination is usually rationalized by some collectivist concept of the rights of the state or the duties of the citizen. The difference in the attitudes toward military programs between young men and defense contractors may be substantially attributable to the specific use of the draft to command manpower resources.

This analysis of bureaus that are discriminating monopsonists leads to the following behavioral hypothesis:

> Some bureaus, specifically those that operate in the budget-constrained region and face increasing prices for specific factors, may exercise factor price discrimination. They have a larger budget and output of services (and a lower average budget per unit of output) than other bureaus with similar demand and cost conditions that pay competitive factor prices. Such factor price discrimination is most likely to be used on those specific factors which are weakly represented by the officers of the sponsor organization.

More complex bureaus than the elementary bureau discussed in this chapter may also be discriminating monopsonists. The general effects of factor price discrimination among the several types of bureaus, however, appear to be similar. Our discussion of the bureau which is a discriminating monopsonist, then, will be sufficient, and all further elaborations on the elementary bureau will assume the competitive purchase of factors.

6

Production Behavior

What combination of factors or processes will a bureau use to produce the equilibrium output of service? Does a budget-maximizing bureau have any incentive to be efficient? If so, under what conditions? These questions are investigated by considering an elementary bureau which can use either one or both of two processes that produce the same service. The model for this bureau is represented by the following equations and constraint:

$$B = a(Q_1+Q_2) - b(Q_1+Q_2)^2, 0\le(Q_1+Q_2)\le\frac{a}{2b}, \tag{6.1}$$

$$TC_1 = c_1Q_1+d_1Q_1{}^2, \quad 0\le Q_1, \tag{6.2}$$

$$TC_2 = c_2Q_2+d_2Q_2{}^2, 0\le Q_2, \text{ and} \tag{6.3}$$

$$B \ge TC_1+TC_2. \tag{6.4}$$

The production problem for a bureau is to find the level of the processes Q_1 and Q_2 that maximizes B, subject to the budget constraint (6.4).

Constrained maximization problems of this nature are best solved by the Lagrange multiplier method. For this problem this method involves formulating the function,

$$Z = a(Q_1+Q_2)-b(Q_1+Q_2)^2 - \lambda[a(Q_1+Q_2)$$
$$-b(Q_1+Q_2)^2-(c_1Q_1+d_1Q_1{}^2) \tag{6.5}$$
$$-(c_2Q_2+d_2Q_2{}^2)].$$

Differentiating this function with respect to Q_1 and Q_2 yields,

$$\frac{\delta Z}{\delta Q_1} = a-2bQ_1-2bQ_2-\lambda(a-2bQ_1-2bQ_2-c_1-2d_1Q_1) = 0 \tag{6.6}$$

and

$$\frac{\delta Z}{\delta Q_2} = a-2bQ_1-2bQ_2-\lambda(a-2bQ_1-2bQ_2-c_2-2D_2Q_2) = 0. \tag{6.7}$$

53

Solving the equality of (6.6) and (6.7) yields the budget–maximizing combination of Q_1 and Q_2:

$$Q_1 = \frac{c_2 - c_1}{2d_1} + \frac{d_2}{d_1} Q_2, 0 \leq Q_1, Q_2. \qquad (6.8)$$

This combination of processes Q_1 and Q_2, however, is also the minimum cost combination for any level of output, although no prior assumption is made that the bureau has any interest in efficiency. (This could be proved by minimizing $[TC_1 + TC_2]$ for any level of $[Q_1 + Q_2]$. The proof is simple and is not given.) At these values of Q_1 and Q_2, the marginal costs per unit of output of both processes are the same. This conclusion generalizes to any number of processes: the budget-maximizing combination of processes in the budget-constrained region, also the most efficient combination, is that for which the marginal cost per unit of output is equal for all processes used. The solution for Q_2 and B is found by substituting (6.8) for Q_1 in (6.1) and (6.2) and solving for the equality of budget and total costs.

This solution, however, applies only to a bureau for which the equilibrium output is in the budget-constrained region. For a bureau operating in the demand-constrained output region, the combination of processes used to produce the bureau's service is completely indeterminate within the range of costs necessary to remain in this region. The indeterminacy of production processes gives the bureau considerable discretion to use factors most strongly represented by the sponsor officers responsible for reviewing the bureau's activities. For example, without concern for the additional costs, installations may be located and contracts placed with companies located in the districts represented by the most important review officers. (A budget-constrained bureau would, at least, have mixed incentives about such activities.) This works to undermine the normal incentive of the review officers to detect and correct the inefficient behavior in the demand-constrained region.

It should be recognized that a budget-constrained bureau has a budget-maximizing incentive to use an efficent combination of only those factors and processes available to the bureau. If individual bureaus are not permitted to use the full range of substitute processes, they will maximize within the range of alternatives they have, and several bureaus using substitute processes will be efficient in combination only if the common review group has some incentive to be efficient. (The behavior of competitive bureaus reviewed by a common committee is discussed in Chapter 15.) The Department of Defense, for example, should not be expected to choose the most efficient combination of military and diplomatic processes to achieve national security objectives. The Department of Health, Education, and Welfare should not be expected to choose the most efficient combination of expenditure programs and tax provisions to achieve welfare goals. Educators should not be expected to choose the most efficient combination of vocational training and apprentice programs to improve labor skills. This problem is sometimes attributed to a doctrinal identification with certain production processes, but it is as easily explained by budget maximization by individual bureaus within a constrained range of production processes.

A recognition of this problem has often led to suggestions that the range of control of individual bureaus be expanded to include all substitute processes. Such suggestions reflect a misunderstanding of the primary problem of bureaucracy. A grouping of substitute processes into a single bureau increases the opportunity for the bureau to choose an efficient combination, but it also increases the bureau's monopoly power and the consequent oversupply of output. The combination of improved efficiency and more nearly optimal supply can better be achieved by other arrangements (more on this in Chapter 15).

Some elementary bureaus, specifically those that operate in the budget-constrained region, have a budget-maximizing incentive to seek out and use the minimum cost combination of factors or processes (available to the bureau) at the equilibrium level of output. The primary reason for concern about these bureaus is not that of efficiency in the supply of the equilibrium output (unless some dominant process is not available to the bureau), but that the output is too large. This conclusion is somewhat modified by the analysis in Chapter 10 concerning the effects of the time-distribution of expenditures. Other bureaus, specifically those that operate in the demand-constrained region, are indifferent to a wide range of factor or process combinations.

Several observers of bureaus have been intrigued by evidence that some bureaus manifest both economizing and spendthrift behavior, working diligently to find more efficent methods of producing some service and wasting a vast amount of resources on some other service. This analysis suggests that an elementary bureau with a single service will exhibit only one or the other of these characteristics, but a bureau which supplies more than one service may exhibit both characteristics.

These characteristics of the production behavior of a bureau will be better understood if we use a numerical example. Consider an elementary bureau with two possible production processes, represented by the following equations and constraint:

$$B = 150(Q_1 + Q_2) - .5(Q_1 + Q_2)^2, \quad 0 \leq Q_1 + Q_2 \leq 150, \quad (6.9)$$

$$TC_1 = 50Q_1 + .5Q_1^2, \qquad\qquad 0 \leq Q_1, \quad (6.10)$$

$$TC_2 = 75Q_2 + .25Q_2^2, \qquad\qquad 0 \leq Q_2, \quad and \quad (6.11)$$

$$B \geq TC_1 + TC_2. \quad (6.12)$$

First, let us consider the output and budget of this bureau if it used only one or the other of these processes. In either case, the output is in the budget-constrained region. If only process 1 is used, the output is $\left[\dfrac{150-50}{.5+.5}\right] = 100$. In this case, the budget is $[150(100)-.5(100)^2] = 10,000$, and the minimum total cost of this output is the same. The average budget and cost per unit of output is 100. The factor surplus generated by use of this process (if the costs increase as a result of increasing factor prices) is $\left[\dfrac{.5}{2}(100)^2\right] = 2500$. If only process 2 is used, the output is $\left[\dfrac{150-75}{.5+.25}\right] = 100$. The budget and minimum total costs are also 10,000, and the corresponding factor surplus is $\left[\dfrac{.25}{2}(100)^2\right] = 1250$. The average budget and cost per unit of output for process 2 is also 100. At this level of demand, the bureau would be indifferent about the use of one or the other of these processes. As sponsor officers representing factor interests, however, would probably prefer process 1, the bureau would probably choose this process to assure their support in the budget review.

Next, consider the output and budget of this bureau if both processes are used. From (6.8) the budget-maximizing combination of Q_1 and Q_2 is

$$Q_1 = \frac{75-50}{2(.5)} + \frac{.25}{.50}Q_2 = 25 + .5Q_2. \tag{6.13}$$

Substituting this expression for Q_1 in (6.9) yields

$$B = 150(25+.5Q_2+Q_2) - .5(25+.5Q_2+Q_2)^2 \tag{6.14}$$

$$= 3,437.5 + 187.5Q_2 - 1.125Q_2{}^2.$$

Substituting this expression for Q_1 in the sum of (6.10) and (6.11) yields

$$TC_1 + TC_2 = 50(25+.5Q_2) + .5(25+.5Q_2)^2 \tag{6.15}$$

$$+ 75Q_2 + .25Q_2{}^2$$

$$= 1562.5 + 112.5Q_2 + .375Q_2{}^2.$$

Solving for the equality of (6.14) and (6.15) yields the quadratic equation,

$$1.5Q_2{}^2 - 75Q_2 - 1875 = 0. \tag{6.16}$$

The larger root of (6.16), which is the budget-maximizing levels of Q_2, is 68.3. From (6.13), the budget-maximizing level of Q_1 is

$$Q_1 = 25 + .5(68.3) = 59.2. \tag{6.17}$$

Notice, in this case, that Q_2 (for which the marginal costs increase less rapidly) is larger than Q_1, although the same amount would be used in the single-process case. The sum of Q_1 and Q_2 is thus 127.5, compared to an output of 100 if only one or the other process is used. The total budget (and minimum total costs) at this output level is

$$[150(127.5) - .5(127.5)^2] = 10{,}996, \tag{6.18}$$

compared to a budget of 10,000 using only one process. The average budget and cost per unit of output is 86.2 compared to 100 if only one or the other process is used. Again, if the increasing costs are due only to increasing factor prices, the factor surplus generated by process 1 is $\left[\dfrac{.5}{2}(59.2)^2\right] = 875$, and the factor surplus generated by process 2 is $\left[\dfrac{.25}{2}(68.3)^2\right] = 583$ for a total factor surplus of 1458, smaller than if only process 1 is used and larger than if only process 2 is used. This numerical example is easily generalized to a case of more than two processes, but the qualitative conclusions are identical.

Budget maximization, for bureaus operating in the budget-constrained output region, is completely consistent with cost-minimizing production behavior at the equilibrium level of output. Efficient behavior by the bureau, in this condition, will increase both its budget and output and will reduce the average budget per unit of output. It will also lead to relatively greater use of factors or processes for which the marginal costs increase less rapidly (compared to the use of only one process) and may, consequently, reduce the factor surplus. This may lead some officers of the sponsor organization to discourage such behavior by bureaus.

It should be recognized that improved efficiency (reflected in the lower average budget per unit of output) will be realized *only* at a higher budget and output level, where the average and marginal value of the output is also lower. As long as a bureau can fully exploit its position as a monopoly supplier of a service, improvements in efficiency generate additional net benefits only to those who have the highest relative demands for the service. A bureau may substantially reward good managers and good analysts, but one should not necessarily expect any group other than those who have high demands for the service of the bureau itself to gain by their efforts. The most recent experiments in public administration —systems analysis and program-budgeting—are already part of the tools of the budget-maximizing bureaucrat.

This initial analysis of the production behavior of an elementary bureau leads to the following behavioral hypotheses:

> Some bureaus, specifically those in the budget-constrained output region, seek out and use the minimum cost combination of the available factors and processes to supply the equilibrium output. Factors or processes will be used in a combination such that the marginal cost per unit of output for all factors used will be the same. Improvements in

efficiency lead to both a higher budget and output, but to a lower average budget per unit of output. At the efficient combination of factors or processes relatively more of those processes for which the marginal costs increase less rapidly are used, compared to the use of only one process. Improvements in efficiency may generate either more or less factor surplus.

Some bureaus, specifically those in the demand-constrained output region, are characterized by indeterminate production behavior. These bureaus may or may not use efficient combinations of factors or processes, but there is no incentive inherent in the bureaucratic form that leads them to seek out and use efficent combinations. For these bureaus, more efficient factor combinations will not lead to any change in their budget, output, or factor surplus.

Further consideration of an elementary bureau's production behavior is included in the analysis of the effects of demand and cost changes in Chapter 8, and in the analysis of the effects of the time-distribution of costs presented in Chapter 12.

7

Comparison of
Organizational Forms

A better understanding of the consequences of the bureaucratic organization of economic activity can be gained by comparing them with the consequences of other forms of organization that face the same demand and
cost conditions. The relevance of this comparison, of course, is based on
the assumption that a collective organization could potentially purchase
the desired service from any one of the several types of profit-seeking
firms and bureaus. The potential use of profit-seeking firms to supply these
services is primarily dependent on contracting and monitoring problems
rather than on any inherent limitation of the type of goods and services
that can be supplied by such firms. For this comparison, also, the sponsor
organization is assumed to be unable to exercise its power as a monopoly
buyers of these services.

Demand and Cost Conditions

Consider the behavior of several types of organizations facing the following demand and cost conditions: The collective organization's demand for
some service is represented by the budget-output function

$$B = 200Q - .5Q^2, \quad 0 \le Q < 200. \tag{7.1}$$

The minimum total costs of producing this service, in the absence of factor
price discrimination, are represented by the cost-output function

$$TC = 75Q + .25Q^2, \quad 0 \le Q. \tag{7.2}$$

If the increasing marginal cost is attributable only to the increasing price of
specific factors, those profit-seeking and bureaucratic monopolies which
exercise factor price discrimination will face minimum total costs represented
by the cost-output function

$$TC = 75Q + .125Q^2, 0 \le Q. \tag{7.3}$$

59

Some more familiar functions derived from the above include the following: The marginal valuation or demand function faced by a profit-seeking monopoly or competitive industry is

$$V = 200 - 1.00Q, 0 \le 200. \tag{7.4}$$

The total revenue function of the profit-seeking monopoly is

$$VQ = R = 200Q - 1.00Q^2, 0 \le Q < 200. \tag{7.5}$$

The average cost function of a profit-seeking monopoly which is not a discriminating monopsonist, the marginal cost function of a discriminating monopsonist, and the long-run supply function of a competitive industry is

$$C = 75 + .25Q, 0 \le Q. \tag{7.6}$$

These functions provide sufficient quantitative information for a static comparison of the behavior of several forms of organization. The equilibrium conditions for a profit-seeking monopoly and competitive industry are provided by the classic theory of the (profit-seeking) firm. The equilibrium conditions for bureaus are described in Chapters 5 and 6.

Equilibrium Conditions

A profit-seeking monopoly supplies an output at a price which maximizes profits or *net* revenues, in this case, the difference between (7.5) and either (7.2) or (7.3). For a profit-seeking monopoly that is not a discriminating monopsonist, the net revenues are

$$R - TC = (200 - 75)Q - (1.00 + .25)Q^2, 0 \le Q \le 200. \tag{7.7}$$

The equilibrium output of this monopoly is the value of Q that maximizes (7.7). This value is found by setting the first derivative of (7.7) equal to zero and solving for Q; the reader can verify that the equilibrium output of this monopoly, given these demand and cost conditions, is 50. Similarly, a profit-seeking monopolist that is also a discriminating monopsonist will supply an output which maximizes the difference between (7.5) and (7.3). The equilibrium output of this monopoly is found by the same method and, in this case, is 55.6.

A group of profit-seeking competitive firms supplies an output such that the demand price equals the supply price, in this case, the level of Q for which (7.4) and (7.6) are equal. For

$$200 - 1.00Q = 75 + .25Q, \tag{7.8}$$

the value of Q and the equilibrium output supplied by a competitive industry are 100.

A bureau, according to the theory developed here, supplies an output which maximizes the approved budget subject to the constraint that the budget must be equal to or greater than the minimum total costs. Then equilibrium output of a bureau will be either the value of Q that maximizes (7.1) (if the bureau is in the demand-constrained region) or the value of Q for which (7.1) and either (7.2) or (7.3) are equal (if the bureau is in the budget-constrained region). In this case the equilibrium output of a bureau which pays competitive factor prices is in the budget-constrained region as

$200 < \left[\dfrac{2(.5)75}{.5 - .25} \right] = 300$. The value of Q for which (7.1) and (7.2) are equal and,

thus, the equilibrium output of this bureau, is $\left[\dfrac{200 - 75}{.5 + .25} \right] = 166.7$. Similarly,

in this case a bureau that is also a discriminating monopsonist is just at the margin of the budget-constrained and demand-constrained output

regions as $200 = \left[\dfrac{2(.5)75}{.5 - .125} \right]$. The value of Q that maximizes (7.1) as well as

the value of Q for which (7.1) and (7.3) are equal and, thus, the equilibrium output of this bureau which is also a discriminating monopsonist is

$$\left[\frac{200}{2(.5)} \right] = \left[\frac{200 - 75}{.5 + .125} \right] = 200. \tag{7.9}$$

Output and Budget Comparisons

Table 7.1 presents the equilibrium output and several related variables for the several types of organizations facing the above demand and cost

Table 7.1 Equilibrium levels of output and other variables for several forms of organization facing the same demand and cost conditions

Product Market	Monopoly		Competitive	Bureau	
factor price	uniform	discriminating	uniform	uniform	discriminating
Equilibrium values					
Output	50	55.6	100	166.7	200
Revenues					
Total	$7,500	$8,025	$10,000	$19,444	$20,000
Average	150	144.4	100	116.7	100
Marginal	100	88.9	100	33.3	0
Costs					
Total	4,375	4,553	10,000	19,444	20,000
Average	87.5	81.9	100	116.7	100
Marginal	100	88.9	100	158.3	125
Profits	3,125	3,472	0	0	0
Collective surplus	1,250	1,543	5,000	0	0
Factor surplus	313	0	1,250	3,472	0

conditions. Definitions of several terms may improve the reader's understanding of the table. The term "profits" refers to the net revenues in addition to the minimum payments to the managers and owners of capital necessary to maintain their employment by the firm. The term "collective surplus" suggests a traditional meaning to economists, but in this case refers to the difference between what the collective organization, given its alternatives and internal decision rules, would be willing to pay for the equilibrium level of service and what it in fact pays to the organization supplying the service. (The concept of the net benefits accruing to the collective organization and the distribution of these net benefits is clarified in Chapter 14.) The equilibrium levels of output are in units of service supplied to the collective organization. The equilibrium levels of the other variables are all in monetary units, such as thousands of dollars.

The traditional concern about profit-seeking monopolies is that they supply too little output. It has long been known that a profit-seeking monopoly which pays competitive factor prices and faces linear demand and marginal cost functions will supply an equilibrium output just one-half of that supplied by a competitive industry facing the same demand and cost conditions. At the equilibrium level of output by the profit-seeking monopolist, the marginal value of the service to the collective organization (which equals the average revenue to the monopoly) is higher than the marginal cost to the monopoly. An increase of output beyond the profit-maximizing level, therefore, would increase the total net value of the service. For these demand and cost conditions a profit-seeking monopoly that pays competitive factor prices would generate a sum of profit plus collective surplus around 88 percent of that generated by a competitive industry. A profit-seeking monopoly that exercises some factor price discrimination will absorb some of the factor surplus, supply a somewhat larger output, and generate somewhat larger profits and collective surplus.

At the equilibrium level of output by a competitive industry, the marginal value of the service to the collective organization (which equals both the average and marginal revenue to the competitive firm) is equal to the marginal cost (and, in industry equilibrium, the average cost) to the competitive firm. This level of output maximizes the sum of the net value of the service to the collective organization and the owners of factors. For this reason, for most purposes, the competitive supply of a service is the norm against which the supply by other forms of organization should be judged.

For these demand and cost conditions, a bureau that pays competitive factor prices will supply an equilibrium output around two-thirds *higher* than a competitive industry. At this level of output, the marginal value of the service to the collective organization (which equals the marginal budget to the bureau) is lower than the marginal cost to the bureau. A reduction of the output from this budget-maximizing level would thus increase the total net value of the service. This bureau will generate no profits and no net benefits to the collective organization. At the higher output level, however, the bureau generates a much larger factor surplus than a competitive industry.

For these conditions, a bureau that fully exploits the opportunities for factor price discrimination (in effect, one which discriminates on both the product and factor market) will supply an output twice that of a competitive industry and will generate no net value to either the sponsor or to owners of factors[1] It is interesting to note that, from revealed behavior, this bureau appears to be as efficient as a competitive industry, that is, it supplies the service at the same average cost to the collective organization. This level of average cost, however, is realized only at an output level twice that of the competitive industry, and at this level the marginal value is zero and is much lower than the marginal cost to the bureau. Let us say again that the main reason for concern about bureaus (in the budget-constrained region) is not efficiency at the equilibrium level of output, but the oversupply of services.

Supply and Cost Conditions

A comparison of the supply and cost conditions is also helpful. A profit-seeking monopoly has no supply function; it will sell output at a uniform price such that the marginal revenue equals marginal cost. A bureaucratic monopoly also has no separate supply function; it exchanges increments of output for the marginal value of each increment to the collective organization up to an output level such that the minimum total costs exhaust the available budget or the marginal value of the increment is zero. In effect, a bureau's supply function is identical to the sponsor's demand function up to the point of equilibrium output and is undefined beyond that. In a sense, a bureau also has no separate marginal cost function. The incremental payment to factors will be the same as the marginal value to the collective organization, because the difference between this value and the minimum incremental cost at the equilibrium level of output will be financed from the collective surplus appropriated at lower output levels. Only if a bureau is efficient at lower output levels, for whatever reason, is the incremental payment to factors equal to the minimum marginal cost.

One implication of this condition is that an analyst may not be able to identify a bureau's minimum cost function from proposed budget and output combinations. All this would yield is a bureau's estimate of its sponsor's marginal valuation function. In the static case all bureaus appear to have declining marginal costs (because the proposed budget and output combinations are based on the bureau's estimate of the sponsor's marginal valuation function) and, in a sense, they do—independent of the slope of the

---

1. These conclusions are clarified and somewhat modified in Chapter 14.

minimum marginal cost function[2] An estimate of a budget-constrained bureau's minimum marginal cost function may conceivably be made by comparing two bureaus which supply the same service or by comparing the actual budget and output of a bureau over time (more on this later). An estimate of a demand-constrained bureau's minimum marginal cost function, however, must be constructed from detailed estimates of the production function and factor costs, creating an extraordinary demand for analysis under conditions in which the bureau has no incentive to cooperate in providing the relevant information.

In summary, for different reasons, both profit-seeking and bureaucratic monopolies operate in output regions that are non-optimal. The substitution of a bureau for a profit-seeking monopoly, however, solves few problems. Such a substitution would redistribute income from the owners of the monopoly and those who finance the collective organization to those with relatively high demands for the service and to the owners of specific factors, but would reduce the aggregate net value of the service.

Behavioral Hypotheses

This static comparison of the budget and output behavior of an elementary bureau with that of profit-seeking forms of organization leads to the following hypotheses:

1. A bureau will supply an output up to twice that of a competitive industry faced by the same demand and cost conditions.
2. At the equilibrium level of output, a bureau will generate smaller net benefits than a competitive industry but, in the absence of factor price discrimination, a larger factor surplus. This suggests that the owners of specific factors will be stronger advocates of the bureaucratic supply of a service than will most beneficiaries of the service[3]
3. At the equilibrium level of output, a bureau may appear to be nearly as efficient as a competitive industry (in terms of average cost per unit of output), but this average cost is realized only at the higher output level, where the marginal value of the service is less than the marginal cost.

---

2. Again, an incorrect inference may have been generally drawn from the observed behavior of bureaus. Some economists have inferred from the apparently declining marginal costs of bureaus that a bureaucratic form of organization may be necessary to supply serivices for which the marginal costs are declining. This analysis suggests that the supply of *any* service by a bureau will suggest declining marginal costs—regardless of the slope of the minimum marginal cost function!

3. The early opposition of the U.S. postal unions to the creation of a postal corporation is one recent example. The continuing opposition of professors and public school teachers to profit-seeking schools is a more long-standing example of such self-serving behavior.

4. The minimum marginal cost function of a bureau, like that of a profit-seeking monopoly, will not be revealed by its budget and output proposals. The budget and output combinations proposed by a bureau will suggest that marginal costs decline with output, regardless of the slope of the minimum marginal costs.

8

Effects of Changes in Demand and Cost Conditions

Basis for Evaluating the Effects of Changes

The equilibrium conditions for a bureau, for given demand and cost conditions, provide the basis for evaluating the effects of changes in these conditions. Similarly, the equilibrium conditions for a competitive industry, for the same demand and cost conditions, provide the basis for comparing the effects of the same demand and cost changes on bureaus and on a competitive industry.

A brief review of some of our earlier discussion provides the model for evaluating and comparing these marginal effects. This evaluation is specific to an elementary bureau that pays competitive factor prices and, again, that faces a passive sponsor. Let us consider again the model of the elementary bureau represented by the following functions and constraint:

$$B = aQ - bQ^2, \ 0 \le Q < \frac{a}{2b}, \tag{8.1}$$

$$TC = cQ - dQ^2, \ 0 \le Q, \text{ and} \tag{8.2}$$

$$B \ge TC. \tag{8.3}$$

Table 8.1 summarizes the equilibrium output and budget, for these demand and cost conditions, of a budget-constrained bureau, a demand-constrained bureau, and a competitive industry.

As we have demonstrated, the equilibrium output and budget of a bureau are higher than for a competitive industry facing the same demand and cost conditions. In the case of constant marginal costs ($d = 0$), both the equilibrium output and the budget of a bureau are just twice that of a competitive industry. The effects of changes in demand and cost conditions are demonstrated in this chapter by evaluating the derivatives of the equilibrium conditions presented in Table 8.1 and by graphical display of some numerical examples.

66

Table 8.1 Equilibrium output and budget conditions

	Q	B
Bureau		
Budget-Constrained		
$a < \dfrac{2bc}{b-d}$ $\left.\begin{array}{l} d \neq o \end{array}\right.$	$\dfrac{a-c}{b+d}$	$\left(\dfrac{a^2-ac}{b+d}\right) - \left(\dfrac{a^2b-2abc+bc^2}{b^2+2bd+d^2}\right)$
$d = 0$	$\dfrac{a-c}{b}$	$\dfrac{ac-c^2}{b}$
Demand-Constrained		
$a \geq \dfrac{2bc}{b-d}$	$\dfrac{a}{2b}$	$\dfrac{a^2}{4b}$
Competitive Industry		
$d \neq 0$	$\dfrac{a-c}{2b+d}$	$\left(\dfrac{a^2-ac}{2b+d}\right) - \left(\dfrac{2a^2b-4abc+2bc^2}{4b^2+4bd+d^2}\right)$
$d = 0$	$\dfrac{a-c}{2b}$	$\dfrac{ac-c^2}{2b}$

Demand Shifts

A uniform shift in the demand or marginal valuation function for a service is represented by a change in the parameter a. The general effects of a shift in the demand for a service on the output and budget of a bureau and a competitive industry are given in algebraic terms in Table 8.2.

In the budget-constrained region, the output of a bureau will increase by an amount equal to a constant $\left(\dfrac{1}{b+d}\right)$ times the demand increase. The rate of increase in the output of a bureau will always be higher than for a competitive industry for the same conditions. The output (and budget) of a bureau with constant marginal costs $(d = 0)$ will grow at twice the rate of a competitive industry. The budget per unit of output, for both a bureau and a competitive industry, will increase only by the amount of the increase in minimum unit costs. (For $d = 0$, the second derivative of the budget with respect to the demand shift is zero.)

In the demand-constrained region, the output of a bureau will increase by an amount equal to a constant $\left(\dfrac{1}{2b}\right)$ times the demand increase. This rate of increase of a bureau's output will generally be higher than for a competitive industry; for constant marginal costs, however, the rate of increase of a bureau's output in this region will be equal to that of a competitive industry. A bureau's budget per unit of output increases continuously with increasing demand, independent of the characteristics of the minimum marginal cost function.

Table 8.2 Effects of a demand shift

	Q	B
Bureau		
Budget-Constrained		
$a < \dfrac{2bc}{b-d}$ $\begin{cases}\dfrac{\partial Q}{\partial a}, \dfrac{\partial B}{\partial a}\end{cases}$	$\dfrac{1}{b+d}$	$\left(\dfrac{2a-c}{b+d}\right) - \left(\dfrac{2ab-2bc}{b^2+2bd+d^2}\right)$
$\dfrac{\partial^2 Q}{\partial a}, \dfrac{\partial^2 B}{\partial a}$	0	$\left(\dfrac{2}{b+d}\right) - \left(\dfrac{2b}{b^2+2bd+d^2}\right)$
Demand-Constrained		
$a \geq \dfrac{2bc}{b-d}$ $\begin{cases}\dfrac{\partial Q}{\partial a}, \dfrac{\partial B}{\partial a}\end{cases}$	$\dfrac{1}{2b}$	$\dfrac{a}{2b}$
$\dfrac{\partial^2 Q}{\partial a}, \dfrac{\partial^2 B}{\partial a}$	0	$\dfrac{1}{2b}$
Competitive Industry		
$\dfrac{\partial Q}{\partial a}, \dfrac{\partial B}{\partial a}$	$\dfrac{1}{2b+d}$	$\left(\dfrac{2a-c}{2b+d}\right) - \left(\dfrac{4ab-4bc}{4b^2+4bd+d^2}\right)$
$\dfrac{\partial^2 Q}{\partial a}, \dfrac{\partial^2 B}{\partial a}$	0	$\left(\dfrac{2}{2b+d}\right) - \left(\dfrac{4b}{4b^2+4bd+d^2}\right)$

These effects of an increase in demand on the output and budget of a bureau, for a specific numerical example, are illustrated by Figure 8.1. For this example, the threshold of budget-constrained and demand-constrained regions is at a value of $a = 300$.

A bureau, like a profit-seeking monopoly, will often find it rewarding to attempt to shift its demand function. The increased budget that would result from a demand shift is particularly high in the demand-constrained output region. And the costs of such promotional activity for a bureau are relatively low, as it can focus its efforts on the small number of officers of the sponsoring organization rather than on the general beneficiaries of the service supplied. One would expect bureaucrats to spend a significant part of their time on various promotional activities, primarily with respect to their bureau's sponsor, supported by those who have the highest relative demand for the service and the owners of specific factors used by the bureau. These partial effects of demand shifts also suggest that government expenditures are likely to be one of the more variable components of national economic activity.

The effects of demand shifts on the output and budget of a specific bureau are in addition to the more aggregative self-generating increases, due to a general increase in the bureaucracy, which have concerned several scholars. Ludwig von Mises expressed a prevalent concern about the political consequences in a democracy of the government's employing a substantial proportion of the labor force; he felt that legislators who represented

Figure 8.1   Effects of Increased Demand

concentrations of public employees and owners of other factors used by the government could not be expected to exercise a critical review of the bureaucracy.[1]

More recently an interesting argument has surfaced from the controversy concerning the U.S. "military-industrial complex": At the margin of high military expenditures, it is probably *easier* for a bureaucrat responsible for a civil program to increase his budget, as this increase would require a smaller proportionate increase in taxes. Similarly, large civil expenditures may make it easier to increase the military budget. This phenomenon, understandably, causes some ambivalence on the part both of those who favor and of those who oppose a transfer of tax revenues from military to civil programs. Representative governments are probably either spenders or economizers, and a substantial transfer of tax revenues from one use to another may not be politically feasible.

One other self-generating effect of a general increase in the bureaucracy

1. Von Mises, *Bureaucracy,* p. 81.

appears not to have been noticed: An increase in the bureaucracy that requires an increase in tax rates probably also increases the supply of bureaucrats. Taxes, remember, are levied against personal money income which is the dominant form of compensation in profit-seeking organizations. An increase in taxes reduces the relative rewards of managing a profit-seeking organization compared to the rewards, more of which are not taxed, of managing a bureau, and this should increase the supply of bureaucrats for any monetary salary.

These more aggregative causes of the size and growth of bureaus and bureaucracy are beyond the scope of this book. They are, nonetheless, a reason for serious concern. This brief discussion suggests that the equilibrium conditions for the bureaucracy as a whole are more complex and, possibly, less stable than those for individual bureaus.

Changes in the Demand Slope

A change in the slope of the demand or marginal valuation function for a service is represented by a change in the parameter b. A low value of this parameter represents a relatively "elastic" demand for the service, and a high value represents a relatively "inelastic" demand. An increase in b thus reduces the "elasticity" of the demand for the service. The partial derivatives of the equilibrium output and budget of a bureau with respect to b are difficult to interpret because an increase in b, for a given value of a, reduces both the elasticity and the absolute level of demand; for this reason no table of the partial derivatives with b is presented. The separate effect of a reduction in the elasticity of demand, for a given absolute level of demand, is best evaluated by increasing both a and b by amounts which, in effect, rotate the demand function in a clockwise direction around the point of the competitive equilibrium. The effects of a rotation of the demand function on the output and budget of a bureau, for a specific numerical example, are illustrated by Figure 8.2. The indicated combinations of the parameters a and b are such that the output of a competitive industry, for the same cost conditions, would be constant at a level of 100 for each combination; the total revenues and costs of a competitive industry would also be constant at a level of 10,000. For this example, the threshold of the budget-constrained and demand-constrained output region is at the combination of $a = 236.7$ and $b = .683$.

A bureau that faces a highly elastic demand function (a low value of b) produces an output only slightly higher than a competitive industry at a budget per unit of output that is also only slightly higher. In the budget-constrained output region, the equilibrium output of a bureau will increase in response to a reduced elasticity of demand. The budget per unit of output will increase only by the amount of the increase of the minimum unit costs.

In the demand-constrained region, the equilibrium output of a bureau

Figure 8.2   Effects of Reduced Elasticity of Demand

will decline in response to a reduced elasticity of demand, the total budget will increase, and the budget per unit of output will increase rapidly— independent of the characteristics of the cost function. The effect of a reduced elasticity of demand may be the best explanation of the observations which led to "Parkinson's Law."[2] Parkinson observed that the staffs of the British Admiralty and Colonial Office increased over a period during which there was an obvious reduction in output. He interpreted this as indicating that bureaus grow exponentially with time, independent of the demand for their output. No purpose is served by being stuffy about "Parkinson's Law" because it reflects an important insight; the corollary

2. Parkinson, *Parkinson's Law and Other Studies in Administration.* This book includes a number of important insights about bureaucracy but, unfortunately, Parkinson's wit and large lay readership have made it too easy for scholars to overlook or discount his insights.

about bureaus, however, has an ambiguous theoretical basis and is not consistent with the behavior of many bureaus. The same phenomenon— declining output and increasing staff (and budget)—may be best inter- preted as the special case of the response of a demand-constrained bureau to a reduced elasticity of demand for its services.

The total budget of a bureau will increase monotonically, in both output regions, with reductions in the elasticity of demand—under conditions in which both the output and budget of a competitive industry are constant. This suggests that a bureau could often find it rewarding to try to reduce the elasticity of the demands for its service by promotional activities which suggest that there is a public "need" or a military "requirement" that must be met at all costs. (Can you imagine a public discussion about collective programs being carried on without the use of these terms?) The acceptance of a "requirement" for a service by the sponsor organization, however, will assure both that the required output will not be achieved and that the budget will truly be "at all costs." A more important suggestion is that an individual bureau operating in a highly competitive output market (for which the elasticity of demand to any one bureau providing a service is high) would both supply a nearly optimal level of output at an efficient budget per unit of output. However, the present environment of bureau- cracy—with severe constraints on the creation of new bureaus or new services by existing bureaus, and the passion of public administration reformers to consolidate bureaus with similar services—seems diabolically designed to reduce the competition among bureaus and to increase the inefficiency and, not incidentally, the budget of the bureaucracy.

Cost Shifts

A uniform shift in the minimum marginal cost function for a service is represented by a change in the parameter c. The general effects of a shift in the minimum costs for a service on the output and budget of a bureau and a competitive industry are given in algebraic terms in Table 8.3.

In the budget-constrained region, the effects of a cost shift on the output and budget of a bureau are almost symmetric with the effects of a demand shift. The output of a bureau will increase by an amount equal to a constant $\left(\dfrac{1}{b+d}\right)$ times the reduction in parameter c. The output of a bureau for which the minimum marginal costs are constant ($d = 0$) will grow at twice the rate of a competitive industry for the same downward shift in costs. The budget of a bureau will initially increase quite rapidly and then less rapidly for equal successive reductions in the parameter c. The budget per unit output will not decline so much as the shift in the cost function, because of the induced in- crease in output. In the demand-constrained region, further reductions in the

Table 8.3 *Effects of a cost shift*

	Q	B
Bureau		
Budget-Constrained		
$a < \dfrac{2bc}{b-d}$ $\begin{cases} \dfrac{\partial Q}{\partial c}, \dfrac{\partial B}{\partial c} \end{cases}$	$-\dfrac{1}{b+d}$	$-\left(\dfrac{a}{b+d}\right)+\left(\dfrac{2ab-2bc}{b^2+2bd+d^2}\right)$
$\dfrac{\partial^2 Q}{\partial c}, \dfrac{\partial^2 B}{\partial c}$	0	$-\dfrac{2b}{b^2+2bd+d^2}$
Demand-Constrained		
$a \geq \dfrac{2bc}{}\begin{cases} \dfrac{\partial Q}{\partial c}, \dfrac{\partial B}{\partial c} \end{cases}$	0	0
Competitive Industry		
$\dfrac{\partial Q}{\partial c}, \dfrac{\partial B}{\partial c}$	$-\dfrac{1}{2b+d}$	$-\left(\dfrac{a}{2b+d}\right)+\left(\dfrac{4ab-4bc}{4b^2+4bd+d^2}\right)$
$\dfrac{\partial^2 Q}{\partial c}, \dfrac{\partial^2 B}{\partial c}$	0	$-\dfrac{4b}{4b^2+4bd+d^2}$

minimum costs will not increase either the equilibrium output or the budget. These effects of a shift in the minimum cost function on the output and budget of a bureau, for a specific numerical example, are illustrated by Figure 8.3. For this example, the threshold of the budget-constrained and demand-constrained output regions is at a value of $c = 50$.

These effects suggest that a new bureau (for which the parameter a has just recently become larger than the parameter c) will be very cost-conscious, because a bureau's budget is very sensitive to costs when a is only slightly larger than c. Those new bureaus that are successful in achieving some reduction in costs will experience a rapid increase in their budgets.[3] Because subsequent reductions in costs do not increase a bureau's budget by so much as the initial reduction, an older bureau will have less incentive to identify and implement further possible cost reductions. These effects also suggest that a bureau subject to an exogenous increase in costs will become more cost-conscious because the sensitivity of a bureau's budget to costs increases as c increases relative to a. The characteristic purging of the overhead staff when demand falls or costs increase is a manifestation of this effect; these reductions in staff could have been made earlier, but the incentives for a bureau to economize are lower when demand is high relative to costs. Once a bureau has reached the demand-constrained output

3. The rapid growth of some new bureaus has also been observed by Downs, but he explains this growth as the consequence of the initial domination of a new bureau by zealots and by the desire to achieve an "initial survival threshold." See Downs. *Inside Bureaucracy*, p. 9 *et seq.* I don't find Downs's explanation very satisfactory. Most new bureaus are dominated by zealots, and some don't grow. Downs also does not explain what determines the initial survival threshold for a specific bureau.

Figure 8.3   Effect of Increased Costs

region, it becomes completely uninterested in any potential cost reductions and insensitive to any cost increases which do not reduce output below this region. Again, a bureau supplying a single service will be in one or the other of these conditions. A bureau supplying several services, such as the Department of Defense, should be expected to attempt to reduce costs on the budget-constrained services and to assure that expenditures are sufficiently high to exhaust the obtainable budget on demand-constrained services.

Changes in the Slope of the Minimum Marginal Cost Function

A change in the slope of the minimum marginal cost function for a service is represented by a change in the parameter d. A low value of this parameter represents a relatively elastic minimum marginal cost function, and a high value represents a relatively inelastic function. An increase in d thus reduces the elasticity of the minimum marginal cost function. As with the parameter b, the partial derivatives of the output and budget of a bureau with respect to d are difficult to interpret, because an increase in d, for a given value of c, both reduces the elasticity and increases the absolute value of the minimum marginal costs. The separate effect of a reduction in the elasticity of this function, for a given absolute level of minimum costs, is best demonstrated by reducing c and increasing d by amounts that, in effect, rotate the minimum marginal cost function in a counterclockwise direction around the point of competitive equilibrium. The effects of such a rotation of the minimum marginal cost function on the output and budget of a bureau, for a specific numerical example, are illustrated by Figure 8.4. The indicated combinations of the parameters c and d are such that the output of a competitive industry, for the same demand conditions, would be constant at a level of 100 for each combination. The total revenues and costs of a competitive industry would also be constant at a level of 10,000. For this example, the threshold between the budget-constrained and demand-constrained output regions is at a combination of $c = 100$ and $d = 0$.

In the budget-constrained region, the equilibrium output of a bureau

PARAMETERS

$a = 200$
$b = 0.5$
$c = $ VARIABLE
$d = $ VARIABLE

Figure 8.4   Effects of Reduced Elasticity of Marginal Costs

which pays competitive factor prices will decline in response to an increase in the slope of the minimum marginal cost function, under conditions where the output of a competitive industry would be constant. A bureau's budget will also decline in response to a (compensated) increase in parameter d, but relatively slowly. (Over the range indicated in Figure 8.4, a bureau's output would decline by 40 percent and the budget by only 16 percent.) The budget per unit of output would thus increase in response to a higher slope of this function. Both the output and budget of a bureau are invariant to changes in the slope of the minimum marginal cost function in the demand-constrained region.

These effects suggest that a bureau may have an incentive to use production processes with a higher marginal cost at lower output levels and a lower marginal cost at higher output levels. (This is also demonstrated in the earlier section on production behavior. As shown in Chapter 12, this effect is also reinforced by the effects of the time-distribution of costs.) The increased budget that would be generated by a reduction in the slope of the minimum marginal cost function, however, is small, and this incentive may be offset by pressure from those sponsor officers who represent the interests of specific factors. Again, in the demand-constrained region, a bureau's response to changes in production and cost conditions is indeterminate.

The conduct of the war in Viet Nam by the U.S. military may be an example of these effects. My impression is that the initial conduct of the war in 1965 reflects the effects specific to the budget-constrained region. In this period, the U.S. commander committed the dominant proportion of his resources to the logistic base and to combat-support forces; this strategy had higher marginal costs at low output levels and lower marginal costs at higher output levels. By 1967 the war appeared to have moved into the demand-constrained region; production behavior was both indeterminate and most inefficient, and the marginal value of output to the sponsor was zero. Beginning in March 1968, the war appears to have returned to the budget-constrained region. And again, the apparent strategy is to delay the withdrawal of the logistic and combat-support forces in order to maintain a low marginal cost at higher output levels. As U.S. participation in this war draws to an end, much of the support for continuing the war, not surprisingly, comes from the military bureaus and the owners of those specific factors not subject to factor price discrimination. Maybe the field manuals for U.S. commanders are based on Parkinson rather than Clausewitz.

Behavioral Hypotheses

In summary, the more important hypotheses concerning the effects on the output and budget of elementary bureaus from changes in demand and cost conditions are the following:

1. The output and budget of a bureau operating in the budget-constrained region will always grow faster than those of a competitive industry faced by the same increase in demand. For constant marginal costs, the rate of increase of both output and budget will be twice that of a competitive industry. The output of a bureau operating in the demand-constrained region will generally grow faster than a competitive industry; when marginal costs are constant, however, the rate will be the same. In this region the budget of a bureau will grow proportionately with the square of the demand increase. Bureaus operating in either region should be expected to engage in promotional activities to increase the demand for their service.

2. The output and budget of a bureau operating in the budget-constrained region will increase in response to a reduced elasticity of a demand for its service. In the demand-constrained region the output will decrease, but the budget will increase in response to a reduced elasticity of demand. Bureaus in either region should be expected to engage in promotional activities to reduce the elasticity of demand for their service.

3. The output and budget of a bureau operating in the budget-constrained region will always increase at a faster rate than for a competitive industry faced by the same uniform reduction in marginal costs. For constant marginal costs, the rate of increase of output will be twice that of a competitive industry. The budget of a bureau will increase quite rapidly in response to an initial reduction in marginal costs and then less rapidly to equal successive reductions. Bureaus operating in this region have an incentive to identify and implement cost-reduction practices. In the demand-constrained region, the output and budget of a bureau are invariant to the level of marginal costs.

4. The output and budget of a bureau operating in the budget-constrained region will increase in response to an increased elasticity of the minimum marginal cost function. Bureaus in this region should be expected to choose production processes with a lower marginal cost at higher output levels. In the demand-constrained region, both the output and budget of a bureau are invariant to the slope of the minimum marginal cost function.

IV

Variations on the Basic Model

9

Nonprofit Organizations

Several variations on the basic model of a bureau are evaluated in the next four chapters. All the evaluations in these chapters are focused on the static equilibrium conditions, with only a limited discussion of the effects of parameter changes on these conditions. All the other assumptions of the basic model are maintained. Specifically, a bureaucrat is assumed to maximize the budget of his bureau subject to the usual constraint, a bureau is assumed to pay competitive factor prices and to be a monopoly supplier, and the sponsor is assumed not to have the incentive or opportunity to exercise its position as a monopoly buyer. (The consequences of relaxing these last two assumptions are evaluated in later chapters.)

A short evaluation of the behavior of a nonprofit organization that is entirely financed by sales revenue will both illuminate the earlier evaluation of an elementary bureau and provide the basis for evaluating a mixed bureau which is financed both by a grant and by sales revenue. A nonprofit institution, like the special case of a bureau, is assumed to maximize its budget subject to the constraint that the budget must be sufficient to cover the total costs of the service supplied—for the same reasons as in the bureaucratic environment. Unlike a bureau, the nonprofit organization considered in this chapter has no sponsor and receives its entire financing from the sale of a service at a per-unit rate.

A Nonprofit Organization That Sells at a Uniform Price

Let us consider a nonprofit organization which supplies a single service and faces the following demand function for this service:

$$P = a - 2bQ, \ 0 \le Q < \frac{a}{2b}. \tag{9.1}$$

where

$P \equiv$ price at which marginal unit of service is sold.

The total revenue function for this organization, given that the same price is charged for all units of the service, is

$$PQ = R = aQ - 2bQ^2, \ 0 \leq Q < \frac{a}{2b}. \tag{9.2}$$

The total cost function, assuming no factor price discrimination, is

$$TC = cQ + dQ^2, \ 0 \leq Q. \tag{9.3}$$

And this nonprofit organization is by its nature constrained by the condition that sales revenue must be equal to or greater than the total costs at the equilibrium level of output.

$$R \geq TC \tag{9.4}$$

The equilibrium conditions for a nonprofit organization financed entirely from sales may also be in either a budget-constrained or demand-constrained region. Maximization of the revenue function (9.2) yields an upper level of $Q = \left[\dfrac{a}{4b} \right]$. Solving for the equality of the revenue function (9.2) and the cost function (9.3) yields a lower level of $Q = \left[\dfrac{a-c}{2b+d} \right]$. The threshold between these regions, where the above levels of Q are equal, is where $a = \left[\dfrac{4bc}{2b-d} \right]$.

The equilibrium output for a nonprofit firm which sells a service at a uniform price and is entirely financed from sales thus is

$$Q = \begin{cases} \dfrac{a-c}{2b+d} & \text{for } a < \dfrac{4bc}{2b-d} \\[3mm] \dfrac{a}{4b} & \text{for } a \geq \dfrac{4bc}{2b-d}. \end{cases} \tag{9.5}$$

From the demand function (9.1) the uniform price at which the equilibrium level of output is sold is determined to be

$$P = \begin{cases} a - \left(\dfrac{2ab - 2bc}{2b+d} \right) & \text{for } a < \dfrac{4bc}{2b-d} \\[3mm] \dfrac{a}{2} & \text{for } a \geq \dfrac{4bc}{2b-d}. \end{cases} \tag{9.6}$$

And, from the revenue function (9.2), the revenues of a nonprofit organization at the equilibrium level of output are determined to be

$$R = \begin{cases} \left(\dfrac{a^2 - ac}{2b+d}\right) - \left(\dfrac{2a^2b - 4abc + 2bc^2}{4b^2 + 4bd + d^2}\right) & \text{for } a < \dfrac{4bc}{2b-d} \\[4mm] \dfrac{a^2}{8b} & \text{for } a \geq \dfrac{4bc}{2b-d}. \end{cases} \qquad (9\,7)$$

In the budget-constrained region, the equilibrium conditions for a nonprofit organization that sells its service at a uniform price are identical with those of a competitive industry, facing the same demand and cost conditions, in industry equilibrium! On reflection, this should not be too surprising. For a competitive industry, the absence of profits in industry equilibrium (net of the opportunity cost of capital and management) is a consequence of profit-maximizing by individual firms and free entry. For a nonprofit organization, the same output, price, and revenue conditions are the consequence of budget-maximizing behavior and the constraint that revenues must cover costs. Competitive firms are assumed to be profit-seeking but become nonprofit firms in industry equilibrium. A nonprofit organization is assumed to be budget-maximizing but acts like a competitive industry in equilibrium. In some cases, of course, a nonprofit organization will be able to command capital, land, and management resources at a lower price (owing primarily to tax conditions) than a competitive industry supplying the same service; then the output of a nonprofit organization will be higher, the price will be lower, and the revenues may be either higher or lower (depending on the slope of the demand function).

A strictly nonprofit organization financed entirely by the sale of output at a uniform price, and operating in the budget-constrained region, will thus both supply the optimal level of output and do so at a minimum cost per unit of service. There still may be a basis for social concern about organizations that, by design, are nonprofit. Cultural conditions may lead budget-maximizers to choose an easy life at a lower level of output than profit-maximizers, and budget maximization may not be such a strong condition for survival of the organization. Also, it is often difficult to enforce a strict nonprofit status. In some cases, a nonprofit organization will act more like a profit-seeking monopoly, spending the difference between revenues and the minimum total costs as perquisites to the managers and employees of the organization. Both of these conditions suggest that a nonprofit organization financed entirely by the sale of output at a uniform price will supply a slightly lower output at a slightly higher price than a competitive industry facing the same demand and cost conditions. For conditions such that the budget-maximizing motivation is as strong as the profit-maximizing motivation and the tax auditors are sharp in identifying non-monetary perquisites as personal income, the equilibrium output, price, and budget conditions of a nonprofit organization operating in the budget-constrained region should be about the same as for a competitive industry. Most nonprofit organizations probably operate in the budget-constrained region. The general opportunity for free entry among nonprofit organizations increases the elasticity of demand faced by each organization relative to the elasticity of the population demand for the services supplied by these organizations. The equilibrium conditions for a nonprofit organization thus are usually, but not uniformly, consistent with those of a competitive industry.

Some nonprofit organizations operate in the demand-constrained region. The monopoly power of these organizations is usually due to restrictions on entry, to the control of a superior production process, or to a unique command of factors at a lower price. For a nonprofit organization operating in the demand-constrained region, the equilibrium output, price, and revenues are entirely dependent on demand conditions and are independent of cost conditions. These organizations supply a lower output at a higher price and have higher revenues than would a competitive industry facing the same conditions. The total revenues of these nonprofit organizations are higher than the minimum total costs at the equilibrium level of output, and such organizations have no incentive to seek out or implement possible means to reduce costs. Similar to those of a bureau operating in the demand-constrained region, the production processes of these nonprofit organizations are indeterminate except to assure that the payment to factors is sufficient to exhaust the maximum available revenues. In contrast to that of a bureau, however, the equilibrium output of these organizations is lower than would be supplied by a competitive industry. My guess is that this is a relatively rare condition among nonprofit organizations, because of the opportunities for entry, but most of us can probably identify some university, hospital, research organization, or cultural organization with behavior characteristics of nonprofit organizations in the demand-constrained region.

A Nonprofit Organization That Is a Discriminating Monopoly

Many nonprofit organizations, as a consequence of the nature of the service they sell, have the opportunity to charge different prices for different units of the same service. This is a common practice of universities and hospitals. Such opportunities will generally be exploited because price discrimination by a nonprofit organization leads to an increase of both output and budget. For the same demand function as in (9.1), the total revenue function for a nonprofit organization which charges the maximum possible price for each unit of service is

$$R = aQ - bQ^2 \quad 0 \le Q \le \frac{a}{2b}. \tag{9.8}$$

A nonprofit organization that is a discriminating monopolist in the sale of its service may also be in either a budget-constrained or a demand-constrained region. The level of Q that maximizes the revenue function (9.8) is the upper level of $\left[Q - \dfrac{a}{2b}\right]$. Solving for the equality of the revenue function (9.8) and the minimum total cost function (9.3) yields the lower level of $Q = \left[\dfrac{a-c}{b+d}\right]$. The threshold of these two regions is where $a = \left[\dfrac{2bc}{b-d}\right]$. The equilibrium level of output of a nonprofit organization that is a discriminating monopolist thus is

$$Q = \begin{cases} \dfrac{a-c}{b+d} & \text{for } a < \dfrac{2bc}{b-d} \\[3mm] \dfrac{a}{2b} & \text{for } a \geq \dfrac{2bc}{b-d}. \end{cases} \tag{9.9}$$

From the demand function (9.1) the price at which the *last* unit is sold is

$$P = \begin{cases} a - \dfrac{2ab - 2bc}{b+d} & \text{for } a < \dfrac{2bc}{b-d} \\[3mm] 0 & \text{for } a \geq \dfrac{2bc}{b-d}. \end{cases} \tag{9.10}$$

The price of all inframarginal units, of course, will be higher. From the revenue function of a discriminating monopolist (9.8), the total revenues are

$$R = \begin{cases} \left(\dfrac{a^2 - ac}{b+d}\right) - \left(\dfrac{a^2 b - 2abc + bc^2}{b^2 + 2bd + d^2}\right) & \text{for } a < \dfrac{2bc}{b-d} \\[3mm] \dfrac{a^2}{4b} & \text{for } a \geq \dfrac{2bc}{b-d}. \end{cases} \tag{9.11}$$

In both the budget-constrained and the demand-constrained regions, the equilibrium output and revenues of a nonprofit organization that is a discriminating monopolist are higher than for a nonprofit organization which sells at a uniform price, and the price at which the marginal unit is sold is lower. Also, the equilibrium output and budget of a nonprofit organization that is a discriminating monopolist are identical with those of an elementary bureau facing the same demand and cost conditions. It is probably more difficult, however, perfectly to discriminate among many customers than it is for a bureau financed by a single sponsor. In this case the nonprofit constraint leads a discriminating monopolist to expand output beyond the competitive equilibrium. The marginal unit of service will be sold at a price less than the marginal cost, and the net losses in this range of output will just offset the net surplus revenues at a lower range of output. A bureau exploits a passive sponsor in much the same way that a nonprofit discriminating monopolist exploits its customers and with the same effect.

This discussion suggests that there is an interesting grouping and symmetry of the equilibrium output of different pure forms of organization facing the same demand and cost conditions. For linear demand and marginal cost functions, a profit-seeking monopolist who sells at a uniform price will supply an output just one-half that of a competitive industry. A profit-seeking firm that is a discriminating monopoly will supply the same output as a competitive industry. A nonprofit organization that sells at a uniform price and is in the budget-constrained region will also supply the same output as a competitive industry. And both a nonprofit organization that is a discriminating monopolist and a bureau with a passive sponsor will supply a higher output which, given constant marginal costs, is twice that of a competitive industry.

Two critical characteristics must both be applicable for these latter organizations to be "too large"; the relaxation of *either* (but not both) the nonprofit status or the opportunity to exploit their customers (or sponsor) will bring the output of monopoly organizations supplying a specific service more in line with that of a competitive industry.

The economic behavior of all forms of nonprofit organizations is beyond the scope of this book, but it should be recognized that bureaus which receive some or all of their financing from a grant constitute the largest subset of the larger group of nonprofit organizations.

10

The "Mixed" Bureau

A mixed bureau—one that receives part of its financing from a grant and part from the sale of a service—faces two separate demands for the same service. In effect, a mixed bureau sells the same output to two groups of customers—one group represented by the collective sponsor of the bureau, and the other the group that directly purchases a service at a per-unit rate. An increase in the output of a service inherently increases the output available to both groups by the same amount, so any service supplied by a mixed bureau has the critical characteristic of a "public" service. The demands by these two groups are not resolved into a single budget-output function by bargaining and then reflected in one grant, as is the case with an elementary bureau with a composite sponsor.

Usually, a mixed bureau will have a significantly different type of relation with its sponsor than with its customers. A bureau will usually behave with deference toward its sponsor but, in fact, exploit the sponsor, generating little or no net value by its activities. Conversely, a mixed bureau will usually have an impersonal relation with its customers but, in most cases, will supply a service at a lower cost than its aggregate value to this group.

In some cases, customers of a mixed bureau are, simultaneously or later, the constituents of the collective organization sponsoring the bureau; then a part of the net benefits to the customers is later appropriated by the collective organization and returned to the bureau. A favorite technique of alumni associations, for example, is to ask individuals to return part of the net benefits they accrued as students in the form of donations to their universities. In difficult times leaders of government often make a similar appeal—"Ask not what your country can do for you . . ." and so forth.

An individual, at the same time or at different times, may be both a constituent of the collective sponsor of a bureau and a customer of the bureau. At any one time, however, his relation with the bureau will be dominated by one or the other role. A constituent (and donor) is not primarily motivated by the value of a bureau's service to its customers. And the customers are not primarily motivated by the value of a bureau's service to the constituents of the sponsoring organization.

Consider a mixed bureau which supplies one service. The budget-output function of its sponsor is

$$B = a_1 Q - b_1 Q^2, \ 0 \leq Q < \frac{a_1}{2b_1}. \tag{10.1}$$

The demand function for the bureau's service by its customers is

$$P = a_2 - 2b_2 Q, \ 0 \leq Q < \frac{a_2}{2b_2}. \tag{10.2}$$

For this demand function, the total sales revenue of a bureau which sells its service at a uniform price is

$$R = a_2 Q - 2b_2 Q^2, \ 0 \leq Q < \frac{a_2}{2b_2}. \tag{10.3}$$

For the same demand function, the total sales revenue of a bureau which sells each unit of a service at the maximum possible price is

$$R = a_2 Q - b_2 Q^2, \ 0 \leq Q < \frac{a_2}{2b_2}. \tag{10.4}$$

The minimum total costs of a bureau which pays competitive factor prices is represented by the cost-output function

$$TC = cQ + dQ^2, \ 0 \leq Q. \tag{10.5}$$

For a mixed bureau, the financing constraint is represented by

$$B + R \geq TC. \tag{10.6}$$

The equilibrium output of a mixed bureau may be in any one of five distinct output regions. The sponsor and customer demands jointly influence the level of output in an output region where the marginal value of output to both the sponsor and the customer is greater than zero. The sponsor demand is dominant in an output region where the marginal value of output to the sponsor is greater than zero but the marginal value to the customers is zero; in this region, the customer demand has no effect on the output level unless the bureau is a discriminating monopolist in the sale of output. The customer demand is dominant in an output region where the marginal value to the sponsor is zero but the marginal value to the customers is greater than zero. Within two of these three output regions, there are the two subregions common to an elementary bureau. In the budget-constrained region, a bureau's budget is maximized at an output such that $[B+R] = TC$. In the demand-constrained region, a bureau's budget is maximized at an output that maximizes the sum of $[B+R]$

Using this basic model, we can evaluate the consequences of budget maximization for a mixed bureau's output, price, and budget for both the bureau which sells a service at a uniform price and the bureau which is a discriminating monopolist in the sale of service. Again, this evaluation assumes a passive sponsor and no discrimination on the factor market.

A Mixed Bureau That Sells at a Uniform Price

Some of the services sold by bureaus are easily transferable from one customer to another. This potential ease of transfer applies to the supply of publications, most postal and transportation services, and some cultural and recreational services. Such services are usually supplied on an un-categorical basis—without personal identification of the customer. Even when a bureau is a monopoly supplier of a service, this ease of transfer effectively enforces the sale of this service at a uniform price.

Both sponsor and customer demands are effective when the marginal value to both groups is greater than zero. For the functions (10.1) and (10.2), this output region is bounded by the smaller of $\left[\dfrac{a_1}{2b_1}\right]$ and $\left[\dfrac{a_2}{2b_2}\right]$. The threshold between the budget-constrained and demand-constrained subregions is at $[a_1 + a_2] = \left[\dfrac{2(b_1 + 2b_2)c}{b_1 + 2b_2 - d}\right]$.

Output Region 1. The equilibrium output within the budget-constrained subregion is found by solving the equality of the sum of (10.1) and (10.3) with the total cost function (10.5). This yields

$$Q = \frac{a_1 + a_2 - c}{b_1 + 2b_2 + d}, \quad a_1 + a_2 < \frac{2(b_1 + 2b_2)c}{b_1 + 2b_2 - d}. \tag{10.7}$$

The output of a mixed bureau is *much* larger than would be supplied if the sponsor and customer demands were not combined. An elementary bureau financed only by a grant would supply an output of $Q = \left[\dfrac{a_1 - c}{b_1 + d}\right]$. And a nonprofit organization (or a competitive industry) financed only by the sale of a service would supply an output of $Q = \left[\dfrac{a_2 - c}{2b_2 + d}\right]$. If both a_1 and a_2 are less than c, but $[a_1 + a_2]$ is larger than c, the output of this service would be zero unless the sponsor and customer demands were combined. As expected, the output of a mixed bureau in this region increases with an increase in either the sponsor or the customer demand and decreases with an increase in the minimum marginal costs; the change in the equilibrium output is equal to the constant $\left[\dfrac{1}{b_1 + 2b_2 + d}\right]$ times the increase in demand or reduction in cost.

The equilibrium price to customers in this region is found by substituting the equilibrium output (10.7) into the customer demand function (10.2). This yields

$$P = a_2 - 2b_2\left(\frac{a_1 + a_2 - c}{b_1 + 2b_2 + d}\right). \tag{10.8}$$

An evaluation of the derivatives of this function indicates a number of interesting properties. An increase in the sponsor demand for the service of a mixed bureau reduces the price of the service to customers. The change in price is equal to the constant $\left[-\dfrac{2b_2}{b_1 + 2b_2 + d}\right]$ times the change in the sponsor demand. The reduction in price is always less than the increased marginal value the sponsor is willing to pay for a given output, even if the marginal costs are constant, because the induced increase in output reduces the marginal value to the sponsor. An increase in customer demand, in contrast, increases the price to customers, even if marginal costs are constant. The change in price is equal to the constant $\left[1 - \dfrac{2b_2}{b_1 + 2b_2 + d}\right]$ times the change in customer demand. An increase in customer demand in this region always increases the price, even if marginal costs are constant, also because the induced increase in output reduces the marginal values to the sponsor. As expected, an increase in marginal costs increases the price to customers. The change in price is equal to the constant $\left[\dfrac{2b_2}{b_1 + 2b_2 + d}\right]$ times the change in costs. The increase in price is always less than the increase in costs, even if marginal costs are invariant to output, because the induced reduction in output increases the marginal value to the sponsor.

The equilibrium amount of the sponsor's grant to a mixed bureau is found by substituting the equilibrium output (10.7) into the budget-output function (10.1). This yields

$$B = a_1\left(\frac{a_1 + a_2 - c}{b_1 + 2b_2 + d}\right) - b_1\left(\frac{a_1 + a_2 - c}{b_1 + 2b_2 + d}\right)^2. \tag{10.9}$$

An evaluation of the derivatives of this function indicates the following properties: An increase in the sponsor's demand increases the amount of the grant at an increasing rate. An increase in the customer's demand also increases the amount of the sponsor's grant, but at a decreasing rate. An increase in customer demand for the service of a mixed bureau thus increases the absolute amount of the grant but reduces the proportion of the bureau's financing from this source. And a reduction in marginal costs increases the amount of the grant at an increasing rate.

The equilibrium amount of the revenues from the sale of service is found by substituting the equilibrium output (10.7) into the sales revenue function (10.3). This yields

$$R = a_2\left(\frac{a_1+a_2-c}{b_1+2b_2+d}\right) - 2b_2\left(\frac{a_1+a_2-c}{b_1+2b_2+d}\right)^2. \tag{10.10}$$

An evaluation of the derivatives of this function indicates the following properties: An increase in the sponsor's demand may either increase or decrease the revenue from sales to customers. If the elasticity of the customer demand is high (b_2 is low), an increase in the sponsor's demand will increase the revenue from sales at a decreasing rate. If the elasticity of the customer demand is low, a reduction in the sponsor's demand will increase the revenue from sales at an increasing rate. An increase in the customer demand will always increase the revenue from sales at an increasing rate. And an increase in the marginal costs may also either increase or decrease the revenues from sales. If the elasticity of the customer demand is high, a reduction in marginal costs will increase the sales revenue at an increasing rate. If the elasticity of the customer demand is low, an increase in the marginal costs will increase the revenue from sales at a decreasing rate. A mixed bureau financed primarily from sales at a uniform price and facing an inelastic customer demand would thus be relatively less concerned about a reduction in the sponsor demand or an increase in marginal costs.

And, finally, the equilibrium amount of the total budget of a mixed bureau in this output region is found by substituting the equilibrium output (10.7) into the total cost function (10.5). This yields

$$TC = c\left(\frac{a_1+a_2-c}{b_1+2b_2+d}\right) + d\left(\frac{a_1+a_2-c}{b_1+2b_2+d}\right)^2. \tag{10.11}$$

The properties of this function are rather more simple than those which separately determine a mixed bureau's grant and revenues. An increase in either the sponsor or the customer demand increases the total budget of a bureau; these rates of increase are constant and proportional to the marginal costs if the marginal costs are invariant to output. A reduction in marginal costs increases the total budget of a mixed bureau at an increasing rate. Although changes in demand and cost affect the distribution of the financing of a mixed bureau between the sponsor and the customers in complex ways, the effects of these changes on the total budget are simple, the direction of the effects is expected, and they provide the correct directional incentives.

Output Region 2. In the region where both the sponsor and customer demands are effective, the equilibrium output in the demand-constrained subregion is found by finding the value of Q for which the sum of the budget-output function (10.1) and the total revenue function (10.3) is maximized. Setting the first derivative of the sum of these functions equal to zero yields

$$Q = \frac{a_1 + a_2}{2b_1 + 4b_2}, \; a_1 + a_2 \geq \frac{2(b_1 + 2b_2)c}{b_1 + 2b_2 - d}. \qquad (10.12)$$

In this region, although the equilibrium output is determined only by demand conditions, the marginal value of output to both the sponsor and the customers is greater than zero. The equilibrium output is set at a level where the marginal increase in the sponsor's grant from an increase in output is just equal to the marginal reduction in revenues from the sale to customers. The equilibrium output is higher, and the price is lower, than that which would maximize only the revenue from sales. In this region, a mixed bureau acts like a profit-seeking monopolist which has zero costs, deals with a sponsor as a discriminating monopolist, and sells a service to customers at a uniform price. An increase in either the sponsor or customer demand increases the equilibrium output by the constant $\left[\dfrac{1}{2b_1 + 4b_2} \right]$ times the increase in demand. The output is invariant to cost conditions.

The equilibrium price, grant, revenues, and total budget are found in the same way as in the budget-constrained case. An increase in the sponsor demand reduces the price, and an increase in the customer demand increases the price. An increase in the sponsor demand increases the grant at an increasing rate, and an increase in the customer demand increases the sponsor's grant at a decreasing rate. An increase in the sponsor demand either increases or decreases the revenues from sales to customers, depending on whether the customer demand is elastic or inelastic. An increase in the customer demand increases the revenues at an increasing rate. An increase in either the sponsor or customer demand increases the total budget of a mixed bureau at an increasing rate. In this region the total budget is higher than the minimum total costs, production processes are indeterminate, and the equilibrium output, price, grant, revenues, and total budget are all independent of cost conditions.

Output Region 3. In the output region where the marginal value to the sponsor is zero but the marginal value to customers is greater than zero, the customer demand is dominant but, because of the characteristic relation of a bureau with its sponsor, the sponsor's demand still has a small marginal effect on a bureau's behavior. For the functions (10.1) and (10.2) this output region is where $\left[\dfrac{a_1}{2b_1} \right] \geq Q < \left[\dfrac{a_2}{2b_2} \right]$. This region has no demand-constrained subregion, because, as the customer demand grows relative to the sponsor demand, the output of a bureau approaches that of a nonprofit organization with no grant.

In this region, a mixed bureau basically treats the sponsor's grant as a lump-sum payment, independent of the bureau's behavior. In a profit-seeking firm, a lump-sum payment does not change its behavior, as it does not change the marginal conditions. A lump-sum grant to a mixed bureau operating in this region, however, does change its behavior. The amount

of the sponsor's grant is $\left[\dfrac{a_1{}^2}{4b_1}\right]$, the maximum amount that can be extracted

from the sponsor at a marginal value of zero. We find the equilibrium output
by equating the sum of this fixed grant and the total revenue function (10.3)
to the total cost function (10.5) and solving the resulting quadratic equation
for Q. This yields

$$Q = \frac{(a_2-c)+\sqrt{(a_2-c)^2+\dfrac{a_1{}^2(2b_2+d)}{b_1}}}{2(2b_2+d)}. \qquad (10.13)$$

In the absence of a grant, a nonprofit organization (or a competitive industry)

that sells a service at a uniform price supplies an output of $\left[\dfrac{a_2-c}{2b_2+d}\right]$. A

mixed bureau that receives a lump-sum grant supplies an output only slightly
larger than the nonprofit institution that is financed entirely from sales. The
effect of a grant on output in this region is smaller than in the region where
both demands are effective, because the induced increase in output does not
induce an addition to the grant. And, as in the previous case, a grant may
reduce the revenues from sales if the customer demand is inelastic. In this
region an increase in the sponsor demand increases the output by only a
small amount but at an increasing rate. An increase in the customer demand
or a reduction in marginal costs increases the output at a slightly declining
rate. The equilibrium price is only slightly lower than for a nonprofit organization financed entirely from sales. A lump-sum grant may increase the total
financing of a mixed bureau by either more or less than the amount of the
grant, depending on the elasticity of the customer demand.

Output Regions 4 and 5. In the output region where the marginal value
to the sponsor is greater than zero but the marginal value to customers is
zero, the sponsor demand is dominant. In this region, unless the bureau
can discriminate among customers in the sale of a service, the price and the
sales revenues are zero; a bureau in this region, financed entirely by a
sponsor's grant, behaves just like an elementary bureau which does not
have the opportunity to sell its service. An increase in the customer's
demand, unless it increases the marginal value of the bureau's output above
zero, has no effect on the bureau's output or budget. In the limit, thus, a
mixed bureau for which the sponsor demand is high relative to the customer
demand is identical to an elementary bureau.

Some graphic examples help illustrate the effects of changing demand
conditions on the output and sources of financing of a mixed bureau.
Figure 10.1 illustrates the effects of increases in the sponsor demand on the
output, grant, and revenues of a mixed bureau. For values of a_1 from 0 to
105, the equilibrium conditions are in the output region where both demands

Figure 10.1   Effects of Increased Sponsor Demand

are effective and the output is budget-constrained; the revenues from sales increase and then decrease, and the sum of the grant and revenues is equal to total costs. For values of a_1 from 105 to 150, both demands are effective and the output is demand-constrained; revenues from sales decrease to zero, and the sum of the grant and revenues is greater than the minimum total costs. For values of a_1 from 150 to 300, the sponsor demand is dominant and the output is budget-constrained; revenues are zero and the grant is equal to total costs. For values of a_1 above 300 (not shown on Figure 10.1), the bureau is in a demand-constrained region where the grant is larger than the minimum total costs.

Figure 10.2 illustrates the effects of increases in the customer demand on the output, grant, and revenues of a mixed bureau. For values of a_2 from 0 to 105, the equilibrium conditions are in the output region where both demands are effective and the output is budget-constrained; both the grant and revenues increase rapidly in this region and the sum of the grant and revenues equals total costs. For values of a_2 from 105 to 150, both demands are effective and the output is demand-constrained; the grant increases only slowly in this region and the sum of the grant and the revenues is larger than the minimum total costs. For values of a_2 above 150, the customer demand is dominant; the sponsor's grant is constant and the sum of the grant and revenues equals total costs.

A separate illustration of the effect of cost increases is not necessary. In the budget-constrained regions, the effect of a cost increase is the same as the effect of a reduction of either of the jointly effective demands or of the dominant demand. In the demand-constrained regions, the equilibrium conditions are invariant to changes in costs.

A mixed bureau that sells a service at a uniform price may generate substantial net benefits to customers and, given the payment of competitive factor prices, to the owners of factors. In the output region where both demands are effective, the net benefits generated by a mixed bureau are substantially larger than those generated by any form of organization facing only the customer demand. (This is not the case in the other output regions.) This effect, however, is due only to the addition of the sponsor

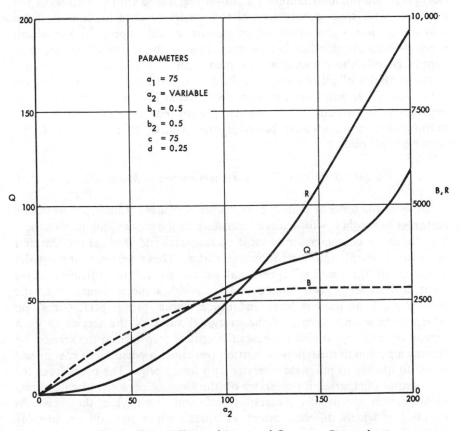

Figure 10.2   Effects of Increased Customer Demand

and customer demands. A competitive industry facing the same aggregate demand would generate higher net benefits. A mixed bureau is thus still not the most efficient form of organization to supply a service in response to the combined sponsor and customer demands. A collective organization, for example, could choose to express its demands by offering a per-unit subsidy to profit-seeking firms to augment the supply of a service. A numerical example later in this chapter illustrates the effect of expressing the sponsor demand through various forms of organization.

It is difficult to understand why collective organizations usually express their demands for a service that could be marketed by a grant to a mixed bureau. A partial explanation may be the general problem of defining the desired output sufficiently to offer a subsidy or to contract for the supply of the service. This problem is not resolved by giving a grant to a bureau, but it is more easily overlooked. A part of the reason may be that bureaus also perform the role of organizing, propagandizing, and collecting funds from the constituency of the collective organization. Maybe the identification of alumni associations, parent-teacher associations, patrons of the arts, etc., with specific bureaus makes it easier to raise funds than if the donors do not know what organizations would supply to subsidized service—even at some loss in efficiency. Maybe the choice of bureaucratic supply is only the consequence of insufficient contemporary experience with the effects of other forms of subsidy with which to compare the performance of bureaus. In any case, mixed bureaus are an important form of organization—particularly in the supply of educational, welfare, and cultural services—and their behavior and relative efficiency need to be better understood.

A Mixed Bureau That Is a Discriminating Monopolist

Many of the services sold by bureaus are not easily transferred from one customer to another. A difficulty of transferring the service among customers is a dominant characteristic of most educational and medical services and of some cultural and recreational services. These services are usually supplied on the basis of a personal or categorical identification. This identification serves two functions. It provides some information to the bureau (such as income level, insurance status, group preferences) on which to base an estimate of the marginal value of the service to each person or category. It also increases the cost of transferring the service, by forcing a person to misrepresent himself (on either a personal or categorical basis) to qualify to purchase a service at a lower price. The procedures for segregating the market for a service on the basis of personal or categorical identification are usually remarkably efficient, even when the service is supplied at widely different prices. A bureau which has some monopoly power in the supply of a service which cannot easily be transferred will usually exploit this opportunity for price discrimination, because it permits the expansion of both the output and the budget beyond the equilibrium level in the absence of price discrimination.

A mixed bureau supplying a single service under conditions which permit price discrimination has an output and budget identical to that of a monopoly bureau which has two sponsors. The process of estimating and appropriating the total value that a sponsor and the customers are willing to pay for a service are different, but the results are the same. The output of a mixed bureau that is a discriminating monopolist in the sale of a service may also be in any one of five regions.

Output Region 1. Both the sponsor and customer demands are effective when the marginal values to both groups is greater than zero. For the functions (10.1) and (10.2), this output region is bounded by the smaller of $\left[\dfrac{a_1}{2b_1}\right]$ and $\left[\dfrac{a_2}{2b_2}\right]$. In this region the output of a bureau is always budget-constrained. A separate demand-constrained subregion does not exist within the constraints of a positive marginal value to both the sponsor and customers.

In this region, the equilibrium output is found by solving for the equality of the sum of (10.1) and (10.4) with the total cost function (10.5). This yields

$$Q = \frac{a_1 + a_2 - c}{b_1 + b_2 + d} \tag{10.14}$$

This output is the same as if the demands by two sponsors for the same service are combined, and is larger than would be supplied if the service were sold at a uniform price and is also much larger than would be supplied if the sponsor and customer demands were not combined. The output of a mixed bureau in this region increases with an increase in either the sponsor or the customer demand and decreases with an increase in the minimum marginal costs; the change in the equilibrium output is equal to the constant $\left[\dfrac{1}{b_1 + b_2 + d}\right]$ times the increase in demand or reduction in cost.

The price at which the marginal unit of service is sold is found by substituting the equilibrium output (10.14) into the customer demand function (10.2). This yields

$$P = a_2 - 2b_2 \left(\frac{a_1 + a_2 - c}{b_1 + b_2 + d}\right). \tag{10.15}$$

In this case the price at which the marginal unit is sold is lower than if the service were sold at a uniform price, but the average price that customers pay for this service is higher. An increase in the sponsor demand reduces the price of the marginal unit, usually by somewhat less than the increased amount the sponsor is willing to pay for a given output. An increase in the customer demand increases the price of the marginal unit, even if marginal costs are constant. And an increase in the marginal costs increases the price of the marginal unit, usually by less than the increase in costs.

The equilibrium amount of the sponsor's grant is found by substituting the equilibrium output (10.14) into the budget-output function (10.1). Similarly, the equilibrium amount of the revenues from sales is found by substituting the equilibrium output (10.14) into the total revenue function (10.4). These functions have the expected symmetric properties: An increase in the sponsor's demand increases the amount of the grant at an increasing rate. An increase in the customer demand also increases the grant, but at a decreasing rate. Similarly, an increase in the customer demand increases the revenues at an increasing rate, and an increase in the sponsor demand increases the revenues at a decreasing rate. And a reduction in marginal costs increases the amount of both the grant and revenues at an increasing rate. In this case, any increase in the demand for the service of a mixed bureau from one source increases the amount but reduces the proportion of the total financing from the other source. In this subregion, the total financing of a mixed bureau is found by substituting the equilibrium output (10.14) into the total cost function (10.5). The properties of this function are the same as for a mixed bureau that sells at a uniform price. In this region, a mixed bureau supplies the equilibrium output at the minimum total cost, but only at an output level which exhausts the potential net benefits to both the sponsor and the customers. In the absence of factor price discrimination, a mixed bureau that is a discriminating monopolist generates a larger factor surplus than one which sells at a uniform price.

Output Regions 2 and 3. The customer demand is dominant in an output region where the marginal value to the sponsor is zero but the marginal demand to the customers is greater than zero. Again, for the functions (10.1) and (10.2), this output region is where $\left[\dfrac{a_1}{2b_1}\right] \leq Q < \left[\dfrac{a_2}{2b_2}\right]$. This region has both budget-constrained and demand-constrained output regions. In both subregions, the bureau receives a lump-sum grant equal to $\left[\dfrac{a_1{}^2}{4b_1}\right]$, independent of its behavior.

In the budget-constrained subregion, the equilibrium output is found by equating the sum of the lump-sum grant and the total revenue function (10.4) to the total cost function (10.5) and solving the resulting quadratic equation for Q. This yields

$$Q = \frac{(a_2 - c) + \sqrt{(a_2 - c)^2 + \dfrac{a^2(b_2 + d)}{b_1}}}{2(b_2 + d)}. \tag{10.16}$$

For the same conditions, this output is substantially larger than for a mixed bureau which sells at a uniform price. This output is only slightly larger than for a nonprofit organization that receives no grant but is a discriminating monopolist. The general effects of changes in demand and cost conditions on the output of this bureau are the same as in the non-discriminating case. The price of the marginal unit is only slightly lower than in the absence of a grant. In this case, a lump-sum grant also increases the revenues from sales, so the total financing increases by more than the amount of the grant.

In the output subregion that is constrained only by the customer demand, the equilibrium output is that which maximizes the revenue from sales. For a discriminating monopolist, this level of output is where the marginal value to the customers is zero. For this case, then

$$Q = \frac{a_2}{2b_2}. \tag{10.17}$$

For the same conditions, this output is substantially higher than for a mixed bureau which sells at a uniform price. In this subregion, the output, price, grant, and total financing are independent of both the sponsor's demand and the cost conditions. The output increases by the constant $\left[\dfrac{1}{2b_2}\right]$ times the change in the customer demand. The price of the marginal unit is zero. The total revenue from sales is $\left[\dfrac{a^2}{4b_2}\right]$ and thus increases with the customer demand at an increasing rate. The total financing is equal to the lump-sum grant plus the revenue from sales and is higher than the minimum total costs. In this case a lump-sum grant to a mixed bureau has no effect on a bureau's behavior except to add to the resources which are wastefully expended.

Output Regions 4 and 5. For a mixed bureau that is a discriminating monopolist, the equilibrium conditions in the output region dominated by the sponsor demand are completely symmetric with those in the region dominated by the customer demand. The reason for this is that the effects of the sponsor and customer demand, in this case, are the same as the effects of demands of two sponsors for the same service. The total revenues from sales are treated as if they are a lump-sum payment. In the budget-constrained subregion, the equilibrium output is

$$Q = \frac{(a_1 - c) + \sqrt{(a_1 - c)^2 + \dfrac{a_2{}^2(b_1 + d)}{b_2}}}{2(b_1 + d)}. \tag{10.18}$$

In the demand-constrained subregion, the equilibrium output is

$$Q = \frac{a_1}{2b_1}. \tag{10.19}$$

And all of the effects of changes in demand and cost conditions on a mixed bureau's behavior are completely symmetric with the previous case. The opportunity to discriminate among customers leads a profit-seeking monopoly to behave like a competitive industry. Price discrimination leads a mixed bureau to behave like an elementary bureau financed by two sponsors.

Mixed bureaus that are discriminating monopolists pose the same welfare problems as do elementary bureaus. They do not generate net benefits to either the sponsor or the customers. However, because they supply a larger output than a mixed bureau that sells at a uniform price and operates in the absence of factor price discrimination, they generate a larger factor surplus. The primary support for such price discrimination by mixed bureaus should thus be expected to derive from the employees and the owners of other specific factors used by these bureaus.

Comparison of Organizational Forms

The behavior of mixed bureaus is probably best illustrated by comparison with the behavior of other forms of organization facing the same demand and cost conditions. By its nature a mixed bureau supplies a service in response to the combined demands of a collective organization and the customers. The demand of the collective organization is characteristically manifested by a grant to a bureau of some specified total amount in exchange for some expected total level of output.

For some services, however, collective organizations sometimes choose to represent their demand by the offer of a per-unit subsidy. The subsidy rate reflects the marginal value of the service to the collective organization and thus may vary with the level of output. The per-unit subsidies are usually offered to any number of organizations (and, sometimes, different types of organizations) supplying the service desired. In any given period, a collective organization offering such a per-unit subsidy determines what per-unit subsidy it is prepared to offer but does not, as is the case in its relations with a bureau, make a joint determination of the total budget and an expected total level of output. Such per-unit subsidies, as a consequence, sometimes create awkward financial problems for the collective organization, because the uncertainty of the service supplied in response to the per-unit subsidy creates uncertainty in the organization's budget. In general, the relations between a collective organization and the organizations supplying a service in response to a per-unit subsidy are rather impersonal and, at least potentially, transitory; this contrasts with the rather intimate and continuous relations between a collective organization and a bureau.

In this section I shall compare the behaviors of several forms of organization supplying a service in response to the combined demands of a collective organization and the customers. The demand of the collective organization is represented by a per-unit subsidy in its relations with a profit-seeking monopoly, a competitive industry, or a nonprofit organization and by a grant in its relations with a bureau. For each of the monopoly forms, the effects of price discrimination in its relations with customers are also evaluated. All of these organizations are assumed to pay competitive factor prices.

Let us consider a collective organization for which the budget-output function for a specific service is

$$B = 200Q - .5Q^2, \quad 0 \leq Q < 200. \tag{10.20}$$

This function determines the amount of the grant to a bureau as a function of the level of service supplied. For this function the marginal value function is

$$S = 200 - Q, 0 \leq Q < 200. \tag{10.21}$$

This function determines the amount of the per-unit subsidy the collective organization is prepared to offer to any organization (other than a bureau) as a function of the total level of service supplied by all organizations. For this service, the customer demand at every level of output is assumed to be equal to the demand of the collective organization and is represented by

$$P = 200 - Q, 0 \leq Q < 200. \tag{10.22}$$

This function determines how much customers are willing to pay for a marginal unit of the service as a function of the total level of output. For any organization eligible for the subsidy, the total demand function is represented by the sum of (10.21) and (10.22). For any organization or group of organizations supplying this service, the minimum total cost function is

$$TC = 175Q + .25Q^2, \quad 0 \leq Q. \tag{10.23}$$

The equilibrium level of output for a profit-seeking monopoly and a competitive industry are determined as described in Chapter 7 (and in any economic text). The equilibrium levels of output for a nonprofit organization and for a mixed bureau are determined as described in the previous chapter and earlier in this chapter.

For the above conditions, only a small amount of this service would be supplied in response to the customer demand only. A profit-seeking monopolist that sells at a uniform price would supply an output of 10. A profit-seeking discriminating monopolist would supply an output of 16.7. A competitive industry or a nonprofit monopoly which sells at a uniform price would supply an output of 20. And a nonprofit discriminating monopolist would supply an output of 33.3. The effect on output of combining the demands of the collective organization and the customers is determined by comparing the total output supplied in response to the combined demands with the above figures. For a mixed bureau facing such conditions, the equlibrium output is in a region where both demands are effective and the output is budget-constrained.

For these conditions, Table 10.1 presents the equilibrium output and related variables for several forms of organization.

A profit-seeking monopolist facing linear demand and cost functions and selling at a uniform price, as seen earlier, supplies an output just one-half that of a competitive industry. For the conditions represented in Table 10.1, a monopolist earns substantial profits and generates some net benefits to the sponsor, customers, and owners of factors. Only from the viewpoint of the owners of this firm is this a preferred form of organization to supply this service. A collective organization may prefer to subsidize the supply by a monopolist to dealing with a bureau, even though a substantial part of the subsidy ends up in profits, but the competitive and nonprofit forms generate an even larger surplus. Customers would prefer the supply by any other form of organization that sells at a uniform price. And the owners of factors would prefer the supply by any other form. Because a monopolist supplies an output where the marginal value is higher than marginal cost, an expansion of output would generate a larger total surplus.

A profit-seeking monopolist will exploit the opportunity for price discrimination because it generates even higher profits. Price discrimination leads to a higher output and a lower price of the marginal unit. A collective organization would probably support the exercise of price discrimination; it leads to a larger total subsidy but also generates larger net benefits. Customers would, again, prefer the supply by any available form of organization that sells at a uniform price, and owners of factors would prefer a discriminating monopolist only to one that sells at a uniform price. Because this monopolist would also supply an output at which the marginal value is higher than the marginal cost, a further expansion of output would generate a larger total surplus.

A competitive industry is again the norm against which the other forms should be judged. At the competitive output, the marginal value is equal to the marginal cost, and thus this output generates the largest total surplus. In this case it is interesting to note that the output supplied in response to the combination of the equal demands by the collective organization and the customers is five times the output that would be supplied in response to the customer demand only. In industry equilibrium no profits (above the opportunity costs of capital and management) are generated. This output generates the largest possible surplus to both the collective organization and the customers. Owners of factors would prefer the supply of a service by a competitive industry only to the supply by a profit-seeking monopoly.

A strictly nonprofit monopoly (or a set of nonprofit firms) that sells at a uniform price and is in the budget-constrained region would have the

Table 10.1 *Equilibrium levels of output and other variables for several forms of organization facing multiple demands and the same cost conditions*

Organization	Monopoly		Competitive	Nonprofit		Bureau	
output price	*uniform*	*discriminating*	*uniform*	*uniform*	*discriminating*	*uniform*	*discriminating*
Equilibrium values							
Output	50	64.3	100	100	128.6	128.6	180
Subsidy	$7,500	$ 8,724	$10,000	$10,000	$ 9,184	0	0
Grant	0	0	0	0	0	$17,449	$19,300
Revenues	7,500	10,791	10,000	10,000	17,449	9,184	19,300
Costs	9,375	12,283	20,000	20,000	26,633	26,633	39,600
Profits	5,625	7,232	0	0	0	0	0
Collective surplus	1,250	2,067	5,000	5,000	8,265	0	0
Consumer surplus	1,250	0	5,000	5,000	0	8,265	0
Factor surplus	313	516	1,250	1,250	2,452	2,452	4,050

same equilibrium output and other values as a competitive industry. The combination of the nonprofit status and the opportunity to exercise price discrimination, however, changes this conclusion. A nonprofit monopoly sells the same output to the collective organization at a uniform per-unit subsidy and to customers at the demand value of each unit. A nonprofit monopoly exploits this opportunity because it leads to a higher total budget. At the higher level of output possible with price discrimination, the marginal value is less than the marginal cost, so the total surplus value generated is lower than for a competitive industry. A nonprofit discriminating monopolist, however, generates the largest possible surplus to the collective organization and a larger factor surplus than any organization other than a discriminating bureau. The discriminating nonprofit monopoly form is particularly prevalent in the supply of educational, medical, cultural, and recreational services, and the primary support for the supply by this form should be expected to derive from the collective organization and the owners of factors.

For equal demands by the collective organization and the customers, a mixed bureau that sells at a uniform price would supply the same output as a nonprofit discriminating monopolist. The only difference is the distribution of the total financing and of the surplus value. A mixed bureau, in effect, sells the same output to the collective organization at the demand value of each unit and to the customers at a uniform price—just the opposite of the nonprofit discriminating monopolist. This reverses the distribution of financing between the collective organization and the customers and transfers the net benefits from the collective organization to the customers. The total net benefits generated by this form are lower than those generated by a competitive industry. This form generates the largest possible net benefits to the customers, however, and a larger factor surplus than any form except a discriminating bureau. A state university with a uniform net tuition (this appears to be increasingly rare) or a government printing office are examples of such mixed bureaus. The collective organization providing the grant to these mixed bureaus should be expected to prefer some other form of organization to supply these services, and the primary support for supply by this form should be expected to derive from the customers and the owners of factors.

A mixed bureau that, in effect, discriminates in the sale of a service to both the collective organization and the customers will supply the largest output. For constant marginal costs, this output will be just twice that of a competitive industry. At the high output supplied by a discriminating bureau, the marginal value is much lower than the marginal costs, and the total surplus value is the lowest of any form of organization. This bureau generates no net benefits to either the collective organization or the customers. At the high output level, however, it generates the largest factor surplus of any form. Only the employees and the owners of specific factors used by this bureau should be expected to prefer the supply of a service by this form. For this reason, for example, university professors are unlikely to be objective judges of the best means to subsidize the supply of higher education services.

General Implications of Mixed Bureaus

In summary, mixed bureaus are a prevalent but non-optimal form of organization to supply a service in response to the combined demands of a collective organization and the customers. From a welfare point of view, the primary problem of a mixed bureau is attributable to the exchange of a total grant for a total expected output. Any service that can be effectively marketed to customers, however, would permit the collective organization to express its demand through a per-unit subsidy. And a nonprofit monopoly (or a set of nonprofit organizations) that sells at a uniform price in response to a per-unit subsidy and the customer demand would essentially generate the competitive solution. This suggests that collective organizations and, sometimes, customers would strongly prefer the use of per-unit subsidies rather than institutional grants to augment the supply of a service. Collective support for education would thus be represented by tuition vouchers rather than by supplying public schooling. For low-income housing, rent vouchers would be given to low-income families rather than their being moved into public housing. For cultural and recreational services that are also marketed, uniform ticket subsidies would replace grants to the bureau.

One administrative problem of per-unit subsidies is the problem of budget-planning by the collective organization, and this problem may have restricted the more general use of this form of subsidy. The potential returns to the collective organization of using per-unit subsidies rather than sponsoring a captive bureau, however, are high, and some effort to reduce or alleviate the budgeting problem—by means such as better estimates of the output effect of the subsidy, borrowing, and non-price rationing—are worthwhile. Even with the use of per-unit subsidies, the collective organization and the owners of factors are likely to disagree with the customers about whether price discrimination should be permitted. The collective organizations and the owners of factors should be expected to encourage price discrimination where possible, even though it reduces the total net benefits and reduces the net benefits to consumers. As the more important of these collective organizations also have the legislative powers, it may be difficult to pass legislation to restrict the use of price discrimination by nonprofit monopolies.

11

The Multi-Service Bureau

All our discussion so far has focused on bureaus which supply only one service. Most bureaus, however, supply two or more services. This chapter evaluates the behavior of a multi-service bureau, specifically to determine whether its behavior is any different from the sum of the behavior of separate bureaus each supplying a single service. Here a bureau is assumed to be a monopoly supplier of the several services, to face one or more passive sponsors from which it receives its total financing, and to pay competitive factor prices. The model developed is specific to a bureau that supplies two services, but the results are easily generalized to bureaus that supply more than two services.

A bureau that supplies two services faces two different budget-output functions, whether from one or more sponsors. There may be no relation between the sponsor's demand for the two services. This bureau also has two different minimum total cost functions, and there may also be no relation between the costs of supplying the two services. As is demonstrated here, a bureau has an incentive to supply two or more services which differ in either demand or cost characteristics, even if there are no demand or cost relationships between the services.

Let us consider a bureau which supplies two services. The budget-output function for one service is

$$B_1 = a_1 Q_1 - b_1 Q_1^2, 0 \le Q_1 \le \frac{a_1}{2b_1}. \tag{11.1}$$

The budget-output function for the second service, either from the same or another sponsor, is

$$B_2 = a_2 Q_2 - b_2 Q_2^2, 0 \le Q_2 \le \frac{a_2}{2b_2}. \tag{11.2}$$

In this case, the demands for the two services are completely independent.

106

The minimum total cost function for the first service is

$$TC_1 = c_1 Q_1 + d_1 Q_1{}^2, \quad 0 \le Q_1, \tag{11.3}$$

and the minimum total cost function for the second service is

$$TC_2 = c_2 Q_2 + d_2 Q_2{}^2, \quad 0 \le Q_2. \tag{11.4}$$

The minimum total costs of the two services are also completely independent. This two-service bureau faces a budget constraint represented by

$$B_1 + B_2 \ge TC_1 + TC_2. \tag{11.5}$$

In the budget-constrained output region, the output problem of this bureau is to find the level of the output of the two services that maximizes $[B_1 + B_2]$ subject to the budget constraint (11.5). This problem is best solved by the Lagrange multiplier method, in a way similar to that in which the production problem in Chapter 6 is solved. This method translates a constrained maximization problem into an unconstrained maximization problem by formulating the function

$$Z = a_1 Q_1 - b_1 Q_1{}^2 + a_2 Q_2 - \lambda [a_1 Q_1 - b_1 Q_1{}^2 \tag{11.6}$$
$$+ a_2 Q_2 - b_2 Q_2{}^2 - (c_1 Q_1 + d_1 Q_1{}^2 + c_2 Q_2 + d_2 Q_2{}^2)].$$

The derivatives of this function with respect to Q_1 and Q_2 are evaluated, and the equality of the two derivatives is solved for the combination of Q_1 and Q_2. For the general case where d_1 and $d_2 > 0$, this yields the following budget-maximizing combination of Q_1 and Q_2:

$$Q_1 = \frac{a_1 c_2 - a_2 c_1}{2[(b_1 c_2 + a_2 d_1) + 2(b_1 d_2 - b_2 d_1)Q_2]} \tag{11.7}$$

$$+ \left\{ \frac{b_2 c_1 + a_1 d_2}{[b_1 c_2 + a_2 d_1 + 2(b_1 d_2 - b_2 d_1)Q_2]} \right\} Q_2.$$

For the specific case where d_1 and $d_2 = 0$, this yields the less complex solution

$$Q_1 = \frac{a_1 c_2 - a_2 c_1}{2 b_1 c_2} + \frac{b_2 c_1}{b_1 c_2} Q_2. \tag{11.8}$$

As a numerical example later demonstrates, this budget-maximizing combination of Q_1 and Q_2 in this region is different from that which would be supplied by independent bureaus supplying each service.

At this combination of Q_1 and Q_2, the ratio of the marginal increase in the budget over the marginal increase in total costs for a small increase in Q_1 is equal to the ratio of the marginal increase in the budget over the marginal increase in total costs for a small increase in Q_2. This conclusion generalizes to the supply of any number of services. For a bureau supplying n services the necessary condition for the budget-maximizing combination of the services is thus

$$\frac{\delta^B 1/\delta Q_1}{\delta^{TC} 1/\delta Q_1} = \frac{\delta^B 2/\delta Q_2}{\delta^{TC} 2/\delta Q_2} = \cdots = \frac{\delta^B n/\delta Q_n}{\delta^{TC} n/\delta Q_n}. \tag{11.9}$$

In the two-service case, given the budget-maximizing combination of Q_1 and Q_2, the solution for Q_2 and $[B_1 + B_2]$ is found by substituting (11.7) into (11.1) and (11.3) and solving for the equality of the total budget and total costs for the combination of both services. For the general case where d_1 and $d_2 > 0$, this leads to a quartic equation in Q_2 which is difficult to solve. For the special case where $d_1 = d_2 = 0$, this leads to a quadratic equation in Q_2 with a single positive root.

In the demand-constrained output region, the output problem of this bureau is to find the level of output of the two services that maximizes $[B_1 + B_2]$. In this region, unless the demands for the two services are related, the joint solution for Q_1 and Q_2 is the same as the separate solution. For the functions (11.1) and (11.2), the equilibrium level of each service is that for which the marginal value is zero. This solution generalizes to any number of services if the demands are independent. The equilibrium level of Q_1 is $\left[\dfrac{a_1}{2b_1}\right]$ and for Q_2 is $\left[\dfrac{a_2}{2b_2}\right]$, whether these services are supplied by the same or separate bureaus. As is general in this region, the output level is independent of cost conditions, and the total budget is larger than the minimum total costs.

Some Representative Examples

Several numerical examples illustrate the properties of the budget-maximizing solution for the combination of Q_1 and Q_2. These examples are restricted to the budget-constrained region, because the demand-constrained solution, in the absence of interdependent demand functions, is the same as in the separate case.

First, let us consider the case of a bureau that supplies two services for which the budget-output functions are the same but the total cost functions are different. The relevant functions are the following:

$$B_1 = 200Q_1 - .5Q_1^2, \quad 0 \le Q < 200, \tag{11.10}$$

$$B_2 = 200Q_2 - .5Q_2^2, \quad 0 \le Q < 200, \tag{11.11}$$

$$TC_1 = 125Q_1 + .25Q_1^2, \quad 0 \le Q, and \tag{11.12}$$

$$TC_2 = 175Q_2 - .25Q_2^2, \quad 0 \le Q < 350. \tag{11.13}$$

The marginal cost of Q_1 increases with the output level, and the marginal cost of Q_2 decreases with the output level. If these two services are supplied by separate bureaus, the output of both Q_1 and Q_2 would be 100, the budget (and total costs) for both Q_1 and Q_2 would be $15,000, and the combined budget of the two bureaus would be $30,000.

A single bureau supplying both services would choose a different output combination and achieve a higher budget. From (11.7) the budget-maximizing combination of Q_1 and Q_2 is

$$Q_1 = \frac{5,000 + 12.5Q_2}{137.5 - .5Q_2}. \tag{11.14}$$

Substituting (11.14) in (11.10) and (11.12) and solving for the equality of $[B_1 + B_2]$ and $[TC_1 + TC_2]$ yields a complicated quartic equation in Q_2. Solving this equation by iteration yields a level of $Q_2 = 125.5$ and from (11.14) a level of $Q_1 = 88$.[1] At these outputs of Q_1 and Q_2, the total budget and total costs of a bureau supplying both of these services are $30,950. The sponsor is willing to grant a budget of $13,725 for this level of Q_1, but the bureau (unknown to the sponsor) needs to spend only $12,925 to supply this output. Conversely, the sponsor is willing to grant a budget of $17,225 for this level of Q_2, but the bureau spends $18,025 for this output, offsetting the surplus on Q_1.

This example illustrates a number of interesting characteristics of the behavior of a multi-service bureau: A bureau supplying two services with identical demand conditions but different cost conditions has an equilibrium budget higher than the sum of the budgets of separate bureaus supplying each service. The primary reason for this is that the budget constraint (11.5) applies to the sum of the budgets and total costs of the two services. The bureau offers to supply two (or more) services for a single budget. The inability of the sponsor to identify or control the expenditures for each service permits the bureau to expand one service relative to another to increase the total budget. A multi-service bureau supplies a smaller output of a service for which the marginal costs increase more with output and a larger output of a service for which the marginal costs increase less than do separate bureaus supplying each service. The net surplus generated on the first service is used to finance the expanded output on the second. These properties are independent of any relation between the demand or cost conditions of these two services. These characteristics suggest that bureaus should be expected to add other services, independent of any relation in use or production to services presently supplied, for which the slope of the marginal cost function is significantly different in any direction.

1. This solution is checked by the marginal condition (11.9).

$$\text{Since } \frac{\delta B_1/\delta Q_1}{\delta TC_1/\delta Q} = \frac{112}{169} = .66 \text{ and } \frac{\delta B_2/\delta Q_2}{\delta TC_2/\delta Q_2} = \frac{74.5}{112.25} = .66.$$

these values of Q_1 and Q_2 are confirmed as the budget-maximizing solution.

A similar example illustrates the effects of differences in the demand conditions. Let us consider a bureau that supplies two services for which the budget-output functions are different, the total cost functions are the same, and (for simplicity) the marginal costs are constant. The relevant functions are the following:

$$B_1 = 200Q_1 - 1Q_1{}^2, \quad 0 \le Q_1 \le 100, \tag{11.15}$$

$$B_2 = 125Q_2 - .25Q_2{}^2, \quad 0 \le Q_2 \le 250, \tag{11.16}$$

$$TC_1 = 100Q_1 \qquad\qquad 0 \le Q_1, \text{ and} \tag{11.17}$$

$$TC_2 = 100Q_2, \qquad\qquad 0 \le Q_2. \tag{11.18}$$

If these two services are supplied by separate bureaus, the output of both Q_1 and Q_2 would be 100, the budget (and total costs) for both bureaus would be $10,000, and the combined budget of the two bureaus would be $20,000. Again, a bureau supplying both of these services would choose a different output combination and achieve a higher budget. From (11.8) the budget-maximizing combination of Q_1 and Q_2 is

$$Q_1 = 37.5 + .25Q_2. \tag{11.19}$$

Substituting (11.19) in (11.15) and (11.17) and solving for the equality of $[B_1 + B_2] = [TC_1 + TC_2]$ yields a quadratic equation in Q_2. In this case $Q_2 = 150$ and, from (11.19), $Q_1 = 75$. At these outputs, the total budget and total costs of a bureau supplying both of these services is $22,500. The sponsor is willing to grant a budget of $9,375 for this output of Q_1 but the bureau spends only $7,500 to supply this output. Conversely, the sponsor is willing to grant a budget of $13,125 for this output of Q_2, but the bureau spends $15,000 to supply this output, again offsetting the surplus on Q_1.

This case illustrates a number of other interesting characteristics of the behavior of a multi-service bureau. A bureau supplying two services with different demand conditions and identical cost conditions has an equilibrium budget higher than the sum of the budgets of separate bureaus supplying each service. Again, the primary reason for this is the freedom of the bureau to allocate expenditures among services that is due to the supply of several services from a single budget and the inability of the sponsor to know or control the expenditures by service. A multi-service bureau supplies a lower output of a service for which the marginal value decreases more with output and a larger output of a service for which the marginal value decreases less than do separate bureaus supplying each service. Again, the net surplus generated on the first service is used to finance the expanded output of the second. These properties suggest that bureaus should be expected to add other services, again independent of any relation in use or production to services presently supplied, for which the slope of the marginal value function is significantly different in any direction.

General Implications of Multi-Service Bureaus

I have shown the effects of the budget-maximizing motivation for bureaus to add to the range of services supplied and, in the process, become less specialized. Another major motivation for broadening the service line of a bureau is to hedge against the uncertainty of demand and cost conditions for a specific service. Both of these motivations lead to the same type of behavior—the search for services for which the demand and cost conditions are significantly *different* from those of the services presently supplied. Additional services also make it more difficult for the sponsor to estimate the costs of supplying a specific service from the bureau's revealed behavior. Almost any major bureau supplies some service which seems anomalous, in terms of the demands and production processes for the other services supplied. The Army builds and maintains inland waterways. The Department of Agriculture advises urban housewives on family budget-planning. The Department of Transportation provided some military forces in Viet Nam. Defense-sponsored research firms conduct research on poverty programs. These anomalous services are a favorite target of public administration reform and a few of them are, from time to time, transferred to other bureaus where they appear to fit. Such reforms are usually a mistake and reflect a misconception about the conditions conducive to efficiency in a bureaucracy. Attempts to broaden the service line of a bureau will go on, in any case, and will generate other such anomalies. More importantly, the broadening of the service line of one bureau is an essential condition for reducing the monopoly power of other bureaus supplying the same service. And competition in a bureaucracy is as important a condition for social efficiency as it is among profit-seeking firms.

I have demonstrated that bureaus have a budget-maximizing incentive to broaden their service line, even when the demand and cost conditions of the several services are unrelated. This incentive is generally reinforced when the demands or costs are related. A bureau has a strong incentive to be the monopoly supplier of all services which are substitutes in use; as will be shown in the next chapter, this leads to a larger budget than the sum of the budgets of separate bureaus supplying the same or a substitute service. A bureau also has an incentive to supply those services for which there are economies in joint production. There is no necessary homogeneity of the types of services that are related in use with those that are related in production. In a highly competitive bureaucratic environment, bureaus would tend to specialize in the supply of those services for which there are economies of joint production and would become less specialized in those services which are related in use. Only in such a competitive environment could the economies of joint production be appropriated by the collective organization, rather than by the bureau itself.

Bureaus that supply several services that are unrelated in use, however, create a problem for the characteristically bureau-oriented review process. An effective review should consider all services which are closely related in use, and a bureau-oriented review is sufficient only when the bureau is a single-service monopoly. Conceptually, a program budget would provide the basis for reviewing similar services supplied by several bureaus, but this concept has proved difficult to translate into practice. Most public administration reforms—which group bureaus supplying similar services into larger specialized monopoly bureaus—represent attempts to shape the bureaucracy to fit the review process. Such reforms are inherently perverse. In the short run, they increase the monopoly power of the bureaus. Over a longer period, the bureaus will again broaden their service line, and the orthodox criteria of public administration will suggest another (also perverse) reform.

In contrast, a program-budgeting system represents an attempt to shape the review process to the present and evolutionary conditions in the bureaucracy. Such a review system recognizes the competition among bureaus to supply similar services and exploits this competition to achieve more effective control by the collective organization and a more efficient bureaucracy. In the long run, a program-budgeting system promises to be more stable and more effective than organizational reforms. At the present time, the concepts of program budgeting are in danger of a premature death as a consequence of a generous application of verbal fertilizer (a cruder term would be more appropriate) by its advocates, the inertia of the legislatures, and the resilience of the bureaucracy. Alas!

12

Effects of the
Time-Distribution of
Expenditures

All of our discussion to this point has assumed that the total cost of a service is expended during a single fiscal period or, more accurately, during a bureaucrat's tenure in a specific position. In a simpler age, when almost all government expenditures were for current operations and maintenance, such an assumption was a more or less accurate description of conditions. Also, in a bureaucracy in which bureaucrats have a long tenure in a specific position, this assumption is sufficient. In most contemporary bureaucratic environments, however, a bureaucrat is often confronted by several alternatives with a different time-distribution of expenditures. And, given the mobility of the senior bureaucrats (probably reinforced by the cyclical phenomenon of budget changes suggested in Chapter 4), a bureaucrat recognizes that there is some significant probability that he will no longer be in the same position in the later years of the relevant planning period. In these conditions what choices will a bureaucrat make? Specifically, what combination of production activities will be selected to supply a single service? What combination of services will be supplied? Some related questions are of a more technical nature: Will a bureaucrat use a uniform interest rate to discount future expenditures in the selection of processes or services? What is the effect of the collective organization's preferences between present and future expenditures on a bureau's behavior?

Some elaboration of the central motivational assumption discussed in Chapter 4 is necessary to provide the basis for understanding the behavior of a bureau in these conditions. In the traditional theory of the firm, the owner-manager is assumed to maximize the present value of the firm; he chooses among activities with a different time-distribution of revenues and expenditures, using an interest rate which is equal to his marginal cost of capital. Even in large corporations, a substantial part of the income of senior managers is in the form of stock options. In such organizations a manager can maintain or sell his property rights in the firm, independent of

113

the decision to maintain or change his managerial position. Consequently, these managers are significantly motivated by the expected future profits of the firm, as these affect the present value of the manager's property rights; processes and products that maximize the manager's wealth will be selected, even at the cost of lower profits during his tenure as a manager.

A bureaucrat's "property rights," however, are specific to his managerial position, and any value of these rights can be appropriated by the bureaucrat only during his tenure in the position.[1] These rights cannot be sold, and very little of their value accrues to a former bureaucrat. Only the rather ephemeral rewards of prestige and personal satisfaction last longer than a bureaucrat's tenure in office, and these rewards are only loosely related to the performance, budgets, and problems of a bureau after his tenure. Consistent with the general budget-maximizing assumption, the coterminous relation of a bureaucrat's rewards and his position implies that a bureaucrat will maximize the total budget of his bureau *during his tenure as head of the bureau.* The implication of this assumption for a bureaucrat's choice of processes and services is developed in this chapter. This expanded motivational assumption may seem unduly strong; some bureaucrats are certainly motivated by the expected conditions of a bureau after their tenure. Again, however, the value of this assumption should be judged by the predictive power of the resulting behavioral hypotheses.

Investment Behavior

Let us consider a bureau that could use one or both of two processes which produce the same service. The two processes have different costs in each of two periods. The first period is the expected remaining tenure of the bureaucrat in his present position. The second period is the entire period following the bureaucrat's expected remaining tenure. The budget-output function for the service is

$$B = a(Q_1 + Q_2) - b(Q_1 + Q_2)^2, \quad 0 \leq (Q_1 + Q_2) < \frac{a}{2b}. \tag{12.1}$$

In this case, B equals the budget that the collective organization would be willing to grant to the bureau in period 1 only if no future grant would be necessary to finance the supply of this service. In a condition where there is a variable distribution of the budget between the two periods,

$$B = B_1 + kB_2, \tag{12.2}$$

1. I am indebted to Louis DeAlessi for this critical insight. See Louis DeAlessi, "Implications of Property Rights for Government Investment Choices," *American Economic Review,* March 1969, pp. 13–24. His article anticipates the major qualitative conclusions of this section concerning the investment behavior of a bureau.

where $B_1 \equiv$ budget in period 1,

$B_2 \equiv$ budget in period 2, and

k = collective organization's "discount rate" on B_2.

If all of the expenditure in period 2 were in the year following period 1, the discount rate k would be equal to $\left[\dfrac{1}{(1+r)^t}\right]$, where r is the marginal borrowing rate of the collective organization, and t is the length of period 1 – the expected remaining tenure of the head of the bureau. The discount rate on B_2 is thus known only to the bureaucrat and is a negative function of both r and t. From (12.1) and (12.2), the budget available in period 1 is

$$B_1 = a(Q_1 + Q_2) - b(Q_1 - Q_2)^2 - kB_2, \; 0 \le (Q_1 + Q_2) < \frac{a}{2b^2}. \quad (12.3)$$

The minimum total cost functions in each period are

$$C_1 = c_{11}Q_1 + c_{12}Q_2, \; 0 < Q_1, Q_2, \text{and} \quad (12.4)$$

$$C_2 = c_{21}Q_1 + c_{22}Q_2, \; 0 < Q_1, Q_2. \quad (12.5)$$

For simplicity, the marginal costs of both processes in both periods are assumed to be constant. And the relevant budget constraints are

$$B_1 \ge C_1, \text{and} \quad (12.6)$$

$$B_2 \ge C_2. \quad (12.7)$$

The production problem in this case is to find the levels of Q_1 and Q_2 which maximize (12.3) subject to the constraints (12.6) and (12.7). Given constant marginal costs for both processes, this leads to a pure solution in either Q_1 or Q_2. The level of Q_1 or Q_2 may be in either a budget- or demand-constrained region.

In the budget-constrained region,

$$Q_1 = \frac{a - c_{11} - kc_{21}}{b}, \; a < 2c_{11} + kc_{21}, \quad (12.8)$$

2. One sees from (12.3) that one way to increase the budget in period 1 is to understate the costs of either process in period 2. Whether this represents unconscious optimism or a conscious lie, there is very little protection against such underestimates if the bureaucrat is not around in period 2.

and in the demand-constrained region,

$$Q_1 = \frac{a - kc_{21}}{2b}, \qquad a \geq 2c_{11} + kc_{21}. \tag{12.9}$$

Similarly, in the budget-constrained region,

$$Q_2 = \frac{a - c_{12} - kc_{22}}{b}, \quad a < 2c_{12} + kc_{22}, \tag{12.10}$$

and in the demand-constrained region,

$$Q_2 = \frac{a - kc_{22}}{2b}, \qquad a \geq 2c_{12} + kc_{22}. \tag{12.11}$$

The solution to the production problem is to choose either Q_1 or Q_2 at the above levels — whichever leads to a larger budget in period 1.

The effect of maximizing the period 1 budget on the choice of production processes with different time-distributions of expenditures is best illustrated by the conditions for which a bureaucrat is indifferent between the two processes. A strict wealth maximizer (or cost minimizer) would be indifferent between the two substitute processes only when the present value of the cost of the two processes is equal; for (12.4) and (12.5) above, this is where

$$c_{11} + kc_{21} = c_{12} + kc_{22}. \tag{12.12}$$

A bureau is indifferent between two processes, in contrast, only when both of the processes lead to the same budget during period 1. If both processes are budget-constrained, a bureau is indifferent between two processes when

$$c_{11}(a - c_{11} = kc_{21}) = c_{12}(a - c_{12} - kc_{22}). \tag{12.13}$$

Only in this case, and only when the costs of both processes are identical in each period, is a bureau indifferent between two processes with the same present value. If Q_1 is budget-constrained and Q_2 is demand-constrained, a bureau is indifferent between two processes for which

$$4c_{11}(a - c_{11} - kc_{21}) = (a - kc_{22})^2. \tag{12.14}$$

Conversely, if Q_1 is demand-constrained and Q_2 is budget-constrained, a bureau is indifferent between two processes for which

$$(a - kc_{21})^2 = 4c_{12}(a - c_{12} - kc_{22}). \tag{12.15}$$

And, if both processes are demand-constrained, a bureau is indifferent between two processes for which

$$(a - kc_{21})^2 = (a - kc_{22})^2. \tag{12.16}$$

In this last case, a bureau will choose the process with the lower cost in period 2, regardless of the relative costs in period 1.

A bureaucrat with an expected tenure shorter than the period for which expenditures are made on the processes he selects uses, in effect, a different interest rate on every investment decision, depending on the specific time distribution of expenditures for each alternative. The implicit interest rate used by a bureaucrat may be *negative* and is always less than the marginal borrowing rate of the collective organization. As a consequence, for any given marginal borrowing rate, a bureaucrat always chooses more capital-intensive production processes than would be efficient at that rate.[3]

The effects of the time-distribution of expenditures on a bureau's choice of production processes are illustrated for a representative case by Figure 12.1. For this case, the parameters of the budget-output function are constant. A value of $K = .5$ is used to represent the discount rate for a marginal borrowing rate to the collective organization of 10 percent and an expected remaining tenure for the bureaucrat of seven years; the same value of k, of course, is consistent with higher borrowing rates and shorter tenures or lower borrowing rates and longer tenures. The cost of Q_1 in period 2 is constant and is always lower than the cost of Q_2 in that period. The distribution of the cost of Q_2 between period 1 and period 2 is a variable, but the present value of the cost of Q_2 is constant at a value of 100. The horizontal scale indicates the proportion of the present value of the cost of Q_2 expended in period 2. The left ordinate scale indicates the present value of the cost of Q_1 at which a bureau, for this case, would be indifferent between Q_1 and Q_2. At any lower present value of Q_1 in this range, selection of Q_1 would lead to a larger budget in period 1. This left scale is dependent on k but is independent of the combination of the marginal borrowing rate and the bureaucrat's tenure for any value of k. The right ordinate scale indicates the implicit interest rate, for this case, at which a bureau is indifferent between Q_1 and Q_2; this scale is specific to an expected remaining tenure of seven years.

This chapter now provides the context for the earlier discussion of the production behavior of an elementary bureau. As demonstrated in Chapter 6, the production behavior of a bureau in a budget-constrained output region is likely to be efficient, but only when all of the costs of the alternative processes are expended during a bureaucrat's expected remaining tenure. When some part of the cost of production activities is expended in a period after a bureaucrat's expected remaining tenure, the choice of pro-

3. Several institutional conditions sometimes weaken this strong assertion. The underpricing of other resources can lead to an undercapitalization of the supply of some services supplied by bureaus; conscripted military manpower, public-domain land, and the frequency spectrum are examples of such underpriced resources. The mechanics of the budget cycle also lead to the implicit use of a wide range of interest rates. Investment decisions made early in the cycle reflect the use of a more or less consistent rate. Toward the end of the budget cycle, the implicit interest rates may be very high or very low, depending on whether the budget is tight or loose, respectively. Gordon Tullock suggests that the political power of employees may also reduce the general tendency to overcapitalize; owners of other factors, however, also have political power, so it is not clear that the political power of factor owners uniformly biases the combination of labor and capital.

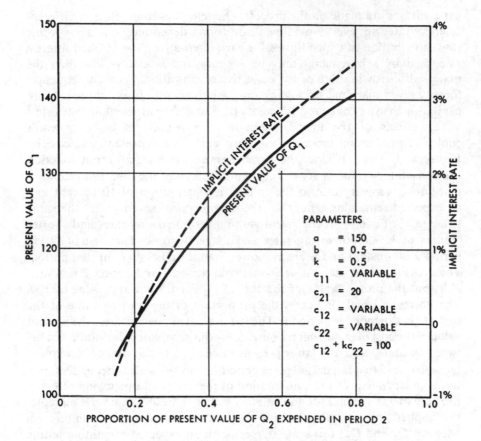

Figure 12.1   Effect of Time Distribution of Q_2 Expenditures on the Present Value of Q_1 and the Implicit Interest Rate at Which Bureau Is Indifferent Between Q_1 and Q_2

duction processes is efficient only when the time-distributions of costs for the alternative processes are identical; for the case represented by Figure 12.1, this condition exists only at the value of .1 on the horizontal scale. In any conditions such that the time-distributions of costs of alternative processes are different, a bureau will choose processes with a higher cost in the early years up to some maximum present value greater than that of processes with a large proportion of expenditures in later years.

Figure 12.1 indicates that the more divergent the time-distribution of costs, the higher the present value a bureau will pay for processes with a larger proportion of costs in the early years. Also, the more divergent the time-distributions of costs, the higher the implicit interest rate at which a bureau is indifferent between alternative processes. The interest rate at which a bureau is indifferent between two processes with only slightly different time-distributions of costs may even be negative. And for any divergence the implicit interest rate is lower than the marginal borrowing rate of the collective organization. For the case represented by Figure 12.1, the implicit interest rate ranges from around −1 percent to 4 percent, although the marginal borrowing rate of the collective organization is 10 percent.

A number of interesting behavioral hypotheses are suggested by this evaluation. Only for processes for which the expenditure period is shorter than the expected remaining tenure of the bureaucrat should bureaus be expected to make investment decisions based on present value calculations using the marginal borrowing rate of the collective organization. For processes with a longer expenditure period, a bureaucrat should be expected to make the investment decisions based on the expected time-distribution of expenditures. These decisions will reflect the use of different implicit interest rates, depending on demand conditions for the service, the time-distribution of expenditures, and the bureaucrat's expected remaining tenure. In such conditions, the production processes selected will have higher costs in the early years than is efficient at the marginal borrowing rate of the collective organization. Another consequence is that such investment decisions cannot be delegated to lower-level managers or resolved by analysis of the objective conditions—since a critical parameter in such decisions is the bureaucrat's expectations of his remaining tenure, and this he is unlikely to reveal. For long-term investment decisions, bureaucrats will usually insist on seeing estimates of the time-distribution of expenditures, because the present value of these expenditures (at any interest rate) does not convey sufficient information for his decision.

This chapter also casts doubt on the value of the extensive, confusing literature on "the" normative rate of interest. This literature has been singularly unproductive in producing a consensus among either economists or government officials concerning either the criteria or the measurement of the "correct" rate to use on government investment decisions, although many economists, myself included, have strong feelings on the matter. Agreement on any rate, however, would still not improve the efficiency of long-term investment decisions made by bureaus. The concept of a normative rate of interest presumably implies that a directive from the collective organization would lead bureaus to use a uniform rate in making investment decisions. In terms of the model developed here, a directive to use a specific uniform rate would, in fact, influence investment decisions (by changing the parameter k) but would not lead to the use of the directed rate or any other uniform rate for the long-term investment decisions. Again, wishing that a policy be implemented, even if it is widely recognized as correct, does not make it so. Some change in the institutional conditions which influence a bureaucrat's conception of his incentives and constraints—his "property rights," if you will—is necessary to make the present value calculus behaviorally relevant in a bureaucratic environment. Otherwise, for any normative rate, the selection of long-term investments by bureaucrats will not be efficient.

Output and Budget Behavior

The time-distribution of expenditures also influences the output and budget of a single-service bureau. As demonstrated above, the direct consequence of maximizing the budget of a bureau during a bureaucrat's expected remaining tenure is the selection of production processes that are more capital-intensive than are efficient as determined by present value calculations at the marginal borrowing rate of the collective organization. For any budget-output function for a single service, the selection of more capital-intensive production processes leads, in turn, to a lower output of the service than would be supplied on the basis of present value calculations. For any budget in the early years, this also leads to a lower budget in later years.

These effects are best illustrated by the output and budget levels at which a bureau is indifferent between two processes with different time-distributions of expenditures. Such effects are illustrated by Figure 12.2 for the same parameters as in Figure 12.1. Again, the horizontal scale indicates the proportion of the present value of the cost of Q_2 expended in period 2. The output functions indicate the levels of Q_1 and Q_2 that, for these conditions, would generate the same budget in period 1. The B_1 function indicates the budget in period 1 and, of course, is the same for both processes. The B_{21} function indicates the budget in period 2 if process 1 is used, and B_{22} indicates the budget in period 2 if process 2 is used. For all conditions represented in Figure 12.2, the present value of the minimum unit cost of Q_2 is constant at a level of 100 and is lower than the present value of the unit cost of Q_1. Q_2 is budget-constrained at all values below .5 on the horizontal scale and demand-constrained above that level.

Figure 12.2 indicates a number of distrubing properties of the output and budget behavior of a bureau with long-term production processes. On a present value basis, Q_2 would be preferred (for all values on the horizontal scale above .1). Up to some higher cost of Q_1 in period 1, however, a bureau will choose Q_1 over this whole range. The level of output that is supplied is lower than would be supplied on a present value basis. If Q_1 is selected, the output supplied decreases and the difference between Q_1 and Q_2 increases with an increasing divergence of the time-distributions of costs. The budget in period 1 decreases with an increasing divergence, whether process Q_1 or Q_2 is selected. *This may lead bureaus systematically to exclude from consideration alternative processes with relatively lower costs in early years, unless such consideration is forced by the collective organization.* Bureaus prefer small wars now to possible big wars later.

Figure 12.2   Effects of Time-Distribution of Q_2 Expenditures on Output and Budget Levels at Which the Bureau Is Indifferent Between Q_1 and Q_2

Bureaus prefer domestic programs now to a crisis which may never develop.[4] Whatever the preferences of the collective organization between the present and future alternatives, the behavior of a bureau is to over-capitalize and to over-insure relative to certain or possible higher future costs. Finally, selection of Q_1 leads to a decreasing budget in period 2 and

---

4. Of course, it may be entirely appropriate to engage in small wars or domestic programs now to avoid very high future costs. The point of this section is merely that bureaus use too low an interest rate when they have any influence on this choice. In some cases, small wars now may lead to big wars later, and domestic programs now (by inflating expectations) may induce a crisis—in which case the bureaucrat's preferences increase *both* the present and the future budget of the bureau.

selection of Q_2 leads to an increasing budget in period 2 with an increasing divergence of the time distributions of expenditures.

For the above conditions, a competitive industry facing the same demand and cost conditions would select Q_2 and supply an output of 50 for a total present value of \$5,000. In the single case where a bureau is forced to consider the choice between processes with widely divergent time-distributions of costs, a bureau may supply a lower output than a competitive industry in the same conditions, albeit at a higher present value per unit of output.

The combination of services supplied by a multi-service bureau is also influenced by the time-distribution of expenditures. A two-service, two-period model of a bureau has been evaluated, but is not reproduced here; such a model essentially combines the features of the two-service, one-period model and the two-period model of production choices outlined earlier. The generalized solution to this model is not surprising. The necessary condition for the combination of services which maximizes the budget in period 1 is

$$\frac{\delta^B 11/\delta Q_1}{\delta^{TC} 11/\delta Q_1} = \frac{\delta^B 12/\delta Q_2}{\delta^{TC} 12/\delta Q_2} = \cdots = \frac{\delta^B 1n/\delta Q_n}{\delta^{TC} 1n/\delta Q_n}. \qquad (12.17)$$

This model suggests that a bureau supplying two services with a different time-distribution of costs will have a larger budget in period 1 than the sum of the budgets of independent bureaus each supplying one service. Compared to two independent bureaus, a single bureau will supply more of a service with larger relative costs in early years and less of a service with higher relative costs in later years. This model also suggests that a bureau will attempt to broaden its service line, even if the demand and cost conditions are independent, to include services with a widely divergent time-distribution of costs. Again, in any one bureau, this reinforces the bureaucratic preference for activities with relatively higher costs in early years, but this incentive can lead to a reduction in the monopoly power of specialized bureaus and an improvement in the efficiency of the bureaucracy.

General Implications of the Time-Distribution of Expenditures

Casual observation suggests that the investment behavior of bureaus is highly variable but has some bias for capital-intensive processes. This chapter has demonstrated that the investment and output behavior of bureaus faced by activities with different time-distribution of costs will have both of these characteristics. The primary reason that a wide range of implicit interest rates are used in the selection of long-term production processes is that a bureaucrat's choice among these processes depends on the demand conditions for the service, the specific time-distribution of costs, and his expected remaining tenure—conditions that are different for every decision and every bureaucrat. For all long-term choices, maximization of the budget during a bureaucrat's expected remaining tenure does lead to a preference for both processes and services with relatively higher costs in early years. The combination of these conditions generates just the type of behavior suggested by casual observation—a high variability in the implicit interest rates with a general bias for capital-intensive processes. Such behavior appears random only to those who uncritically assume that the present value calculus is relevant to a bureaucrat's choice, independent of the incentives and constraints of his position.

A bureau's investment behavior, in contrast, is strongly determined by the nature of the bureaucrat's position. Most bureaus, except those in the demand-constrained region, have a budget-maximizing incentive to be efficient on short-term resource-allocation decisions. Unfortunately, for long-term investment decisions in an environment where bureaucrats have a relatively short tenure, budget-maximizing behavior appears to be uniformly inefficient. Unless a bureaucrat's rewards can somehow be changed in such a way as to induce him to use the present value calculus, collective organizations should maintain undelegated control of all major, long-term investment decisions. Some changes in the bureaucracy, of the type described in Chapter 18, are necessary to permit the delegation of these decisions without the loss of efficiency.

V

The Government Market
for a Bureau's Services

V

The Government Market
for a Bureau's Services

13

The Behavior of Collective Organizations

General Characteristics

A this point, any further elaboration of a theory of the behavior of bureaus requires the relaxation of the assumption of the passive sponsor. The primary effect of this assumption is that bureaus have the opportunity to appropriate a part of the net benefits to the collective organization to finance the supply of an output larger than that which maximizes the total net benefits.

The assumption of a passive sponsor is consistent with any one of three conditions. (1) The selection processes for the officers of the collective organization and the decision processes and rules within the collective organization may be such that the preferences revealed by the decisions of the collective organization are consistent with budget-maximizing behavior by the bureaus. (2) The collective organization may be indifferent to budget-maximizing behavior by the bureaus; only in this case is the collective organization passive, in the strict sense. Or (3) the preferences of the collective organization may be contrary to budget-maximizing behavior by the bureaus, but the officers may not have sufficient information or authority to prevent such behavior; this is the typical assumption of the public administration literature but does not appear to be based on any objective characteristics of actual collective organizations.

The earlier chapters of this book assumed a passive collective organization but did not address the characteristics of such organizations that might lead to this condition. They also assumed that a collective organization has a budget-output function for each service but did not examine how such a function is determined. These problems must now be examined to complete a theory of the behavior of bureaus faced by collective sponsors with the specific characteristics of representative government. This extension is necessary both to address the positive questions about the behavior of bureaus that do not have an exclusive monopoly in the supply of a service and to address the normative questions about the representative governments through which public services are financed.

Collective organizations, of course, are not passive, in the strict sense. Many people work very hard to select officers for collective organizations. Many officers work very hard, and most officers undoubtedly identify their personal interests, at least in part, with their perception of the public interest. There are often good reasons to be skeptical about whether the public interest is served by their activities, but there is seldom any purpose served by being cynical about their motivations. The beginning of wisdom in the study of collective organizations, from country clubs to national states, is the recognition that the officers of such organizations, like bureaucrats, are men with quite personal objectives and with limited capacities. The personal objectives of such officers include both selfish and benevolent elements, in different proportions, and it may be that the selection process for officers of collective organizations is such that those selected are more strongly motivated by benevolent considerations than are their constituents. The officers, however, even when motivated by benevolent considerations, are men who are neither omniscient nor omnipotent. They are inherently neither philosopher-kings nor, in the modern terminology, Pareto-optimizers.[1]

The behavior of collective organizations and the degree to which they serve the interests of their constituency depend on several characteristics: (1) the opportunities and costs for a person to transfer his membership among collective organizations; (2) the processes for selecting officers of the collective organization; (3) the processes for dividing the activities of the collective organization among its officers; and (4) the decision rules of

---

1. Economists, at least, should recognize the paradox in their typical assumptions about the motivations of people in their private and public activity. Nathan Rosenberg expressed this most aptly:

"The history of the economist's treatment of political behavior and policy making presents a curious and not entirely edifying spectacle. The eighteenth-century origins of our discipline are steeped in a conception of human behavior which was uncompromisingly self-interested and egoistic. The keynote was perhaps set by Mandeville who assured his readers that 'there is nothing so universally sincere upon Earth, as the Love which all Creatures, that are capable of any, bear to themselves.' As a counterpart to this view, the possibility of disinterested, to say nothing of altruistic, behavior on the part of all public officials was treated with at least skepticism and more often contempt. Adam Smith made withering references to 'that insidious and crafty animal, vulgarly called a statesman or politician,' and David Hume accepted it 'as a maxim, that, in contriving any system of government, and fixing the several checks and controls of the constitution, every man ought to be supposed to be a *knave*, and to have no other end, in all his actions, than private interest.' Yet somehow or other, economists allowed themselves to be saddled with a Benthamite legislator whose own preference function played no role in political decision-making and whose adroit use of the felicific calculus enabled him to calculate that wondrous ambiguity, 'the greatest happiness for the greatest number.' Perhaps even more astonishing than his ability to make this calculation was the assumption that he would in fact legislate accordingly" (Nathan Rosenberg, "Efficiency in the Government Sector: Discussion," *American Economic Review*, May 1964, pp. 251–252).

the collective organization. Almost all the literature on the behavior of collective organizations assumes that an individual has no choice whether to be a member of such organizations (the costs of transferring membership are infinite) and focuses on the effects of the three political characteristics.[2] These four characteristics differ substantially among collective organizations and, as a consequence, the behavior of collective organizations may be much more heterogeneous than the behavior of profit-seeking institutions or bureaus.

The costs of transferring membership among churches or country clubs is small; the costs of moving in order to be served by another local government are somewhat larger; and these costs increase at each higher level of government. A variety of processes and voting rules are used to select officers of collective organizations, and for some organizations the officers are effectively self-perpetuating. Some small collective organizations act as a body, but most collective organizations divide some of the activities among committees which are selected in various ways. Many collective organizations make decisions on the basis of a majority approval of some quorum of the officers, but some decisions are based on a different decision rule or a different quorum. For this reason, even the taxonomic phase of political science has proved difficult.

The behavior of bureaus sponsored by significantly different types of collective organizations should be expected to be quite different. Actually, this does not present so much of a problem as it might appear. Most of the variance in the political characteristics of collective organizations are among private collective organizations and local governments. Among these organizations, however, there is one important uniform characteristic —the cost of transferring membership or moving in order to be served by another local government is small. As a consequence, the demand for services financed by any one of these smaller collective organizations is very elastic, because the slope of the demand function to each organization is determined more by the distribution of the costs of transferring membership or moving than by the population demand for the service. The maximum net benefits that a bureau financed by a private functionally specialized collective organization could appropriate is the aggregate cost of transferring membership. The maximum net benefits that all bureaus financed by a multi-service local government could appropriate is the aggregate cost of moving. The casual member of a church or country club has little reason to be concerned about the political characteristics of the organization, because his costs of transfer are low. The renter-employee has little reason to be concerned about the political characteristics of local government, because his costs of moving are low. Conversely, it should not be surprising

2. Choice of membership among collective organizations should be distinguished from the choice of membership among groups (such as political parties) within a collective organization. There is a good deal of literature, of course, on party affiliation and recruitment.

that church organizations are dominated by the doctrinaire and local governments by property-owners, because their costs of transfer or moving are higher.

One effect of the low cost of transfer and the consequent high elasticity of the demand for the services of each organization is that the behavior of bureaus financed by these organizations are fairly homogeneous— independent of the political structure of the organizations. As demonstrated in Chapter 8, a bureau facing a highly elastic demand for its service will supply the service at or near the minimum total cost at an output only slightly higher than the optimal. One should not expect any form of organization, therefore, to provide local services at a *uniformly* lower cost than the cost at which these services are now supplied by private or local government bureaus. The automobile and an efficient housing market are probably the strongest contributors to the responsiveness and efficiency of local government.

The life of an owner of a competitive firm or of a local bureaucrat is not an easy one, but this need not be the basis for public concern. I suspect that part of the "fiscal crisis of the cities" is a quite understandable yearning for the monopoly power and easier life of their big brother bureaucrats at higher levels of government. Local politics are still important to most people in isolated communities and to local property-owners in any community. In fact, local government is likely to be more efficient the more it is dominated by local property-owners (who have an interest in maximizing the value of their property); for this reason there may be a good case for *restricting* the franchise in local governments to those who own property in the community. In our increasingly mobile age, when most people live in metropolitan areas with many political jurisdictions, local politics are increasingly irrelevant. And there is increasingly *less* reason to be concerned about the bureaucratic supply of local services except for those groups for whom residential location is restricted by racial discrimination or economic conditions.[3]

There is more reason to be concerned about the bureaucratic supply of services financed by higher levels of government. The higher the costs of moving, the more the demand for services financed by any level of government approximates the population demand for these services. In the limiting case—an authoritarian national state that effectively prohibits

3. An understanding of the political economy of federalism has been surprisingly slow to develop. The most important early contribution was by Charles Tiebout, "A Pure Theory of Local Expenditures," *Journal of Political Economy* LXIV (October 1956), 416–24. Some of the more perceptive recent contributions include the following: Bryan Ellickson, "Metropolitan Residential Location and the Local Public Sector" *Econometrica,* July 1970 (abstract); Mancur Olson, "The Principal of 'Fiscal Equivalence': The Division of Responsibilities among Different Levels of Government," *American Economic Review,* May 1969, pp. 479–487; Vincent Ostrom, "Operational Federalism: Organization for the Provision of Public Services in the American Federal System," *Public Choice* VI (Spring 1969), 1–18; J. Roland Pennock, "Federal and

emigration—the demand for services financed by the national state is equal to the population demand for these services, and the consequent lower elasticity of demand permits more exploitation by the bureaucracy. It is no accident that the most bureaucratic states have the most authoritarian controls on emigration. It is also no accident that international population flows are uniformly in the direction from more bureaucratic to less bureaucratic nations, with some people finding ways to evade the authoritarian controls even at high personal cost. The higher the cost of moving, the more important are the political characteristics of collective organizations as determinants of the responsiveness and efficiency of bureaus. Fortunately, for analytic purposes the political characteristics of the regional and national governments in the United States and other Western nations are surprisingly homogeneous. Officers of these governments are elected by regional constituencies, usually from only two significant candidates for each position. The review and program formulation activities of the government are performed primarily by service-specialized committees. And decisions are usually approved by majority vote of a specified quorum of the officers. These are the primary characteristics of governments that influence their behavior relative to their sponsored bureaus. For purposes of this analysis it does not make much difference whether the chief executive is directly elected or is selected by the legislature.

The following discussion is thus primarily focused on the relation between either state or national governments and the bureaus supplying services financed by these governments. At the present time, most of the expenditures by bureaus are financed by these higher levels of government. And the higher cost of moving among these governments makes the performance of bureaus sponsored by these governments a matter for greater concern.

Ideal Behavior: The Normative Model

The most explicit model of what private and public goods and services *ought* to be supplied is developed in the economic literature. Briefly, this model states that goods and services should be supplied at a level such that

---

Unitary Government—Disharmony and Frustration," *Behavioral Science* IV (1959), 147–157; Jerome Rothenberg, "Local Decentralization and the Theory of Optimal Government," *The Analysis of Public Output,* (New York: Columbia University Press, 1970), 31–58; Gordon Tullock, "Federalism: Problems of Scale," *Public Choice* VI (Spring 1969), 19–30; and Robert Wood, *Suburbia* (Boston: Houghton Mifflin Co., 1958).

This recent literature suggests that the responsiveness and efficiency of local governments (more than 80,000 in the United States) are due primarily to people's opportunity to select their government by moving—rather than, as suggested by Robert Dahl, because of their greater opportunity to participate in politics at this level.

the *difference* between the total value to all people of each good or service and the total cost to all people is maximized.[4]

For private goods (for which the use of the good by one person precludes its use by another person at the same time), the general solution to the problem of optimal supply is indicated on Figure 13.1. For analytic purposes, assume there are three groups of customers of equal size, the demands for a specific private good among customers within each group are homogeneous, and the demand functions for the three groups are represented by V_1, V_2, and V_3. For private goods, the aggregate demand function ΣV is the sum of the quantities that would be purchased by the three groups at each price.[5] The total amount of the good that would be supplied at each price is represented by the supply function C. The output of this private good that maximizes the difference between the total value of the good (the area under ΣV) and the total cost of the good (the rectangle for any V and q combination intersecting C) is at Σq, where the aggregate marginal value is equal to the price. The distinguishing characteristic of the optimal supply of private goods is that different quantities of the good are supplied to the several groups at the same price. The first group is supplied an amount q_1 at a price v and a total cost vq_1, and similarly for the other groups. The total expenditure by the three groups equals $v \cdot \Sigma q$.

For public services (for which the use of the service by one person does not reduce the amount available for use by another person at the same time), the general solution to the problem of optimal supply is indicated on Figure 13.2. The demand functions for each group are the same as in Figure 13.1. For public services, however, the aggregate demand function ΣV is the sum of the price that each group would be willing to pay for each quantity.[6] Again, the total amount that would be supplied at each price is represented by the supply function C. The output of the public service that maximizes the difference between the total value and the total cost of the service is at q, again where the aggregate marginal value is equal to the price. The distinguishing characteristic of the optimal supply of public service is that the same quantity of the service is supplied to the several groups at different prices.

4. Economists may be more familiar, and more comfortable, with the marginal conditions for the optimal supply. In marginal terms, briefly, goods and services should be supplied such that the marginal value of each good to each individual is equal to the price to each individual. The marginal conditions imply the total condition; the reverse, however, does not necessarily hold, because the distribution of the net benefits of the optimal level of the good may not be consistent with the marginal conditions.

5. In the upper value region, the aggregate demand function is identical to the demand function for the third group. In the lower value region, the slope of the aggregate demand function is always lower than that for any group.

6. In the lower value region, the aggregate demand function is identical to that for the third group. In the higher value region, the slope of the aggregate demand function is always higher than that for any group. A comparison of the slopes of the aggregate demand function for private and public services, given the same group demand functions, gives operational content to the phrase "private wants and public needs."

Figure 13.1   Optimal Supply of a Private Good or Service

The first group is supplied a quantity q at a price v_1 and a total cost v_1q, and similarly for the other groups. The total expenditures for the three groups equals $q \cdot \Sigma v$.

The above exposition of the characteristics of the optimal supply of private goods and public services briefly summarizes a rich theoretical literature dating back to the nineteenth century (although the provincial community of English-speaking economists rediscovered the characteristics of the optimal supply of public services only in the middle 1950's). By themselves, however, these characteristics do not identify the nature of the institutions and collective activities that would lead to the optimal supply of these goods. One or more of the following types of collective activities are necessary to supply any amount of either private or public services: (1) the definition and enforcement of property rights and contracts; (2) fiat measures requiring or prohibiting certain activities, enforced by civil or criminal penalties; (3) subsidy or taxation of private activities; and/or (4) governmental supply of the good or service. The appropriate focus of political economy is the identification of which one or combination of the collective activities would generate the most nearly optimal supply of each private and public service.

Economists continue to find new ways to prove that competitive industries, operating in an environment of well-defined property rights, supply the optimal amount of strictly private goods at the minimum possible cost. The concepts of private and public services, however, do not map

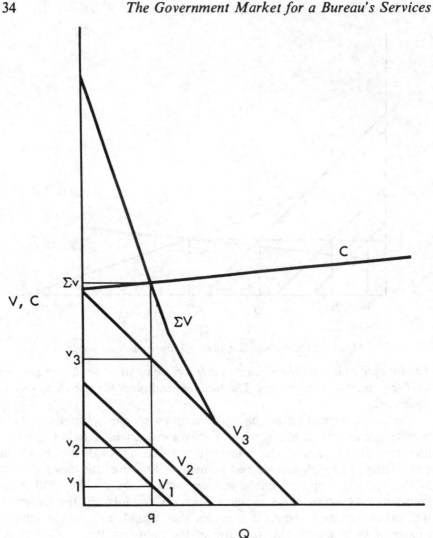

Figure 13.2   Optimal Supply of a Public Service

neatly against actual goods and services, and it is increasingly recognized that many goods have both private and public characteristics. In most nations, both private and public institutions supply goods with both private and public characteristics. And there is no body of literature that reflects any consensus about the institutions and policies that would generate the optimal amount of mixed private and public services or of pure public services. The normative model of what goods and services should be supplied, in short, does not by itself provide a normative model of the form and activities of government that would generate the optimal supply of services with public characteristics.

In contemporary Western nations, the population has a substantial influence on the form and activities of their governments, either through moving or through representative political processes. One would hope, in these conditions, that the normative model of what public services ought to be supplied would also have some predictive power about what governments, in fact, do. Unfortunately, I believe, the normative model has very little predictive power about the behavior of governments at a level where the costs of movement are high. (In contrast, the normative model of what private goods ought to be supplied has a great deal of predictive power about the behavior of private firms.) The continued existence of representative national governments is not sufficient evidence that government activity is consistent with the normative model. The absence of mass emigration, separatist movements, or revolution indicates only that a government is, at least, barely acceptable. But the difference between barely acceptable and optimal governments includes most of the governments in the world.

In conditions where emigration is very costly, the primary reasons why the existing forms of representative government do not necessarily generate optimal behavior are the following:

1. The election processes generate very little information about the population's demands for specific public services. Legislators are usually elected by regional constituencies in a two-candidate election. (The direct election of chief executives differs primarily in the size of the constituency.) A candidate is elected on the basis of the *package* of the candidate's positions on issues, estimates of the candidate's effectiveness in influencing the decision on this package of issues, attitudes toward the aggregate activities of government, and, undoubtedly, personal characteristics of the candidate and purely random considerations.

Even if the candidate's package of positions on issues is explicit and the only consideration of the voters, the election of one candidate indicates only that a majority of voters prefer one package of positions to another. In recent years, casual observation suggests that the candidates' positions on issues are increasingly obscure and are of declining importance in the voters' considerations. In any case, on any one issue, the elected legislator or chief executive may have an entirely incorrect estimate of the voters' preferences. A two-candidate election provides about as much information on the population preferences as would the selection of a fixed diet for a several-year period from a menu which includes only two fixed diets, where the price and some of the elements of the diet are obscure, the capability of the chef is uncertain, a bar girl and a rock group are distracting one's attention, and there is only one place to eat in a very large region. Moreover, the process for selecting the two menus assures that they will be similar.

A selection from a larger number of candidates combined with proportional representation would improve the quality of the information on voter preferences but would solve only part of the problem. The opportunity to choose which particular government (or restaurant) to provide a specific service would further improve the information on preferences even if the voter had no direct influence on the services offered by a particular government. Some of the ingenuity devoted to the analysis of political processes should probably be devoted to the design of a system of service-specialized competing governments from which people could choose to provide the public services they prefer.

2. The elected officers of higher-level governments, in most conditions, have very poor information on the minimum total cost to supply a specific service. Monopoly bureaus, like profit-seeking monopolies, do not have an objective supply function and their behavior does not directly reveal their cost conditions. The primary information available to the executive and the legislators are the budget-output proposals by the bureaus, and these are jointly based on the bureau's estimate of the sponsor's demand for a service, the minimum cost of producing the service, and the expected reduction of the budget-output proposal in the sponsor's review process.

Unless there are other organizations that also supply the same or a similar service, the only way the sponsor can estimate the bureau's minimum total cost function is by building up this function from detailed production and factor cost information. Those few legislators who could conceivably make such estimates probably have a relatively high preference for the services of the bureau and, as shown later, would not have the incentive for this task.

This cost information problem is not so acute for private collective organizations and local governments, because there are many other organizations supplying similar services to provide a basis for comparison. Indeed, the primary technique for budget-review at this level is to compare the budget-output proposal of the sponsored bureau with the revealed experience of other organizations. In higher-level governments, the primary budget-review technique is to compare the budget-output proposal of the sponsored bureau with its own revealed experience in prior periods. In a rapidly changing world, historical comparisons, unfortunately, provide a narrower range of relevant comparisons than cross-section comparisons. In any case, the division of the budget-review process among service-specialized committees, as will be demonstrated later, distorts the incentives to improve the estimates of the minimum costs of producing a service.

3. Assuming that the information problem on the demands and costs of public services is resolved (in some yet unidentified way), what characteristics of present governments might conceivably lead the executive and legislators to maximize the difference between the total value of the services to all people and the total cost of the services? There is no apparent characteristic of government (such as the political analog of a stock option)

that would make the motivations of the executive and legislators consistent with maximizing the total net benefits to the entire population. These officers usually cannot directly appropriate as personal income any part of the net benefits.

The behavior of both the executive and the legislators can best be interpreted as the result of maximizing their own personal interests subject to the constraint of reelection. The reelection constraint is important but does not, given that a simple plurality or majority is sufficient for reelection, assure behavior which maximizes the total net benefits to all people, even in the officer's own regional constituency.

For all that, the most dangerous of all politicians is one who is indifferent to his own reelection or the future of his party; this condition, of course, provides an opportunity for both statesmanship and skullduggery but puts the voter in the unfortunate position of being absolutely dependent on the politician's motivations and the constraints on his power. And one man's statemanship may be another man's skullduggery. The reelection constraint substantially reduces the range of discretionary behavior for both the executive and legislators, but does not by itself assure that the politically motivated behavior is in the general public interest.

The model of government designed in Philadelphia in the summer of 1787 has proved remarkably viable, but it was consciously designed to provide the minimal necessary government—to reduce the probability of disastrous behavior by government rather than necessarily to induce optimal behavior. There is increasing and widespread concern that this characteristic of our form of government is breaking down, particularly with respect to the conduct of foreign policy and military activity. But even if the constitutional limits on the executive discretion on these activities are restored, the present forms of representative government do not necessarily induce anything more than a barely acceptable combination of activities by higher-level governments.

In summary, the normative model of what public services should be supplied provides a valuable criterion against which the behavior of all governments can be judged. It does not by itself, however, suggest the nature of the institutions that would induce behavior consistent with it; what is lacking is a positive model of the behavior of political institutions that approaches the richness and power of the models of market institutions. Even in representative governments, unless individuals can select from a set of governments at low cost, the normative model does not have much predictive power. And if individuals can select from a set of governments at low cost, popular control of the individual governments is less important. There is an "invisible hand" in governmental affairs, but it is a helping hand for some, a barely acceptable appendage to many, and a mailed fist for others.

14

A Model of the Review Process in Representative Government

General Characteristics

We must have a positive model of the behavior of the officers of a representative government in their review activities to describe the "market" for a bureau's services. In Chapter 3 the characteristic relation between a bureau and the sponsoring collective organization was described as a bilateral monopoly, and Chapters 5 through 12 developed the monopoly bureau's solution to the determination of the budget and output for a specific service. This chapter develops the representative government's solution to this same problem. A comparison of the monopoly bureau's solution with the monopoly sponsor's solution will indicate whether there exists a single determinate solution or a range of solutions within which the solution is indeterminate. The monopoly sponsor's solution is also necessary if we are later to develop the solution to the budget and output when a bureau is competing with another bureau or a competitive industry for the right to supply a specific service.

Consider the following simplified model of a representative government:[1]

1. The government finances only the supply of pure public services.

2. The government serves a population consisting of three groups, each with a different level of demand for each public service.

3. Each of the three groups elects an equal number of representatives to a legislature. (For present purposes, the size of the population in each of the three groups and the nature of the election processes are irrelevant.)

4. All services are financed out of general revenues. Each of the three

1 After completing the analyses presented in this chapter, I found that Robert Dorfman had recently developed a model of representative government with some important similar characteristics. See Robert Dorfman, "General Equilibrium with Public Goods," *Public Economics*, edited by J. Margolis and H. Guiton (New York: St. Martin's Press, 1969), pp. 247–275.

population groups bears a predetermined constant proportion of any incremental taxes.

5. All activities of the government must be approved by at least a simple majority of the entire legislature.

6. The legislature divides the review responsibilities among committees, one committee for each service. The committees review the budget-output proposals from the bureaus (or from other sources) and recommend a proposed budget and program for approval by the entire legislature.

7. The committees for each service are dominated by representatives of the group with the *highest* relative demand for the service. (One might think it equally plausible that the committees would consist of those representatives who have the highest and lowest demands for a specific service. A characteristic of legislatures, however, is that advocacy is concentrated and opposition is diluted. This is consistent with the observation that committee votes on an issue are more nearly unanimous than the votes of the entire legislature, and the legislature reduce the committee recommendations more often than they increase them.)

8. The review committees recommend programs to the legislature that maximize (their perception of) the net benefits accruing *to the median voter in the region they represent*, subject to the constraint of approval by the entire legislature.

In a strict sense, this is a model of a parliamentary government without a directly elected executive. With a few changes in words, however, it would describe a government headed by an elected executive with no legislature but with a popular referendum on each issue. In any case, this model abstracts from the bargaining between the executive and the legislature and does not directly address the bargaining within the legislature over different issues.

The behavior of this government is evaluated for example conditions consistent with those illustrated by Figure 13.2. First, the optimal level of output of the public service and the optimal distribution of tax charges to the three population groups are determined. Next, the behavior of this government is evaluated, given the supply of the public service by a competitive industry (or the equivalent). And finally, the behavior of the government is evaluated, given the supply of the public service by a monopoly bureau. For both the second and third cases, the effects of two different distributions of tax charges are evaluated. In a later chapter we shall evaluate the supply by a bureau competing with another bureau and with a competitive industry. All these cases refer to the supply of a single public service under the several specified conditions.

The critical information necessary to evaluate these several cases are the demands for the service by each group and the total cost of the service.

These demands and cost conditions are represented by the following general functions:

$$V_1 = a_1 - 2b_1Q, \ 0 \le Q < \frac{a_1}{2b_1},$$

$$V_2 = a_2 - 2b_2Q, \ 0 \le Q < \frac{a_2}{2b_2}, \tag{14.1}$$

$$V_3 = a_3 - 2b_3Q, \ 0 \le Q < \frac{a_3}{2b_3}, \text{ and}$$

$$TC = cQ + dQ^2, \ 0 \le Q. \tag{14.2}$$

The specific values of the parameters of these general functions that are used for these cases are shown below.

Let us consider conditions for which the demands for a specific public service by the three population groups, as perceived by their representatives, are represented by the following marginal valuation functions:

$$V_1 = 20 - Q, \ 0 \le Q < 20,$$

$$V_2 = 30 - Q, \ 0 \le Q < 30, \text{ and} \tag{14.3}$$

$$V_3 = 50 - Q, \ 0 \le Q < 50.$$

In the upper value region where all three demands are effective, the aggregate demand for this public service is thus

$$\Sigma V = 100 - 3Q, \ 0 \le Q < 20. \tag{14.4}$$

The total cost function for this specific service is assumed to be

$$TC = 50Q + .1Q^2, \ 0 \le Q. \tag{14.5}$$

The Optimal Output and Tax Charges

The optimal level of output of a public service is that for which the aggregate marginal value equals the price. For the above conditions, the optimal quantity of this service is the level of Q for which

$$100 - 3Q = 50 + .1Q \tag{14.6}$$

For these conditions the characteristics of the optimal solution are presented in Table 14.1. The specific relevance of this solution is that it maximizes the total net benefits to all groups and that the net benefits to any one group cannot be increased without reducing the net benefits to another group. In this case (with equal demand slopes), the net benefits to each group are the same.

Under most institutional conditions, it is not possible to determine and

Table 14.1 Optimal supply of public service: Example conditions

Groups	Benefits	Taxes	Net Benefits	Q
Low demand	192.5	62.4	130.1	
Middle demand	353.8	223.7	130.1	
High demand	676.4	546.3	130.1	
Total	1,222.7	832.4	390.3	16.1

levy the optimal distribution of tax charges for each service, but only for the package of services financed from a common tax system. An estimate of the optimal distribution of tax charges for each service is operationally relevant only for conditions such that only one public service is supplied by each government, or each service is financed by a separate tax, or if the demand and cost conditions for all services are identical. An estimate of the optimal distribution of tax charges for the above demand and cost conditions is made, however, to provide a basis for comparison with the following cases of the supply of public services with specific institutional characteristics. Conceptually, given knowledge of the demand functions of each group, one can determine the optimal tax charges by setting the unit tax price to each group equal to the marginal value to each group of the common optimal level of output. At this level of output and tax charges, all groups are in equilibrium and no group would prefer either a larger or a smaller amount of this service.

Notice that the optimal distribution of the tax charges for this service is progressive relative to the level of the demand function for the service. The level of the demand function for this service by Group 2 is only 1.5 times that of Group 1, but the optimal tax charge is 3.6 times as large. The level of the demand function by Group 3 is 2.5 times that of Group 1, but the optimal tax charge is 8.7 times as large. The progressive distribution of the optimal tax charges reinforces the characteristic problem—each population group has a strong incentive to understate its true demands for public services.

These characteristics of the optimal solution provide the basis against which the following cases, representing the solution in specific governmental settings, should be compared.

Competitive Supply of Public Services

Now let us consider the solution for several cases for a government with the characteristics described above. First, consider conditions for which there is an objective price schedule at which various quantities of a specific public service are available, and that this price schedule is known by all of the representatives (more accurately, at least by those representatives that include the marginal vote required for approval). This is the case if the public services are supplied by a competitive industry or if there is a sufficient cross-section sample of the budget and output of bureaus supplying this service to provide an objective basis for estimating the minimum cost function. Under these conditions, there is no particular reason to assign the review responsibilities to a committee. The representatives of the middle-demand group include the median vote on any proposal for this service, and the approval by this group is necessary for any majority. If the representatives of this group know the price at which the public service is available, they can deny approval to any proposal other than one which maximizes the net benefits of this group. The only solution here which can command majority approval is the output at which the marginal value of the service to the middle-demand group is equal to the "tax price" to this group, that is, the proportion of incremental taxes paid by this group times the price of the service.

For the first case, let us assume that the total incomes of the three groups are equal and that the tax system is such that the proportions of the incremental taxes paid by the three groups are the same. Thus, any differences in demands among the three groups reflect pure differences in preferences (caused by differences in the composition of the population and economic activity, regional conditions, etc.) at the same income level. For the above conditions, the solution is the level of Q for which the marginal value to the middle-demand group is equal to the marginal tax price to that group.

$$30 - Q = \frac{1}{3}(50 + .2Q) \tag{14.7}$$

The characteristics of the solution for this example are presented in Table 14.2. At the optimal level of output and tax charges, the aggregate marginal value is equal to the price, and the marginal value for each group is equal to the tax price to that group. In this example the quantity of the public service supplied is lower than the optimal quantity; as a consequence, the aggregate marginal value is higher than the price.

The quantity of any public service supplied by a majority decision rule,

Table 14.2 *Competitive supply and equal taxes: Example conditions*

Groups	Benefits	Taxes	Net Benefits	Q
Low demand	171.9	213.5	−41.7	
Middle demand	296.9	213.5	83.3	
High demand	546.9	213.5	333.3	
Total	1,015.6	640.6	375.0	12.5

when the service is supplied at an objective price and the tax price to each group is the same, is equal to the optimal quantity only when the demand for the service by the median voter is equal to the arithmetic mean of the demands by other groups.[2] When the demand by the median voter is lower than the arithmetic mean of the other voters, as in this example, the quantity supplied is lower than the optimal quantity, and conversely, when the demand by the median voter is higher than the arithmetic mean, the quantity supplied will be higher than the optimal quantity. For these conditions, thus, there is no *a priori* reason for majority rule decisions to lead to a uniform undersupply or oversupply of public services. For any government to which public services are available at an objective price, a majority rule decision will make the marginal value equal to the tax price only for the median voter. The marginal value is lower than the tax price for the group with a low relative demand and higher for the group with a high relative demand.

For this case, the total net benefits are somewhat lower than at the optimal quantity of the public service. The group with the lowest demand is absolutely worse off than if none of the public service is supplied. This is not a general conclusion; the low-demand group may have either positive or negative net benefits from the majority rule selection of the quantity, depending on the specific parameters, but the net benefits to this group are always lower than in the optimal case. The net benefits to the middle group are positive but lower than in the optimal case, and the net benefits to the high-demand group are substantially higher. The last conclusion is general for the two conditions of this example.

The general effect of the majority rule selection of the output of a public service, if the service is available at an objective price and the tax price to each group is equal, is thus to benefit the high-demand group at the expense of the low-demand group. Legislators are most likely to exchange votes ("log-roll") on those public services for which the differences in demands are *not* primarily due to differences in incomes. For these, the low-demand group for one service may be the high-demand group for another, and vice versa. As a consequence of this log-rolling, no group is *relatively* better or worse off from the supply of these services; log-rolling, however, typically requires a representative to vote for approval against his own preferences, and the consequent general expansion of these services may make all groups absolutely worse off. The effect of log-rolling is similar to the effect of averaging the bill at a restaurant; each person has an incentive to order a high-priced meal than if the bills were separate. Both bureaus and restaurants, understandably, prefer the averaging of their charges.

2. An interesting "least squares" proof of this is given by Yoram Barzel, "Two Propositions on the Optimum Level of Producing Collective Goods," *Public Choice* VI (Spring 1969), 31–37.

Differences in the demand for most public services among groups in the population are likely to be associated with differences in the incomes of the groups and, consequently, with the proportion of the taxes paid by each group. The effects of a different tax price for each group are evaluated in this second case, again assuming that the public service is available at an objective price. For this case, let us assume that the differences in demand among the three groups for a public service are due only to differences in income, and that the level of the demand function is proportional to the income of each group. The marginal valuation function of each group i is thus represented by

$$V_i = y Y_i - Q \qquad (14.8)$$

where

$$Y_i \equiv \text{income of group } i.$$

Let us assume also that the tax charges to each group are proportional to the income of the group and thus also to the level of demand. Although most national tax systems are nominally progressive, the differential taxation of different forms of income make them effectively proportional for large groups over a wide range of total income. The tax charges to each group i are proportional to the group income, accordingly

$$T_i = r Y_i \qquad (14.9)$$

where

$$T_i \equiv \text{total tax charges to group } i \text{ and}$$

$$r = \text{marginal tax rate on income.}$$

Here, then, the tax share of group i is indicated by the proportion of total income earned by this group. For these conditions, the solution is also the level of Q for which the marginal value by the middle-demand group equals the marginal tax price to that group

$$30 - Q = .3(50 + .2Q) \qquad (14.10)$$

The characteristics of the solution for this example are presented in Table 14.3.

A tax system for which the tax prices are proportional to the relative

Table 14.3 *Competitive supply and proportional taxes: Example conditions*

Groups	Benefits	Taxes	Net Benefits	Q
Low demand	182.9	145.5	37.4	
Middle demand	324.4	218.3	106.1	
High demand	607.4	363.8	243.6	
Total	1,114.7	727.6	387.1	14.2

levels of the demand functions for a service brings the quantity selected by majority rule somewhat closer to the optimal quantity; this is a general conclusion whether the demand of the median voter is above or below the arithmetic mean of the demands of all groups. For this example, the effect of proportional (rather than equal) taxation is to lower slightly the tax price of the middle group and thus to increase the quantity of the public service. The quantity selected, however, is still lower than the optimal, and the aggregate marginal value is higher than the price of the service. Again, the marginal value of the service to the low-demand group is lower than the tax price, the marginal value to the middle group is equal to the tax price, and the marginal value to the high-demand group is higher than the tax price. The total net benefits are very near the maximum possible. The net benefits to all three groups are positive. The net benefits to the low- and middle-demand groups, however, are still lower than with the optimal distribution of tax charges, and the net benefits to the high-demand group are higher than in the optimal case.

The differences in the net benefits generated by the supply of public services for which the differences in demand are primarily due to differences in income are not likely to be evened out by log-rolling on the amount of the several services. The representative of a constituency that is consistently in the low-demand group for a large number of public services has no incentive to trade votes except to try to reduce the tax charges to this group. And the representative of a consistently high-demand group does not need to trade votes with representatives of the low-demand group. A number of scholars have mistakenly concluded that log-rolling is the "invisible hand" which protects the public interest in the supply of public services. Where the differences in demand for public services are random, such vote trading can reduce the difference in the net benefits among the represented groups. Where the differences in the demands for public services are consistent, however, no characteristic of our present political institutions reduces the difference in the net benefits accruing to the high- and low-demand groups.

This example suggests a number of interesting general conclusions: For those public services for which the levels of demand by the several groups are primarily determined by the group incomes, for which the median demand is not far from the arithmetic mean of the group demands, and that are supplied at an objective price, majority rule decision processes and proportional taxation lead to a level of public services near the optimal. Although the solution is near "allocative efficiency," proportional taxation does not generate a "distributional equilibrium." At tax prices proportional to the level of the demand functions of the several groups, the low-demand group would prefer that less of the service be supplied, and the high-demand group would prefer that more be supplied. For a nation with demands for public services that are a strong function of income, a system of progressive taxation is the only way to achieve both allocative efficiency and a distributional equilibrium. Further, the tax structure should be more progressive the higher the sensitivity of demand to income, the greater the differences in group incomes, and the lower the cost of public services.[3]

For those services for which the demands are strongly dependent on conditions other than income, however, a tax system that is proportional or progressive to income is not necessarily proportional or progressive to the demands. For some services, the middle-demand group may be a fairly low-income group, and any system of tax charges which increases with income will lead to the oversupply of these services. Differences in demands for public services that are dependent on other than differences in incomes usually reflect the preferences of specific demographic groups or economic interests. Because people with these special preferences are often regionally concentrated, the strong inference from this evaluation is that the provision of these public services should be assigned to lower-level governments. A progressive national tax system appears to be an appropriate way to finance such services as national defense and general transfer payments, but it seems to be a very poor way to finance such regionally specific public services as flood control, irrigation, crop insurance, urban mass transit, etc. At the national level, the middle-demand groups for these services are often low-income groups, and a national tax system based on income will lead to a substantial oversupply of these services.

Bureaucratic Supply of Public Services

With this background, the more characteristic conditions at higher-level governments—where the public services are supplied by a monopoly

---

3. Buchanan has demonstrated that the income elasticity of the optimal tax charges is equal to (the negative of) the ratio of the income elasticity of demand for public services over the price elasticity of demand, as follows:

$$\eta_T = -\frac{\eta_Y}{\eta_P}$$

See James M. Buchanan, "Fiscal Institutions and Efficiency in Collective Outlay," *American Economic Review*, May 1964, pp. 227–235.

Given the form of the marginal valuation function used in this analysis (14.8),

$$\eta_Y = \frac{yY}{yY-P},$$

$$\eta_P = -\frac{P}{yY-P}, \text{ and, thus}$$

$$\eta_T = \frac{yY}{P}.$$

The income elasticity of the optimal tax charges, thus, is a positive function of the sensitivity of demand to income and of the level of income and a negative function of the price of public services.

bureau and there is thus no objective price at which a service is available—can now be developed. At these levels the review activities are characteristically assigned to service-specialized committees dominated by representatives of the group with the highest relative demand for each service. At the city and county levels of governments the elected representatives more often perform the review activities as a group; this is possible primarily because of the availability of public services to these levels of government at a quasi-objective price. National governments are not necessarily any more complex than local governments in terms of the number of services provided, but the division of the review processes among specialized committees is primarily dictated by the absolute size of the legislature and the complexity of reviewing the budget-output proposals of monopoly bureaus.

A division of the review activities among specialized committees has some obvious advantages but some significant, and less obvious, disadvantages. The composition of the committees is generally not representative of the entire group, and, consequently, the programs and budgets recommended by these committees are generally not consistent with those that would be selected by the entire group acting as a body. For this case, the two critical assumptions are that the committee assigned to review a specific service is dominated by representatives of the group with the highest relative demand for the service and that the committee acts to maximize the interests of the group it represents subject to majority approval by the larger body.

For the general demand and cost conditions represented by (14.1) and (14.2), a committee dominated by representatives of the high-demand group maximizes the net benefits to this group,

$$[a_3 Q - b_3 Q^2] - t_3 [cQ + dQ^2], \tag{14.11}$$

subject to the constraint of approval by a majority of the legislature,

$$[a_2 Q - b_2 Q^2] \geq t_2 [cQ + dQ^2]. \tag{14.12}$$

The first term in (14.11) is the total value of the service to the high-demand group and the second term is the amount of the total cost of the service paid by this group. The net benefits accruing to the high-demand group is the *difference* between these two terms. The first term in (14.12) is the total value of the service to the middle-demand group (which includes the median vote), and the second term is the amount of the total cost of the service paid by this group. The middle-demand group is just indifferent to the provision of the service when the two terms in (14.12) are equal; any level of Q for which the first term of (14.12) is slightly larger than the second term will thus command majority approval of the entire body. The solution to the review committee's problem is the level of Q for which (14.11) is maximized or for which the two terms in (14.12) are equal, *whichever is smaller.* The two solutions to the review committee's problem, thus, are

$$
Q = \begin{cases} \dfrac{a_3 - t_3 c}{2(b_3 + t_3 d)} \\[2mm] \text{or} \\[2mm] \dfrac{a_2 - t_2 c}{b_2 + t_2 d}, \text{ whichever is smaller.} \end{cases} \tag{14.13}
$$

Now all sorts of interesting implications can be developed. *A bureau's best estimate of the budget-output function of a representative government with majority rule is the inverse of the tax share by the group electing the median representative times the budget-output function of that group.* For the above notation, thus,

$$
B = \frac{1}{t_2}\left(a_2 Q - b_2 Q^2\right), \, 0 \le Q \le \frac{a_2}{2b_2}. \tag{14.14}
$$

The second solution to the review committee's problem should now be recognized as identical with the solution of a budget-maximizing bureau in the budget-constrained region.

If the first solution yields a lower level of Q, a review committee dominated by representatives of the high-demand group will recommend a level of Q higher than the optimal level but somewhat lower than the bureau's solution; then there is some conflict between the interests of the review committee and the bureau, and this conflict will be manifested by the bargaining, gaming, and obfuscation of information characteristic of bilateral monopoly relations.

If the second solution yields a lower level of Q, the review committee's solution is identical with the bureau's solution; the committee would prefer a larger output but recommends the largest output that it expects would be approved by a majority of the legislature. Here the review process is a stylized farce with every actor playing his institutional role. The primary purpose of the review is to check whether the bureau has accurately estimated the largest program that would be approved by a majority of the legislature; the review committee may either augment or reduce the bureau's proposal if the bureau has misjudged the attitudes of the legislature, but is unlikely to probe the bureau's activities significantly. Although the formal relationship of a bilateral monopoly is maintained, the actual relationship between this bureau and this review committee is more accurately described by the phrase, "in bed with each other," and the consequent output solution, not surprisingly, is determinate.

The conditions for which the above two solutions are equal have a number of interesting properties. For ease of understanding let us assume that the demand slopes are equal ($b_2 = b_3$) and that marginal costs are constant

($d = 0$). For these conditions the two solutions for Q are equal where

$$(a_3 - t_3 c) = 2(a_2 - t_2 c). \tag{14.15}$$

If the term on the left of (14.15) is lower than the term on the right, the review committee will prefer a lower level of Q than the bureau's solution. If the term on the left is higher, the review committee will select the same level of output as the bureau.

The interests of the review committee and the bureau are thus more likely to be consistent the higher are the relative demands by the high-demand group and the lower is the relative proportion of incremental taxes paid by this group. Review committees dominated by representatives of groups with only a slightly higher demand for a service and who pay higher taxes are likely to be in general conflict with monopoly bureaus.

In contrast, review committees dominated by representatives of groups with a substantially higher demand for a service and paying lower taxes are likely to exercise only the most nominal review of a bureau's budget-output proposal, primarily to assure that the proposal will command majority approval by the legislature. The domination of some committees in the U.S. Congress by representatives of relatively low-income states assures that bureaus supplying services for which the population of those states have a relatively high demand will have friendly reception and only a cursory review.

These properties of the committee review of the budget-output proposal of a monopoly bureau are illustrated by two cases. For the first, let us assume the same demand and cost conditions as in the earlier examples and an equal distribution of the tax charges. This case would be most relevant to services for which the differences in demands are primarily due to conditions other than differences in income. From (14.13) the output solutions are

$$Q = \quad \text{or} \quad \begin{cases} \dfrac{50 - .333(50)}{2[.5 + .333(.1)]} = 31.2 \tag{14.16} \\[2mm] \dfrac{30 - .333(50)}{.5 + .333(.1)} = 25.0, \text{ whichever is lower.} \end{cases}$$

In this example the second solution, which is equal to the bureau's solution, is selected by the review committee because a higher level of Q could not command a majority vote. The characteristics of the solution for this example are presented in Table 14.4.

The output level is substantially above the optimal level, and the aggregate marginal value is below the marginal cost. For the bureaucratic supply of a service and equal tax charges, this is a general conclusion. The marginal value for both the low-demand and the middle-demand group is below the tax price to that group, and the marginal value to the high-demand group is higher than the tax price. The total expenditures for this service, for these conditions, are nearly 60 percent higher than at the optimal level of output. The total net benefits generated are only two-thirds that of the optimal level of output. The low-demand group is absolutely worse off than if none of the service is supplied, and the middle-demand group is indifferent; for an equal distribution of tax charges, the bureaucratic supply of a service usually, but not always, leads to these conclusions. And the net benefits to the high-demand group are three times those generated by the optimal level of supply and tax charges.

Table 14.4 Bureaucratic supply and equal taxes: Example conditions

Groups	Benefits	Taxes	Net Benefits	Q
Low demand	200.0	437.5	237.5	
Middle demand	437.5	437.5	0	
High demand	937.5	437.5	500	
Total	1,575.0	1,312.5	262.5	25.0

In Chapter 5 the elementary bureau is described as appropriating all the net benefits of the collective organization. This example now enables me to make a more accurate statement: For conditions such that the review committee's solution is equal to the bureau's solution, the bureaucratic supply of a service generates some total net benefits, negative net benefits to the low-demand group, no net benefits to the middle-demand group, and substantial net benefits to the high-demand group. Indeed, the generation of net benefits to some group is a necessary condition for the pervasive existence of governments, and the substantial negative and positive benefits from the activities of government-sponsored bureaus is the basis for the strong contrary attitudes of different groups toward the government.

As demonstrated by the case where the interests of the bureau and the review committee are consistent, the bureaucratic supply of public services leads to a substantially larger than optimal output and budget. At this level of output, all of the positive net benefits accrue to the high-demand group, the net benefits to the middle group are zero, and the net benefits to the low-demand group are negative. How can this level of output win majority approval? Why do not most of the representatives of the middle group form a majority coalition with representatives of the low-demand group to oppose programs recommended by the committees that generate zero or negative net benefits to their constituencies?

The reason is clear to those who have studied the behavior of national legislatures: The legislature as a body cannot formulate credible alternatives to expenditure programs recommended by the committees.[4] A large national legislature, as a body, essentially serves as a representative referendum, either approving or failing to approve program recommendations by the bureaus as endorsed by the review committees without the opportunity for significant amendment. Sometimes this is due to the rules and procedures necessary to conduct business in a large legislature, such as formal limitations on debate and amendments. More importantly, when the public services are supplied only by bureaus sponsored at that level of government, the legislature does not have an alternative source of supply of the service that is not responsive to the review committee. This gives the bureau and the review committee the opportunity to forward recommended expenditure programs to the legislature on an either-or, all-or-nothing, take-it-or-leave-it basis. The expenditure program must generate net benefits only to the high-demand group plus the constituencies of one more than half of the representatives of the middle-demand group to be approved by a majority of the legislature. Most legislatures are the captives of their own committees, whose interests, in turn, are usually consistent with the bureaus they purportedly review.

A second case illustrates the effects of a system of tax charges proportional to the level of demand of the three groups. Again, this would be consistent with conditions for which the level of the demand functions are proportional to the income of the groups, and the tax charges are proportional to the level of income. From (14.13) the output solutions for this example are

$$Q = \begin{cases} \dfrac{50 - .5(50)}{2[.5 + .5(.1)]} = 22.7 \\ \text{or} \\ \dfrac{30 - .3(50)}{.5 + .3(.1)} = 28.3, \text{ whichever is smaller.} \end{cases} \tag{14.17}$$

In this example, the first solution is preferred by the review committee, as a higher level of Q would reduce the net benefits accruing to the high-demand group. It should be clear, however, that this solution can be achieved only by some effort by the review committee in estimating the minimum total costs of providing the service. Because a bureau does not willingly reveal such information, the actual solution is likely to be somewhere between the two above solutions. The amount of effort that a review committee devotes to estimating the minimum costs of supplying a service is probably a function of the difference in the net benefits accruing to the high-demand group from these two output solutions. If this difference is small, a committee reviewing a complex and cleverly obscure bureau may

4. The two sources on the behavior of the U.S. Congress which I found most useful are the following: Richard Bolling, *House Out of Order* (New York: E. P. Dutton & Co., 1965); and Lewis Froman, *The Congressional Process* (Boston: Little, Brown & Co., 1967).

find it easy to accept the bureau's solution, as this would still command majority approval by the larger body of representatives. The characteristics of the review committee's solution for this example are presented in Table 14.5.

Here, a proportional tax system reduces the amount of the service supplied. The level of output, however, is still higher than optimal, and the aggregate marginal value is still lower than the marginal cost. Again, for the bureaucratic supply of a public service, this is a general conclusion except for a system of tax charges that is highly progressive relative to the demands for the service. The marginal value of the service to both the low- and middle-demand groups is lower than their tax price, and the marginal value to the high-demand group is higher. The total expenditures for the service are over 40 percent higher than at the optimal level of output.

Table 14.5 *Bureaucratic supply and proportional taxes: Example conditions*

Groups	Benefits	Taxes	Net Benefits	Q
Low demand	200.0	237.6	−37.6	
Middle demand	423.6	356.4	67.2	
High demand	878.1	594.0	284.1	
Total	1,501.7	1,188.0	313.7	22.7

Given that the output is somewhat indeterminate between the two solutions (depending on the effectiveness of the review process), the net benefits generated by both solutions are compared in Table 14.6. For proportional tax charges, the review committee's solution generates somewhat larger total net benefits than if the tax charges are equal. The net benefits to the low-demand group are still negative (although this is not a general conclusion) and the net benefits to both the middle- and high-demand groups are positive. The review committee solution would have no trouble commanding more than a majority vote.

A comparison of the net benefits generated by the review committee's output solution and the bureau's output solution, for the same case, is quite disturbing. The bureau's output solution would command a bare majority vote but would generate much smaller total net benefits. Almost all the difference in net benefits, however, accrues to the low- and middle-demand groups, who are poorly represented in the review process. The difference in net benefits resulting from an effective review represents an increase of only a few percent to the high-demand group best represented in the review but a difference of nearly 90 percent in the aggregate. One can understand why representatives in the review committee sometimes opt for an easier life by endorsing the bureau's solution. One can also understand why the larger group of representatives often feel short-changed by the committee review process. Given the low payoff and the high cost to the review committee of an effective review of a bureau's proposed budget and program, the bureau's budget-maximizing solution to the output of a service seems to be a more general solution than it may at first appear.

Table 14.6 Comparison of the net benefits

Groups	Bureau	Review Committee	Difference
Low demand	−99	−37.6	61.4
Middle demand	0	67.2	67.2
High demand	267	284.1	17.1
Total	168	313.7	145.7

Under such conditions, the committee review process is a farce. The bureaus estimate the largest budget that will be approved by the larger body of representatives and add a few percent based on the historical record of reductions made by the committee. The review committees oblige by making the expected reductions. The larger body of representatives dutifully approve the budget recommended by the committee. Most of the participants in this process, I suppose, believe that they are acting in the public interest. The effect of all this activity, of course, is that the low-demand group (most of whom are relatively poor) is worse off, the middle-demand group is indifferent, and the high-demand group (most of whom are relatively rich) complains about high taxes all the way to the bank.

This chapter may impress some readers as an unfairly harsh indictment of the review process in representative government. The model developed in this chapter, however, does not provide any basis to impugn the motivations or derogate the energy which officers of collective organizations bring to their review activities. My primary purpose here is to develop the conditions for which the interests of the review committees differ from those of the bureau and those conditions for which they are consistent. My most important conclusion here is that, although the interests of the review committee and the bureau are not identical, they are often (maybe, generally) consistent. And, even when they are not consistent, the low incremental benefits to the review committee and the high costs of an effective review often leads the committee to accept the bureau's solution.

When conditions are generally recognized as unsatisfactory, some conspiracy theory—such as "the military-industrial complex"—is usually offered as a simple explanation, along with the implication that the solution to the problem is to "throw the rascals out." Alas, such problems and their solutions should be so simple! Such explanations and solutions often have a widespread appeal, but they are generally wrong. The more disturbing fact is that good men who work very hard at their jobs, in certain institutional conditions, can and do make an awful botch of things. The important challenge is to identify those institutional conditions for which a representative proportion of rascals is tolerable and good men are more effective.

15

Bureaucratic Behavior in a
Competitive Environment

General Considerations

Competition among local governments in providing public services generates a range of alternative service-tax packages from which an individual may choose, primarily by moving. In those areas and for those individuals for whom the costs of moving are low, such competition among local governments (or private collective organizations) assures that the combination of services will be responsive to the preferences of residents and that the services will be supplied at near the minimum cost, regardless of the political structure of the local government and even, as is usually the case, if the services are supplied through each local government by monopoly bureaus. A high elasticity of demand for a service financed by a local government is translated into a high elasticity of demand for the service supplied by a monopoly bureau. For these conditions, the analysis in Chapter 8 suggests that a monopoly bureau supplies a near-optimal level of output of a service at the minimum possible costs.

The costs of moving among national governments, however, are much higher, so the elasticity of demand for services supplied through national governments more nearly approximates the population demand for these services. At this level, the political structure of the government is more important. A competition among bureaus supplying the services financed by a national government at least creates the possibility that the elasticity of demand for the service supplied by any one bureau may be much higher than the population demand for the service, with a consequent improvement in efficiency. As will be seen, however, the effects of competition among bureaus financed by a national government depend very much on the nature of the review process and the political structure of the government. In the governmental setting described in Chapter 14 what are the effects of a competition among bureaus in supplying the same or a similar

155

service? Specifically, who benefits from this competition? Is such competition in the public interest?

The evaluation of the elementary monopoly bureau suggests that the primary problem of the bureaucratic supply of a service is not inefficiency; it is oversupply. In the budget-constrained output region, a budget-maximizing bureau has an incentive to supply the equilibrium output at the minimum total costs, and thus to use the most efficient combination of the available factors and processes. Only in the demand-constrained output region is the total budget larger than the minimum total costs at the equlibrium level of output and only there is a bureau indifferent among factor and process combinations. The more elastic the demand for the service supplied by a bureau, moreover, the more likely that the bureau's output will be in the budget-constrained region. Given the review processes and decision rules of a representative national government as described earlier, does the competition among bureaus also lead to an efficient combination of processes? Given the review process and the requirement for majority approval, does the competition among bureaus correct for the problem of oversupply of a service by a monopoly bureau?

Three general conditions determine the effects of a competition among bureaus or other forms of organization for the supply of a service financed through government: (1) the demand conditions facing one bureau as a function of the supply conditions of another bureau (or other form of organization) supplying the same service; (2) the range of alternatives considered by the review committee and the entire body of representatives; and (3) the criteria for choice at the relevant levels of the review process. The effects of these three conditions are illustrated for cases involving two different review procedures.

Review of Competing Bureaus by a Common Committee

First, consider a case in which two bureaus supply the same service. The two bureaus have somewhat different cost conditions, possibly as a consequence of different sets of inherited assets or the use of different production processes. The budget-output proposals of the two bureaus are jointly reviewed by a committee dominated by representatives of a group with a relatively high demand for the service. This review committee selects the budget and output for each bureau and forwards a total budget and output for the service for approval by a majority of the entire body of representatives.

Assume that the relative demands and tax shares are such that the largest total output of the service that would be approved by a majority of the representatives is smaller than that which would maximize the net benefits to the high-demand group. The budget-output function for the middle-demand group is represented by

$$B_2 = a_2 Q - b Q^2, 0 \leq Q < \frac{a_2}{2b}, \tag{15.1}$$

and the tax-share for this group is t_2. The total budget-output function for the sum of the services supplied by the two bureaus, then, is

$$B = \frac{1}{t_2} [a_2 (Q_1 + Q_2) - b(Q_1 + Q_2)^2]. \tag{15.2}$$

The total budget for the two bureaus must be equal to the sum of the total costs of the two bureaus, where

$$TC_1 = c_1 Q_1 + d_1 Q_1^2, 0 \leq Q_1, \text{ and}$$

$$TC_2 = c_2 Q_2 + d_2 Q_2^2, 0 \leq Q_2. \tag{15.3}$$

Solving the equality of the total budget and the total costs for the output of the bureau supplying Q_1 yields the following quadratic equation:

$$Q_1 = \frac{(a_2 - 2bQ_2 - t_2 c_1)}{2(b + t_2 d_1)}$$

$$\tag{15.4}$$

$$\pm \sqrt{\frac{(a_2 - 2bQ_2 - t_2 c_1)^2 - 4(b + t_2 d_1)[(-a_2 + t_2 c_2)Q_2 + (b + t_2 d_2)Q_2^2]}{2(b + t_2 d_1)}}.$$

The largest root of (15.4) is the largest amount of Q_1 that would be approved for a given level of Q_2. This relation is illustrated for a specific set of parameters in Figure 15.1. If, for example, the output of Q_2 were fixed (by prior legislation or just inertia), this relation indicates the largest output of Q_1 that the legislature would approve. The bureau supplying Q_1 may propose a larger output and budget to the review committee, but the proposal would be reduced to a level such that the combined output of Q_1 and Q_2 would be approved by the legislature.

What combination of Q_1 and Q_2 would the review committee choose if the outputs of both bureaus are variable in the relevant period? The above relation does not, by itself, indicate what outputs the two bureaus would propose. One may be tempted to propose the maximum output that the legislature would approve given that the output of the other bureau is zero, but gaming considerations probably lead them to prefer that their budget proposals not be reduced too much. In any case, the combination of the budget-output proposals by the two bureaus will probably be too large to be approved by the legislature, so the review committee must reduce one or both of the proposals.

Again, the review committee is assumed to act in the interests of the constituents represented by the members of the committee. In this case, the total output of the service that the legislature will approve is lower than

Figure 15.1   Relation of the Ouput of Two Competing Bureaus

that output that maximizes the net benefits to the high-demand group, so the review committee has the incentive to maximize the total *output* that the legislature will approve. Notice that the relation between Q_1 and Q_2 is slightly convex; the sum of Q_1 and Q_2 is thus highest for some interior combination of Q_1 and Q_2. The particular combination of Q_1 and Q_2 that maximizes the combined output and, thus, maximizes the potential net benefits to the high-demand group is also the combination that maximizes the total budget of the two bureaus.

As Chapter 6 showed, the combination of processes that maximizes the total budget of a single bureau in the budget-constrained region is also the most efficient combination of processes. For the specific combination of parameters presented on Figure 15.1, the efficient combination of Q_1 and Q_2 is

$$Q_1 = -50 + 4Q_2. \qquad (15.5)$$

Substituting (15.5) for Q_1 in (15.2) and (15.3), one can solve the equality of the total budget and the total costs for the level of Q_2 and then, using (15.5), for Q_1. For these parameters $Q_1 = 13.3$, $Q_2 = 15.8$, and $[Q_1 + Q_2] = 29.1$. The availability of Q_2 has increased the amount of the service that would be approved by a majority of the legislature from 25 to 29.1; this increases the net benefits to the high-demand group, leaves the middle-demand group just short of indifferent, and increases the negative net benefits to the low-demand group. It should not be surprising that the legislature may be substantially divided on the value of a new process or of a more efficient combination of processes when it leads to further oversupply.

For quite different reasons, thus, a review committee dominated by representatives of the high-demand group, given the same information, will select the same combination of processes from two competing bureaus and the same total output and budget as would a monopoly bureau in the budget-constrained region. In this case the equilibrium combination of processes, the total level of output, and the total budget are invariant to the amount of competition among the bureaus. A review committee, maximizing its own interests, has an incentive to find the most efficient combination of processes and thus to maximize the output of the service that will be approved by the legislature. This is not necessarily an easy task, since the competing bureaus still have an incentive to obscure their cost function, but the review basically replicates the solution of the monopoly bureau in the budget-constrained region, albeit for different motivations. Under these conditions, competition among the bureaus does not make the combination of processes more efficient (as the monopoly bureau's production behavior in this region is also efficient) and does not reduce the oversupply of the service.

Some monopoly bureaus, however, operate in the demand-constrained region, and the difference between their budgets and the minimum costs can be substantial. The interests of a demand-constrained bureau and the review committee are not generally consistent. A bureau acts to maximize its budget and here is not motivated to be efficient. The review committee act to maximize the net benefits to the constituencies they represent, and, whether the level of output preferred by the review committee is higher or lower than the output that would be approved by the legislature, the committee generally prefer that the output be efficiently produced.

There is one condition that may make the interests of a demand-constrained bureau more consistent with those of the review committee: The bureau may take advantage of the indeterminancy of production processes in the demand-constrained region to increase the use of specific factors from the region represented in the review committee. Aside from the representation of specific factor interests, the review committee is generally motivated to probe a demand-constrained bureau to reduce its budget to the minimum costs.

This is always a difficult task for a committee reviewing a monopoly bureau, because it has no contemporary basis for comparison and the bureau's interests are to obscure its production and cost conditions. The review committee generally prefers a competition among bureaus supplying the same or a similar service. This competition induces efficiency in two ways. The higher elasticity of demand faced by each bureau increases the probability that each bureau is in the budget-constrained region where the bureau itself is motivated to be efficient. And the competition among bureaus provides the review committee a contemporary basis for comparison, making it easier to recognize unusually efficient or inefficient performance and to reward or penalize bureaus on this basis.

The effects of the increased efficiency in this case are illustrated in Figure 15.2. A monopoly bureau, facing the demand and cost conditions represented by V_2 and t^2C and not subject to an effective review, supplies an output of $Q = \left[\dfrac{a_2}{2b}\right]$, where the marginal value to the middle-demand group is zero, at a total budget of $B = \dfrac{1}{t_2} \cdot \left[\dfrac{a_2{}^2}{4b}\right]$, where the bracketed term is equal to the total area under V_2. Competition among the bureaus supplying this service in combination with an effective review yields the same total output, $Q = \left[\dfrac{a_2}{2b}\right]$, but reduces the total budget to $B = \left[\dfrac{a_2 c}{2b}\right]$, equal to $\left[\dfrac{1}{t_2}\right]$ times the area under $t_2 c$ out to the equilibrium output.

Compared to the equilibrium conditions of a demand-constrained monopoly bureau, a competition among bureaus changes the equilibrium combination of processes, does not change the combined level of output, and reduces the total budget for the service. Competition among bureaus

Figure 15.2   Effects of Increased Efficiency in the Demand-Constrained Region

thus promotes efficiency but does not reduce the oversupply of the public service. The increased efficiency, however, reduces the total budget for the service and, consequently, increases the net benefits to all groups. Increased efficiency, however achieved, always generates additional net benefits to the high-demand group; only where it does not induce an increase in output does it increase the net benefits to all groups.

In summary, a competition among bureaus reviewed by a common committee dominated by representatives of the high-demand group increases the efficiency of the bureaucracy only relative to demand-constrained monopoly bureaus and does not reduce the general problem of bureaucratic oversupply.

The conclusions of this evaluation of competing bureaus faced by the same review committee, frankly, are somewhat weaker than suggested by my intuition and observations. My personal experience, primarily involving the analysis of military programs, suggests that a monopoly bureau is most unlikely to use so diverse a combination of processes as would several bureaus supplying the same service, probably because of the historical and doctrinal identification of individual bureaus with specific processes (bombers, carriers, artillery, etc.). For some military programs, a diversity of processes can be very important to insure against the possibility of the catastrophic failure of one or more of the processes. This risk-reducing effect of a competition among bureaus is not represented by the rather simple models based on the maximization of some expected value.

In any case, there is usually a substantial range of nearly efficient combinations of processes, and the observation that substantially different processes are used by different bureaus is consistent with a concern about efficiency by both the bureaus and the review authorities. The fact that review officers in both the executive and legislative branches value better analysis and improved information on the bureau's costs indicates only that they are interested, as I have suggested, in finding a more efficient combination of processes. An improvement in efficiency, however achieved, by either the bureau or a review committee, usually benefits only the high-demand group and does not reduce the oversupply of the service. The single dominant characteristic of bureaus and national governments, it appears, is that they are too large.

Review by Committee and the Legislature

One other effect of a competition among bureaus is not suggested by our evaluation of the equilibrium conditions. A review committee will only rarely choose the exact combination of outputs from competing bureaus that is most efficient, even though they are generally motivated to select this combination. In any review cycle, some bureau's output and budget is likely to be larger than is efficient and some other bureau's output and budget will be smaller. The first bureau will be smugly quiet, but the second bureau may appeal to another committee or directly to the larger body of representatives in an attempt to increase its output and budget. The appeal by the second bureau, as a consequence of being accidentally short-changed by the review committee, substantially reduces the monopoly power of the review committee, as the choice among the two bureaus must now be made by the larger body of representatives, and it substantially increases the information available to the legislature on the cost of supplying the public service.

These effects of competition among bureaus supplying the same service, as demonstrated here, can substantially reduce the oversupply of the service, primarily by forcing the resolution of the budget-output proposals of the competing bureaus by the representatives of the middle-demand group rather than by representatives of the high-demand group. The oversupply problem is substantially alleviated only when the representatives of the middle-demand group know the costs of the service and are in a position to offer a significant alternative to the total budget-output proposal of the bureau that is forwarded by the review committee. The representatives of the middle-demand group need not know the costs of all processes which could be used to supply a service or the efficient combination of these processes; as we are demonstrating, a knowledge of the costs of one process or of one source of supply is sufficient to reduce significantly the monopoly power of the bureau and the review committee.

First, let us consider a case in which the representatives of the middle-demand group know the costs of process Q_2 but do not know the costs of producing the substitute Q_1. Such a condition might arise if the bureau producing Q_2 "end-runs" the review committee to increase its budget, if the same or a similar service is supplied through a number of lower-level governments, or if the service is supplied by a competitive industry. The total cost function for Q_2 is

$$TC_2 = 40Q_2 + .4Q_2{}^2, \tag{15.6}$$

and for these conditions is known by the larger body of representatives; for this process, the marginal costs are low at low output levels but increase rapidly with output. The total cost function for Q_1 is

$$TC_1 = 50Q_1 + .1Q_1{}^2. \tag{15.7}$$

For this case Q_1 is supplied by a monopoly bureau and thus the cost function for Q_1 will not be revealed by the bureau's budget-output behaviour.

The marginal costs of the bureau-supplied output are somewhat higher at low output levels and increase only slightly with higher output. This may be the more general case, since Chapter 8 demonstrates that a budget-maximizing bureau using a single process will prefer those production processes with a less rapidly increasing marginal cost. The relevant demand for the bureau's output of Q_1 is the total demand for $[Q_1 + Q_2]$ by the middle-demand group minus the amount of Q_2 supplied. The availability of Q_2 at a known cost substantially increases the elasticity of demand for Q_1 supplied by the monopoly bureau.

The total demand by the middle-demand group, assuming an equal distribution of tax charges, is

$$(Q_1 + Q_2)^P = 30 - .333C. \tag{15.8}$$

From (15.6) the amount of Q_2 available at the marginal cost C is

$$Q_2^S = -50 + 1.25C. \tag{15.9}$$

The demand for the output of Q_1 supplied by the monopoly bureau is thus

$$Q_1^D = (Q_1 + Q_2)^P - Q_2^S \tag{15.10}$$

$$= 80 - 1.583C.$$

From (15.10) the budget-output function facing the monopoly bureau and the review committee is

$$B_1 = 50.537Q_1 - .316Q_1^2. \tag{15.11}$$

This should be compared with the budget-output function which the bureau would face if it controlled the supply of both Q_1 and Q_2:

$$B = 90(Q_1 + Q_2) - 1.5(Q_1 + Q_2)^2. \tag{15.12}$$

Comparing (15.11) with (15.12), we see that the availability of Q_2 at a cost known to the representatives of the middle-demand group both reduces the demand and increases the elasticity of demand facing the bureau. From (15.7) and (15.11) the output solution of the bureau supplying Q_1 is

$$Q_1 = \frac{50.537 - 50}{.316 + .1} = 1.3. \tag{15.13}$$

This should be compared with an output of $Q_1 = 13.3$ when the bureau has a monopoly of both Q_1 and Q_2. An output of $Q_1 = 1.3$ is the largest output that would be approved by majority vote, as any larger output would reduce the net benefits to the middle-demand group below that which would be generated by Q_2 only. The output of Q_2 is found as follows. From (15.8) and (15.13)

$$C = 86.1 - 3Q_2. \tag{15.14}$$

From (15.6)

$$C = 40 + 8Q_2. \tag{15.15}$$

The level of Q_2 for which (15.14) and (15.15) are equal is $Q_2 = 12.1$, and, thus, $[Q_1 + Q_2] = 13.4$. These outputs should be compared with $Q_2 = 15.8$ and $[Q_1 + Q_2] = 29.1$ if the bureau has a monopoly of both Q_1 and Q_2.

It would not pay a bureau supplying Q_2 to end-run the review committee unless the committee had made a substantial error, because the total output determined by the legislature as a body is sufficiently smaller than the output of Q_2 and is also somewhat smaller than at the equilibrium review committee solution. This is not a general case, but it does suggest that a bureau may think twice about informing the legislature about its costs and forcing the output decision to be made by the entire body.

Figure 15.3 illustrates the effects of the output solution by the legislature and the review committee in this case. The availability of Q_2 at known marginal costs t_2C_2 reduces the demand function of the middle-demand group for the output of Q_1 from the line hk to the broken line gjk. At this reduced and more elastic demand, the largest output of Q_1 that the legislature would approve is that for which the area of the polygon $egml$ is equal to the area $efnl$. The availability of Q_2 at a known cost reduces the loss of net benefits caused by the bureaucratic supply of this service from the area

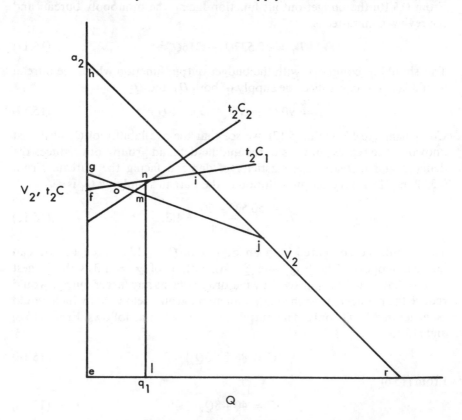

Figure 15.3　Effects of a Good Alternative Source of Supply

of the triangle *fhi* to the area of the smaller triangle *fgo*. One good alternative source of supply available at a known cost greatly reduces the monopoly power of the bureau and the review committee and generates a nearly optimal level of total output of the service.

This solution has a number of interesting properties. The combination of Q_1 and Q_2 is not the most efficient for the combined level of output; the output of Q_1 supplied by the bureau is still almost twice as large as the efficient level. The combined level of output is almost identical to the level that would be selected by the middle-demand group if they knew the costs of both processes. Thus, the primary difference in this output solution from the availability of the output of both processes at known costs involves the combination of Q_1 and Q_2 and not the total level of output. The combined level of output is not optimal; a somewhat lower level of output would generate larger total net benefits. This solution, however, is much superior to the case in which the outputs of both processes are supplied by a monopoly bureau or are jointly reviewed by a review committee dominated by representatives of the high-demand group. A monopoly of both processes leads to large net benefits to the high-demand group, zero net benefits to the middle-demand group, and negative net benefits to the low-demand group. The solution, where the bureau and the review committee have a monopoly only over Q_1, generates larger total net benefits, somewhat smaller net benefits to the high-demand group, positive net benefits to the middle-demand group, and smaller negative net benefits to the low-demand group. This solution is quite close to the optimal solution, even though one (or all but one) of the processes is supplied by a monopoly bureau; it differs from the optimal solution primarily because the median demand is lower than the arithmetic mean of the group demands and because the equal tax charges do not lead to a distributional equilibrium.

Now consider another case where the output of only one process is available at a cost known to the larger body of representatives, and the outputs of other processes are supplied by a monopoly bureau or through a review committee. This output solution is different from the case analyzed above and is dependent on which output is available at a known cost and which outputs are supplied by a monopoly. Because the marginal costs of Q_1 are higher than for Q_2 at low levels of output, the net benefits to the middle-demand group that would be generated by using only Q_1 are lower than in the previous case. This permits the monopoly bureau to expand its output and budget to a level somewhat larger than where Q_2 is available at a known cost. Without developing the calculations, the output solution for this case is $Q_1 = 0 = Q_2 = 19.6$, and, thus, $[Q_1 + Q_2] = 19.6$. This is the largest output, consisting only of Q_2, that generates the same net benefits to the middle-demand group as would the use of Q_1 only. This output solution should be compared with $Q_1 = 13.3$, $Q_2 = 15.8$, and $[Q_1 + Q_2] = 29.1$ if both processes are supplied by a monopoly bureau or through a review committee.

Although $Q_1 = 0$ in this case, the *potential* availability of Q_1 at a known cost substantially reduces the monopoly power of the bureau and the review committee.

Figure 15.4 illustrates the effects of the output solution by the legislature and the review committee. The availability of Q_1 at known marginal costs t_2C_1 reduces the demand function of the middle-demand group for the output of Q_2 from the line *hm* to the broken line *gkm*. At this reduced and more elastic demand, the largest output of Q_2 that the legislature would approve is that for which the area of the polygon *egkln* is equal to the area of the polygon *efjn*. The potential availability of Q_1 at a known cost, even though it is not used, reduces the loss of net benefits caused by the bureaucratic supply of this service from the area of the triangle *fhi* to the area of the smaller triangle *fgo*. An inferior source of supply that is not used reduces the monopoly power of the bureau and the review committee and generates a more nearly optimal output of this service.

This solution is not the most efficient combination of Q_1 and Q_2; the output of Q_2 supplied by the monopoly bureau is around 40 percent higher

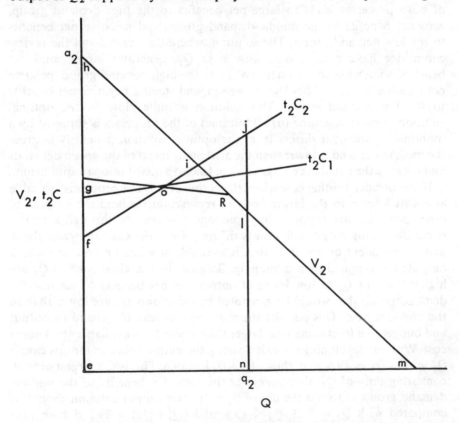

Figure 15.4   Effects of an Inferior Alternative Source of Supply

than would be efficient at this total level of output. The total output is substantially larger than would be selected if the outputs from both processes were available at a cost known to the entire legislature. This output solution is also somewhat larger than the level that would maximize the total net benefits. Even though the source of supply for which the costs are known to the legislature is not used, this solution is substantially superior to the case where the output of both processes is supplied by a monopoly bureau. It is, however, somewhat inferior to the case where Q_2 is available at a known cost; compared with this case, this solution generates smaller total net benefits, larger net benefits to the high-demand group, smaller net benefits to the middle-demand group, and larger negative net benefits to the low-demand group. In general, the availability of output at a known cost from a source of supply with lower marginal costs at low output levels leads to an output solution closer to the optimal than when the output from this process is supplied by a monopoly bureau.

In both of these cases—where the output solution is, in effect, pieced together by the review committee and the legislature—the resulting combination of Q_1 and Q_2 is not the most efficient combination. This is an understandable result of an uncoordinated review process. One should strongly resist the siren song of efficiency, however, if the necessary coordination to achieve this efficiency is delegated to a monopoly bureau or a review committee. The combination of outputs selected by the bureau or committee is more likely to be efficient, but the total output level, selected to maximize the budget of the bureau and the net benefits to the high-demand group, will be substantially larger than the optimal level. Again, since the general problem of the bureaucratic supply of services is not inefficiency but oversupply, the delegation of a coordination function to a bureau or a review committee with specialized interests only reinforces this problem. The legislature as a body should be willing to tolerate a good deal of inefficiency as the price of maintaining effective control of the output solution.

Summary Comments on the Effects of Competition

Competition among bureaus in the supply of the same or similar services is generally in the public interest, but the effects depend on the characteristics of the review process.

Such competition is of least value, except possibly to increase the diversity of processes used to produce the service, if its alternative is a budget-constrained monopoly bureau and if the review committee is dominated by representatives of a group with relatively high demands for the service, thus replicating the output solution of a monopoly bureau. In this case, competition among bureaus does not increase the efficiency or reduce the oversupply relative to the solution by a monopoly bureau.

Competition among bureaus is more valuable if the alternative is a demand-constrained monopoly bureau. Competition then increases the efficiency but does not reduce the oversupply relative to the solution by a monopoly bureau; because the increased efficiency reduces total expenditures without changing the output, however, the competition among bureaus generates additional net benefits to all groups.

Competition among bureaus is most valuable just when it generates a procedural problem—when the decision on the outputs and budgets of competing bureaus is not resolved at the departmental and review committee levels and thus must be resolved by the legislature as a body. This increases the amount of cost information available to the legislature and increases the probability that any one bureau may end-run the review committee in an attempt to increase its budget. Any significant source of supply of a service at known costs—whether from an aberrant bureau, from other levels of government, or from a competitive industry—substantially reduces the monopoly power of the bureaus and the review committee, even if this source is not used. The effect of an alternative source of supply at costs known to the legislature depends somewhat on the costs of output from this source at low output levels. In general, however, the availability of a significant alternative leads to a combination of outputs from the several sources that is somewhat inefficient (a monopoly bureau would still supply too large an output), but the total level of output is lower and much closer to the optimal level.

Competition among bureaus reviewed by a common committee is valuable only in special cases. Competition *around* the review committee can increase the total net benefits generated by supply of the service and substantially increase the net benefits accruing to the middle- and low-demand groups. The effects of *one* significant source of supply at costs known to the legislature are quite similar to the effects of all sources of supply being directly evaluated by the legislature. Given this type of competition among bureaus or with other sources of supply, the primary remaining problems for representative government in supplying the optimal amount of a public service are dependent on how well the population demands for public services are known and represented by their representatives, on the relation between the distribution of demands, and on the distribution of tax charges.

16

An Aggregative Model of
Public Services in the
United States

Governments, particularly the national governments of large countries, do not serve many of their constituents very well. The ubiquity of government in both geography and history is evidence only that it benefits some group that is able to control its critical processes. The theory developed in this book suggests that the bureaucratic supply of services, in combination with representative majority rule, does indeed serve the high-demand group quite well at the cost of indifference by some and an absolute loss by others. What are the magnitudes of this problem in the United States? What are the magnitudes of the consequences, the total net benefits, and the net benefits to each group that might be generated by specific changes in the bureaucracy and our political institutions?

Assumptions and Parameters

A set of assumptions and parameters are necessary to transform the very aggregative model developed in Chapter 14 into one specific to conditions in the United States. This model is then used to estimate the approximate magnitude of the effects of bureaucratic supply and representative majority rule and of several specific changes. Most of the qualitative conclusions of this chapter depend only on the form of this model, but the quantitative estimates of the benefits and costs, of course, are dependent on the specific parameters. Both the form and the parameters of this model, I believe, are roughly representative of conditions in the United States, but the reader, of course, should judge this for himself.

First, assume that the governments of the United States finance the supply of one aggregate package of public services. Governments, of course, supply many public services, with many different demand and cost conditions. The first assumption implies only that the demand and cost functions for the aggregate package of public services are stable over some

169

range in the level of these services. This is consistent, in some cases, with a constant distribution of the services in this package, but does not necessarily imply this stronger condition.

Next, assume that the demand for this package of services by each of three groups in the U.S. population is represented by the function

$$Q_i = yY_i - t_iC, \tag{16.1}$$

where $Y_i \equiv$ income of group i, and

$t_i \equiv$ tax share of group i.

The demand function (16.1) has the following properties: The level of the demand function for each group is proportional to the income of the group. This implies an income elasticity of unity at a zero tax price and a monotonically higher income elasticity at higher tax prices.[1] Other conditions being the same, an income elasticity of unity implies that a constant proportion of income is spent for public services at different levels of income. The assumed income effects on demand are roughly consistent with the available evidence. The nearly constant proportion of income by state that is spent by state and local governments suggests a lower bound of around unity on the income elasticity of demand for public services. The long-term increase in the government proportion of GNP since 1929, however, suggests an upper bound of around 2 on the income elasticity of demand.[2]

The demand function for this package of public services by each group is also assumed to have a slope of -1 with respect to the tax price to that group.[3] At best, this is a rough average of the population demand for public services, which probably has a steeper slope because of the vertical aggregation of individual demands, and the lower demand slope faced by many

---

1. The expression for the income elasticity, given a linear demand function, is the following:

$$\eta_Y = \frac{\delta Q}{\delta Y} \frac{Y}{Q} = \frac{yY_i}{yY_i - t_iC}$$

For a given tax price, the income elasticity η_Y decreases with an increase in income. For a given income, the income elasticity η_Y increases with an increase in the tax price.

2. Tullock suggests that the long-term growth in the proportionate size of government is due, not to a high-income elasticity of demand for public services, but to a reduced cost of obtaining special favors from government. He attributes this to a moral phenomenon: a greater willingness to request special favors, that is, a breakdown of the Kantian rule. This is possible, but it is difficult to determine why this has occurred only since 1929 or only in higher-income nations. Operating against this effect, the increased size of the constituency has probably increased the cost of obtaining either special or general favors through political institutions. Until better econometric studies are done, however, any attribution of the growth of government to income or price effects can be only conjectural.

3. The expression for the tax price elasticity, given a linear demand function, is the following:

$$\eta_{t_iC} = \frac{\delta Q}{\delta t_iC} \frac{t_iC}{Q} = - \frac{t_iC}{yY_i - t_iC}$$

For a given tax price, the absolute value of the tax price elasticity η_{t_iC} decreases with an increase in income. For a given income, the absolute value of this tax price elasticity η_{t_iC} also decreases with an increase in the tax price.

units of government owing to the lower cost of moving among these units. It is difficult to find a direct empirical confirmation of this assumption about the effect of the tax price, because governments do not sell their package of services at a uniform price; but, in any case, most of the conclusions of this chapter are not very sensitive to changes in the assumed slopes of the demand functions.

A demand function that is linear in both income and tax price is chosen to reflect my belief that high-income groups are willing to pay a uniformly higher tax price than low-income groups for any common level of public services. Unfortunately, the econometric research that would be necessary to estimate more accurately these income and tax price effects on the demand for public services has not been performed, but it is unlikely that better estimates would significantly change the above assumptions concerning the demand by large groups for the aggregate package of public services.

Next, let us assume that the aggregate tax charges of all levels of government in the United States on each of three groups are proportional to the income of each group. Although this may seem incorrect, it is roughly accurate for broad groups. The tax systems of many states and of the federal government are nominally progressive, but the many types of exemptions and the widespread use of excise taxes make the aggregate effective tax system very nearly proportional for over 80 percent of families.[4]

4. This conclusion, which may be surprising to many readers, is confirmed by the following data:

Taxes and Transfers as a Percent of Income. 1965

	Taxes			Transfers	Taxes
	Federal/				*Less*
	state	*local*	*total*		*Transfers*
Annual Family Income					
Under $2,000	19	25	44	126	−83
$ 2,000– 4,000	16	11	27	11	16
4,000– 6,000	17	10	27	5	21
6,000– 8,000	17	9	26	3	23
8,000–10,000	18	9	27	2	25
10,000–15,000	19	9	27	2	25
Over $15,000	32	7	38	1	37
Total	22	9	31	14	24

Source: *Economic Report of the President, 1969* (Washington, D.C.: 1969).

Over 80 percent of family units in the United States had annual incomes between $2,000 and $15,000 in 1965. In this range, the total tax rate was surprisingly constant at a level of 27 percent. I believe this is the more appropriate basis for comparison than the rate of taxes less transfers, because of the ambiguities concerning who are the beneficiaries (as distinct from the recipients) of transfers.

It should be recognized that this table represents an estimate of the distribution of tax *payments* by income class. It may not adequately represent the distribution of the tax *burden* by income class, because of the different effects of tax shifting. Until such a distribution of tax burdens is available, however, the above distribution is probably the best available. In any case, people may be more aware of their tax payments than their tax burdens.

The combination of this assumption and the assumption concerning the income effects on the demand for public services leads to the derivative assumption that the tax charges are proportional to the level of the demand function for each group. The available data on the distribution of income in the United States can thus be used to estimate both the relative levels of demand for public services by different groups and the relative tax charges.

The distribution of income and taxes, *as it influences the demands for public services as represented by the U.S. Congress,* is determined in the following way: First, the 50 states are ranked on the basis of the 1968 per capita personal income by state, from lowest to highest. For each state the following data are also listed: personal income, population, the number of Representatives, and the number (always two) of Senators. The total personal income and taxes represented by the 145 Representatives of the lowest-income states are determined by aggregating the personal income by state from the state with the lowest per capita income to the state for which the cumulative number of Representatives is the largest less than 145; the personal income of the marginal state is pro-rated based on the proportion of its Representatives that would bring the cumulative number up to 145. The income and taxes represented by this one-third of the Representatives are considered to be the income and taxes of the low-demand group, as represented in the House. The income and taxes of the middle- and high-demand groups, each group also represented by 145 Representatives, are determined in the same way. This procedure is necessary because personal income is not regularly reported by Congressional districts; it, however, *underestimates* the differences in the incomes represented by the lower and upper third of the Representatives, because the differences in personal incomes among the 435 Congressional districts are greater than among the 50 states. The income and taxes of states represented by thirds of the Senators are also determined in the same way, but without this bias.

The results of these calculations, expressed as a percent of the total personal income in the United States, are presented in the first two columns of Table 16.1. The third column presents the arithmetic average of the percentages represented by each third in the House and the Senate. Because the House and the Senate, for most purposes, have equal political power, the average income percentages presented in the third column are used to determine the demand for public services by the three groups, as represented in Congress; the income percentages in this column are also the tax shares of the three groups. For comparison, the percent of personal income by groups representing approximate thirds of voters is presented in the fourth column.

Each third of the Representatives, not surprisingly, represents an almost equal percent of the population and a significantly, but not hugely, different percent of total income; as discussed above, however, the percentages underestimate the differences in income among these groups as represented in the House. Each third of the Senators represents very different percentages of the total population and income. The average of the House and Senate percentages is used as the percent of income of the three groups, as it affects the final choices made by the joint action of the House and the Senate.

The low-demand group, thus, is represented by one-third of the effective votes, includes 27 percent of the population, earns 21 percent of the income, and pays 21 percent of the taxes. The middle-demand group is also represented by one-third of the effective votes, includes 30 percent of the population, earns 29 percent of the income, and pays 29 percent of the taxes. The high-demand group is represented by the final one-third of the effective votes, includes 43 percent of the population, earns 49 percent of the income, and pays 49 percent of the taxes. The distribution of income among these three groups is very close to the 20:30:50 distribution on which the examples in Chapter 14 are based.

Table 16.1 Percent of personal income, taxes, and population by group

Groups	House	As represented by Senate	Average	Voters
	(percentage of U.S. total)			
Low demand				
Income and taxes	26.8	15.7	21.2	15
Population	33.1	20.7	26.9	40
Middle demand				
Income and taxes	33.2	25.6	29.4	28
Population	32.9	27.2	30.0	30
High demand				
Income and taxes	40.0	58.7	49.4	57
Population	34.0	52.1	43.1	30

SOURCE: U.S. Bureau of the Census, *Statistical Abstract of the United States, 1969* (Washington, D.C.: 1969).

It is also interesting to compare these percentages, which result from our present election processes, with what might result if a national unicameral legislature were elected by proportional representation. Assuming that the lowest-income families are slightly underrepresented (owing to ineligibility and lower voting participation) so that the 40 percent of the families with the lowest family income were represented by one-third of the effective votes, the next 30 percent of families by one-third, etc., we see that the percent of income of the three groups as represented by legislators elected by proportional representation would be that indicated in the fourth column. Strangely enough, the distribution of income as represented by equal thirds of the Senators most closely approximates the distribution that might result from proportional representation—a rather coincidental effect of the election of two Senators from each state.

One unexpected effect of the equal voting power of the House and the Senate is to increase the differences in the incomes represented by thirds of the effective votes relative to the distribution in a legislature elected from area constituencies of equal population and to reduce the differences in incomes relative to the distribution in a legislature elected by proportional representation. Because the actual differences in income among the groups as represented in the House are somewhat greater than are indicated in the first column of Table 16.1, the actual income percentages as represented jointly by the House and the Senate are likely to be somewhere between those in the third and those in the fourth column. In the absence of better estimates, however, the income percentages in the third column are the basis for subsequent analysis in this chapter.

The next problem is to scale government. In 1969 the total expenditures by all levels of government in the United States were around $293 billion. This included payments to all government employees of around $115 billion (the national income originating in general government and government enterprises), payments for goods and services purchased from other forms of organization of around $100 billion (the sum of these first two numbers is the total government purchases in the GNP accounts), and transfer payments of around $78 billion. Although these figures are measured quite accurately, there is some ambiguity about what is the most appropriate measure of the amount of resources organized by the government bureaucracy. For purposes of this analysis I have chosen to use a total of $200 billion—the sum of the compensation of the employees of general government (around $100 billion) plus the purchases of goods and services from other forms of organization (also around $100 billion). This total is also approximately equal to the total expenditures of the federal government in 1969. The expenditures by government enterprises are excluded because they are largely financed from the sale of services at a per-unit rate. Transfer payments, other than federal grants to state and local governments, are excluded, because final expenditure of these payments is largely determined by individuals. This is a somewhat arbitrary definition of the expenditures by the government bureaucracy, because it includes the intermediate goods and services produced by private organizations and excludes transfers. A good case could be made for using almost any figure from $100 billion to $300 billion to represent the scale of government in the United States. The proportionate effects of the different characteristics of government that are evaluated in this chapter are independent of the total measure of expenditures that is used.

Next, some assumption is needed to relate the total expenditures of the government bureaucracy to the cost per unit of the package of public services and the number of units of these services. For simplicity, this analysis is based on a cost function of the type

$$TC - cQ \qquad (16.2)$$

where

$$\$200 \text{ billion} = \$20 \text{ billion} \cdot 10 \text{ units}.$$

This cost function has constant marginal and average costs per unit of \$20 billion. The effect of using this type of cost function is that one ignores one of the stronger effects of bureaucracy— the generation of a larger factor surplus to those specific factors used by government. The factor surpluses generated by government are important to explaining some characteristics of government behavior, but consideration of the effects on factor surplus would unduly complicate this final analysis. For a total expenditure by the bureaucracy of \$200 billion and a unit cost of \$20 billion, a total of 10 units of the package of public services would be supplied. The particular combination of \$20 billion per unit and 10 units is chosen only for convenience and has no empirical relevance. The effects of the different characteristics of government described later are substantially invariant to a range of combinations of c and Q, the product of which is \$200 billion.[5]

These assumptions, plus the model of the review process developed in Chapter 14, are sufficient to develop the budget-output functions for each group. Assuming majority rule and bureaucratic supply of public services, we see the largest output that would win approval is the level of Q for which

$$a_2 Q - bQ^2 = t_2 cQ. \qquad (16.3)$$

Solving (16.3) for a_2 yields

$$a_2 = t_2 c + bQ. \qquad (16.4)$$

Substituting the assumed values to t_2, c, b, and Q in (16.4) yields

$$a_2 = .294(20) + .5(10) = 10.880. \qquad (16.5)$$

The assumption that the level of the demand function for public services is proportional to income provides the basis for estimating a_1 and a_3 by multiplying a_2 by the relative shares of income of the low-demand group and the high-demand group, respectively. The value of a_1, thus, is

$$a_1 = 10.880 \left(\frac{.212}{.294}\right) = 7.845, \qquad (16.6)$$

and the value of a_3 is

$$a_3 = 10.880 \left(\frac{.494}{.294}\right) = 18.281. \qquad (16.7)$$

5. One exception to this statement concerns the progressiveness of the optimal tax charges: the lower the unit cost of public services, the more progressive is the optimal tax structure. At the \$20 billion unit cost, all three demands are effective and each group pays some taxes.

These estimates provide the full model necessary for us to estimate the effects of the various characteristics of the present and alternative forms of government. This model includes the budget-output functions and tax shares of the three groups and the total cost function:

$$B_1 = 7.845Q - .5Q^2 \text{ and } t_1 = .212, \tag{16.8}$$

$$B_2 = 10.880Q - .5Q^2 \text{ and } t_2 = .294, \tag{16.9}$$

$$B_3 = 18.281Q - .5Q^2 \text{ and } t_3 = .494, \text{ and} \tag{16.10}$$

$$TC = 20Q. \tag{16.11}$$

The equations (16.8) through (16.11) and the model developed in Chapter 14 now provide the basis for estimating the total benefits, the total tax charges, and the net benefits that accrue to each group from the present and alternative characteristics of government.

This model, it should be recognized, abstracts from some of the more important effects and problems of bureaucracy and government. It accepts the demands for public services, as represented in our political institutions, as an adequate aggregation of individual demands. As mentioned earlier, it does not consider the effects on the factor surplus. It also assumes that all bureaus are perfectly efficient; this would be the case only if all bureaus were in a budget-constrained equilibrium or if the review committees were able to eliminate all of the excess costs of bureaus operating in the demand-constrained region. The efficiency problem of bureaus is still substantial but is not considered in this analysis. Any possible misallocative effects of the tax system are also ignored. This model addresses only those effects of different characteristics of government that operate through the level of output of public services.

Bureaucratic Supply with Majority Rule

The first form of government considered, I believe, closely represents the present characteristics of government in the United States and other Western nations. This government is characterized by the bureaucratic supply of public services, majority rule, and a proportional tax system. The bureau's solution for the aggregate package of public services is assumed to dominate the review committee's solution.[6] The effects of this

6. A strict interpretation of the model developed in Chapter 14 would suggest, given the demand and cost conditions, that the review committee's solution would dominate the bureau's solution. This would be the case if there were a single committee, representing the broad interests of the high-demand group, responsible for reviewing the aggregate package of public services. It is assumed here that the bureau's solution dominates the review committee's solution for each service. This is consistent with the division of review responsibilities among many committees, each dominated by representatives of those with the highest relative demand for each service.

form of government, given the above assumptions, are summarized by Table 16.2.

This form of government does generate some net benefits, but only to the high-demand group (and, realistically, to owners of specific factors). The low-demand group, most of whom are relatively poor, are absolutely worse off as a consequence of this form of government. Within the low-demand group, those who lose most are those who also have high incomes and thus pay high taxes. One can perceptively ask why individuals in this low-demand group do not emigrate. Among the several reasons that most of them do not, even though they are exploited through the institutions of government, are the following: For most of this group the income after taxes and the environmental amenities in the United States are still superior to those in most other nations, the costs of moving are high, and other forms of governments would exploit this group to a comparable degree. When one or more of these conditions do not apply, members of this low-demand group do emigrate. The American colonies were settled by such people and, later, the American West was opened by those who had relatively low demands for the activities of government.

Table 16.2 Bureaucratic supply with majority rule

Groups	Benefits	Taxes	Net Benefits	Q
	(billions of dollars, annually)			
Low demand	$ 30.8	$ 42.4	$−11.6	
Middle demand	58.8	58.8	0	
High demand	132.8	98.8	34.0	
Total	$222.4	$200	$ 22.4	10

The geographical pervasiveness of bureaucracy, however, has created a condition such that the national governments of large, relatively wealthy nations can exploit a substantial part of the "site-rent" of those who have low preferences for the services provided by government. The prospects are not optimistic. When the opportunities for emigration are foreclosed or the alternatives inferior, one potential outlet for such exploited groups, to be blunt, is revolution. If revolution is also effectively foreclosed by the military power of the government, we may increasingly see a new form of emigration—cultural rather than geographic separation. The "hippie" communities are a manifestation of such a cultural emigration to avoid many of the effects of the government and may be a model of the way that an increasing proportion of people will escape the bureaucracy.

A minority of the low-demand group are also relatively wealthy. Among this subgroup those who do not emigrate are likely to be the major contributors to the financing of radical groups, as they were prior to the American Revolution and Civil War. And some of this subgroup will emigrate to less bureaucratic nations, because the economic and environmental advantages for the wealthy here are not sufficiently superior for them to tolerate much exploitation. An alliance of the interests of the exploited poor and a few discontented rich is explosive and is one of the more tragic consequences of the increasing bureaucratization of American life.

The middle-demand group, most of which had annual family incomes of $6,000 to $10,000 during the 1960's, are likely to be indifferent or ambivalent toward the government. This group may be chauvinistic about the country because of economic and environmental advantages, but they will have mixed feelings about the government. They are confused by a conflict between the rhetoric of our political system, which exalts the power of the median voter, and their suspicion that the government is really run by the "Eastern establishment." The recognition by this group that they do not control the formulation of alternatives in our political system sometimes leads to the creation of third-part movements from this group—for example, the Know-Nothings, the Populists, the Wallace movement. The major parties will court such a group, primarily to assure that they do not form an alliance with the low-demand group. Vice President Agnew is the current major party spokesman to "middle America." This middle-demand group is unlikely either to emigrate or to revolt, but they are likely to believe that government could serve them better if only they could exert the influence which their median voting position would presumably indicate.

A government characterized by the bureaucratic supply of public services and majority rule yields positive net benefits only to the high-demand group, most of whom have relatively high incomes, primarily because this group controls the formulation of alternatives. Around 60 percent of the total benefits of the government accrue to this 40 percent of the population that pays around 50 percent of the taxes. Within the high-demand group, the individuals who benefit most are those who also have low incomes and thus pay low taxes. The high-demand group has a strong incentive to maintain control of both the major parties and of the press. Most campaign contributions and party workers will come from this group. Major parties are likely to be dominated by this group, although they will usually select candidates with characteristics more appealing to the middle-demand group. It is a mistake to think of this group as including only the very rich; the annual income of the median family in this group is probably around $13,000, somewhere between, for example, the median income of journalists and that of professors. Some of the very rich, at least those whose income is not dependent on some special activity of government, are likely to be in the low-demand group because they may prefer the more expensive private substitutes for public services. Most of the readers of this book, I suspect, are in the high-demand group and will be understandably upset by many of my conclusions.

This summary of the net benefits of government in the United States is specific to the three broad groups which represent 80 percent or more of the population and does not accurately represent the net benefits which accrue to the tails of the income distribution. The very poor (the lowest 10 percent of families by income) generally have a proportionately low demand for public services; the large transfer payments to this group (relative to their earned income), however, probably generate positive net benefits at this level. The very rich (the highest 10 percent of families by income) generally have a proportionately high demand for public services; the highly progressive tax structure at this level, however, substantially reduces the net benefits to this group. Although the very poor may generally favor big government and the very rich may generally oppose big government, this should not distort one's impression of the net benefits which accrue to the 80 percent of the population that pays roughly proportional taxes.

This form of government, even at the equilibrium level of public services, promotes continuing dissension, controversy, and conflict among the several groups. The marginal value of public services to the low-demand group will be very small or zero and much lower than the marginal tax price to this group. This group would prefer a smaller government. They have no incentive, however, to form an alliance with the high-demand group, and they will have no political power unless they can form an effective alliance with the middle-demand group. The marginal value of public services to the middle-demand group is usually positive but lower than the tax price to this group. This group would also prefer a smaller government but cannot exercise their political power unless they can capture control of the formulation of alternatives submitted to their decisive vote. Although the high-demand group receives all the positive net benefits of government, they usually prefer a larger government than that which will win majority approval. At the equilibrium level of public services, the marginal value of public services to this group is still higher than the tax price to this group. As a consequence, they will try to influence the middle demand group that an even larger government would be desirable. And if the intellectual community, the press, and Presidential commissions that are dominated by this group are successful in increasing the demand for public services by the middle-demand group, the high-demand group will be even better off, the middle-demand group will be no better off, and the low-demand group will be even worse off. This system of government seems perversely designed to break down any community of interests that may have once existed.

This is a gloomy picture of democratic, representative government in the United States. The moderately rich use the acquiescent middle to exploit the moderately poor. The actual situation, however, may be worse than the numbers in Table 16.2 suggest. The difference in the incomes among the represented groups is larger than can be estimated from state data; a larger difference in income would generate larger negative net benefits to the low-demand group and larger positive net benefits to the high-demand group. Also, voting participation increases as a function of income and, thus, with the level of demand for public services. This income effect on voting does not change the distribution of net benefits among the represented groups but does increase the negative net benefits of the lower-income unrepresented group. In both of these conditions, the negative net benefits to the low-demand group and the positive net benefits to the high-demand group are even higher with a consequently greater divergence in their attitudes toward government.[7]

Bureaucratic Supply with a Two-Thirds Rule

The second form of government considered is characterized by the bureaucratic supply of public services, a two-thirds rule, and a proportional tax system. Approval of the budget and output of all public services would thus require the support of at least two-thirds of both the House and the Senate. A two-thirds rule deserves consideration primarily as a means to compensate for the oversupply of public services by bureaus subject only to a majority rule. Given the bureaucratic supply of public services, a two-thirds rule would generate a level of output that would leave the 145th Representative and the 33rd Senator, counting down the list on the basis of the per capita income of their constituencies, just indifferent.

The demand for public services represented by this marginal vote is estimated from the percent of total personal income represented by the one-third of the members of Congress in the range from one-sixth to one-half, counting down the list on the basis of per capita incomes of their constituencies; the two-thirds rule would generate net benefits to one-half of this group and negative net benefits to one-half, and leave the median representative *in this group* indifferent. Using the same technique as for the above cases, we can estimate the percent of personal income represented by this one-third of the members of Congress to be 25.1. For this group, thus, the value of a_4 is

$$a_4 = 10.880 \left(\frac{.251}{.294} \right) = 9.289. \tag{16.12}$$

---

7. It is interesting to compare the analysis of this section with an independent, but supporting, analysis of the conditions which would lead to a "taxpayers' revolt." See James Buchanen and Marilyn Flowers, "An Analytic Setting for a 'Taxpayers' Revolution," *Western Economic Journal* (December 1969), pp. 349–359, and Raymond Jackson, "A 'Taxpayers Revolution' and Economic Rationality," *Public Choice* (Spring 1971), pp. 93–98.

The budget-output function for this group, then, is

$$B_4 = 9.289Q - 5Q^2, \tag{16.13}$$

and the largest level of output that would be approved by two-thirds of the members of Congress, given the bureaucratic supply of public services, thus, is the level of Q for which

$$9.289Q - .5Q^2 = .251(20)Q. \tag{16.14}$$

Solving (16.14) for Q yields $Q = 8.538$ and from the total cost function (16.11) total expenditures and taxes of $170.8 billion. The effects of a uniform use of a two-thirds rule, given the functions in the basic model (16.8) through (16.11), are summarized by Table 16.3 below.

The effects of a two-thirds rule as summarized in Table 16.3 should be compared with the effects of a majority rule as summarized in Table 16.2. A two-thirds rule, it appears, would reduce the budget and output of government in the United States by around 15 percent. Total benefits would be reduced by less than 10 percent, and total net benefits would be increased by around 60 percent.

The net benefits to the low-demand group would still be negative, but the absolute loss to this group would be reduced by half. Small net benefits would accrue to the middle-demand group. The net benefits to the high-demand group would be about the same.

Table 16.3 Bureaucratic supply with a two-thirds rule

Groups	Benefits	Taxes	Net Benefits	Q
	(billions of dollars, annually)			
Low demand	$ 30.8	$ 36.2	$ -5.4	
Middle demand	56.4	50.2	6.2	
High demand	119.6	84.4	35.2	
Total	$206.8	$170.8	$ 36.0	8.538

Although the low-demand group would have a much smaller incentive to emigrate or revolt, they would still prefer a smaller government, because the marginal value of public services to this group is lower than the tax price to this group. The middle-demand group would be somewhat better off with a two-thirds rule but they would also prefer an even smaller government. Most of the net benefits of the government still accrue to the high-demand group.

In this case, a two-thirds rule would slightly increase the net benefits to the high-demand group—the two-thirds rule effectively substituting for a thorough review and reformulation of the bureau's budget and output solution by some aggregate review committee. The high-demand group would be very nearly in equilibrium, preferring neither a smaller nor a larger government. This is not a general case; under most conditions a two-thirds rule would reduce the net benefits of the high-demand group, and this group would prefer a larger government. Given the bureaucratic supply of public services, a two-thirds rule would generally increase the total net benefits of government and reduce the difference in the net benefits which accrue to the several groups.

One of the traditional arguments for majority rule—that it assures a more egalitarian distribution of the net benefits of government—may be entirely wrong. Given the bureaucratic supply of public services, only the high-demand group, most of whom have relatively high incomes, would usually favor majority rule over a two-thirds rule. A two-thirds rule would usually increase the net benefits to the low- and middle-demand groups by enough so that either group could afford to compensate the high-demand group for any loss of net benefits and still be better off.

A two-thirds rule, which is now exercised only on the rare occasions of a Presidential veto, may be the only way partially to correct for the problem of oversupply by the bureaucracy without addressing it directly. The high-demand group, including most of the intellectual community, the bureaucracy itself, and the owners of specific factors used by the government may not favor a two-thirds rule unless they are compensated for any loss in net benefits. A wider understanding of the effects of bureaucracy and majority rule by the low- and middle-demand groups could lead to the more general use of a two-thirds rule without the approval of the high-demand group.

Competitive Supply with Majority Rule

The third form of government considered is characterized by the competitive supply of public services, majority rule, and a proportional tax system. The competitive supply of public services could be achieved by a combination of changes within the bureaucracy, use of private sources of supply, and changes in the review process. These changes would be piecemeal, difficult, and time-consuming, but would not require a change in the more fundamental rule of majority approval.

Given the competitive supply of public services and majority rule, the equilibrium level of public services would be the level of Q which maximizes the net benefits to the middle-demand group.

$$B_2 - T_2 = a_2 Q - bQ^2 - t_2 cQ. \tag{16.15}$$

Given the functions (16.9) and (16.11),

$$B_2 - T_2 = 10.880 - .5Q^2 - .294(20)Q. \tag{16.16}$$

Solving (16.16) for the value of Q that maximizes the net benefits to the middle-demand group yields $Q = 5$ and, from the total cost function (16.11), total expanditures and taxes of $100 billion. A competitive supply of public services, as demonstrated earlier, leads to a level of output and total expenditures that, for constant marginal costs, are just one-half the output and expenditures from a bureaucracy facing the same demand and cost conditions. The effects of this form of government, given the functions (16.8) through (16.11), are summarized by Table 16.4.

A competitive supply of public services with majority rule would lead to a much smaller government than bureaucratic supply or even a two-thirds rule. The total benefits and expenditures are much smaller but the total net benefits are substantially larger than in the previous case. The net benefits to the low- and middle-demand groups are both positive and larger, and the net benefits to the high-demand group are slightly lower than in the previous case.

Table 16.4 Competitive supply with majority rule

Groups	Benefits	Taxes	Net Benefits	Q
	(billions of dollars, annually)			
Low demand	$ 26.7	$ 21.2	$ 5.5	
Middle demand	41.9	29.4	12.5	
High demand	78.9	49.4	29.5	
Total	$147.5	$100.0	$47.5	5

This analysis underestimates the full value of a competitive supply of public services, because the competitive supply would both increase the efficiency and reduce the oversupply relative to monopoly bureaus. The efficiency problem of bureaucracy is still substantial but is not considered in this analysis.

In this case, although the low-demand group has a positive net benefit, it would prefer a still smaller government, because the marginal value of public services is still lower than the tax price to this group. The middle-demand group is in equilibrium, as the marginal value of public services is equal to the tax price to them, given a proportional tax system. Again, although most of the net benefits of government with these characteristics accrue to the high-demand group, they would prefer a larger government because the marginal value of public services to this group is substantially higher than the tax price to this group is substantially higher than the tax price to this group. Both the low- and middle-demand groups should favor the competitive supply of public services. The high-demand group, the bureaucracy, and the owners of specific factors used by government should be expected to oppose the substitution of a competitive supply for the supply by monopoly bureaus. And again, a wider understanding of the processes of government is probably necessary to achieve this change, given the expected opposition by the minority that now controls the critical processes of government and captures all, or almost all, of the net benefits of government.

This chapter demonstrates that *either* a two-thirds rule or the competitive supply of public services would reduce the size of government, substantially increase the total net benefits, and substantially reduce the differences in the net benefits of government among the several groups. Under a proportional tax system, however, none of these three forms of government would achieve a distributional equilibrium, such that each group is just satisfied with the common level of public services supplied. As will be seen in the next section, given the postulated demand function, a progressive tax system is a necessary characteristic of both the optimal level of public services and a distributional equilibrium for each of the groups.

"Optimal" Government with Endogenous Tax Shares

The final form of government considered is the economist's concept of an optimal government. The characteristics of the institutions supplying public services and the decision rules of the government are not specified, and the tax system itself is considered a variable. The primary value of this model of government is its role as an ideal against which the effects of feasible governments and tax systems with specific identifiable characteristics can be compared. This analysis assumes that the demands for public services represented by our present political institutions are an adequate aggregation of individual demands.

The optimal level of public services is that which maximizes the total net benefits to all groups, where

$$[B + B_2 + B_3] - TC =$$
$$[(a_1 + a_2 + a_3)Q - (b_1 + b_2 + b_3)Q^2] - cQ. \qquad (16.17)$$

Given the functions (16.8) through (16.11),

$$[B_1 + B_2 + B_3] - TC = [7.845 + 10.880 + 18.281)Q \qquad (16.18)$$
$$-(.5 + .5 + .5)Q^2] - 20Q.$$

Solving for the level of Q that maximizes (16.18) yields $Q = 5.669$ and, from the total cost function (16.11), total expenditures and taxes of \$113.4 billion. This model also determines the tax shares at which each group would be in equilibrium by setting the tax price to each group to be equal to the marginal value to each group of the common optimal amount of public services supplied. For the middle-demand group, for example,

$$t_2c = a_2 - 2b_2Q \qquad (16.19)$$
$$= 10.880 - 1 \cdot 5.669 = 5.211$$

and

$$t_2 = \frac{5.211}{20} = .261, \tag{16.20}$$

By the same method, the tax share of the low-demand group is found to be .109, and the tax share to the high-demand group is found to be .630.

The effects of an optimal government in the United States, given the functions (16.8) through (16.11), are summarized in Table 16.5.

A comparison of this table with the earlier tables leads to some very interesting conclusions. The optimal level of total benefits, total expenditures, and output of public services is only 10 to 20 percent larger than that which would be generated by the competitive supply of public services, and the total net benefits would be very slightly larger. The optimal government would be around 60 percent of the size of the present government and would generate total net benefits over 100 percent larger.

Table 16.5 Optimal government with endogenous tax shares

Groups	Benefits	Taxes	Net Benefits	Q
	(billions of dollars, annually)			
Low demand	$ 28.4	$ 12.4	$16.0	
Middle demand	45.6	29.6	16.0	
High demand	87.4	71.4	16.0	
Total	$161.4	$113.4	$48.0	5.669

The primary differences between a government with a competitive supply of public services and the optimal government involves the distribution of tax charges and net benefits among the three groups. In a tax system which would achieve distributional equilibrium, the low-demand group, with 21 percent of the income, would pay 11 percent of the taxes. The middle-demand group, with 29 percent of the income, would pay around 26 percent of the taxes. And the high-demand group, with 50 percent of the income, would pay around 63 percent of the taxes. This tax system would thus exempt some of the low-demand group from all general taxes and would be slightly progressive above that level. At the lower optimal level of government, however, *the tax rates on the income of the high-demand group would still be lower than at present.* Another interesting feature of the optimal government is that the net benefits of government would be the same for each group. At the optimal level of government and with this tax system, no group would prefer either a smaller or larger government; the political equilibrium would also be a distributional equilibrium without controversy and tension among the groups on the issue of the scale of government.[8]

At the optimal level of government and with this tax system, the net benefits to the low- and middle-demand groups would be substantially larger and the net benefits to the high-demand group would be substantially smaller than those generated by the bureaucratic supply of public services and majority rule. Any change from the present characteristics of government toward more nearly optimal characteristics should thus be favored by the large majority and strongly opposed by the minority high-demand group that now effectively controls our government and most strongly influences the prevailing attitudes toward government. Bureaucracy and government, however, are creations of man and can be changed, to the benefit of most people, by a wider understanding of the effects of alternative political institutions.

8. This equilibrium, however, may not be too stable. There would still be an incentive for any group to try to reduce its tax charges. If successful, this would probably change the equilibrium level of output of public services

VI

The Alternatives

17

The Basis for Normative Judgments

The Conceptual Process

The problems of bureaucracy and national governments are not due to disinterest or the absence of suggestions for change. Indeed, a characteristic of modern life, at least in democratic nations, is the plethora of prescriptions for what government should or should not do. The offering of such prescriptions is an inalienable right of citizens, a legitimate self-serving activity by those who are specially affected by government, and a professional compulsion of social scientists. In general there are more prescriptions than problems. One recent Presidential candidate was characterized as offering prescriptions for problems that do not exist.

How does one select from among the many prescriptions? Ultimately, the selection will be made by experiment and evaluation whether the experiment, on net, benefits those who have the decisive influence on the government. The costs of experiment in bureaucratic and political institutions, however, are very high. Policies, programs, and organizational changes that were originally conceived as experiments develop a constituency in the bureaucracy, the legislature, and the public. The bureaucratization of experiments increases the costs and extends their life beyond the time at which there is general recognition that the experiment has failed. A cross-section of the programs of any national government includes a large proportion in this category. The selection from among the many prescriptions breaks down into the selection of which new experiments to make and the evaluation of the ongoing experiments. The higher the cost of experimentation, the more important is the selection of new experiments. The lower the cost, the more new experiments will be made and the more important is the evaluation of ongoing experiments. And, in our changing world, most government programs, however successful they may have been in an earlier period, should be regarded as experiments.

The following chapters suggest a set of possible changes in the structure of bureaus and the review process of national governments that, in some sense, would make them "better." Changes in organization and procedures should also be recognized as experiments. The standard way of reducing the costs of such experiments is to make small, piecemeal changes; this is entirely appropriate and, in the absence of a revolution, all that can be expected. Even so, the costs of experiments in public administration are substantial, so the burden of proof should rest on those who offer pre-scriptions for the various perceived ills. A common acceptance of the burden of proof by those who offer such prescriptions would at least reduce the number of prescriptions to a manageable level.

Selection from among the prescriptions suggested in the following chapters, as well as from others, should be based on the following con-ceptual process:

1. The first step is the selection of a normative theory about what ought to be done by some institution or group of institutions in the society. Such a theory merely describes the characteristics of the optimal conditions and does not, by itself, identify the institutions or procedures for achieving these conditions. I am personally prepared to accept, in the absence of an appealing alternative, the standard Pareto criterion for what ought to be done—namely, that every individual (or homogeneous group) should be as "well off" as possible without any other individual's (or homogeneous group's) being "worse off." This criterion has been widely accepted as describing the optimal supply of goods and services for a given distribution of income and wealth but was not considered applicable to evaluating changes in the distribution of income and wealth. Recent extensions in the application of the Pareto criterion to the evaluation of transfer payments, however, have convinced me and others of the more general relevance of this normative theory.[1]

Selection of a normative theory is basically an ethical and intellectual exercise, involving the selection of a criterion for what is "good," and evaluation of the internal logic of the theory. Because I accept the criterion and logic of the normative theory of private and public goods and services, the prescriptions suggested in these chapters are designed to create con-ditions which will more nearly approximate the optimal conditions as defined by this theory than those that now exist.

2. The next step is the selection of a set of positive theories about the behavior of different types of institutions in specified conditions. The primary purpose of this book is to develop a positive theory of the behavior of bureaus and of their collective sponsors, particularly in representative national governments. A positive theory, however, is not proved by the

1. For two recent examples, see Edgar O. Olsen, "A Normative Theory of Transfers," *Public Choice* VI, Spring 1969; and H. M. Hochman and J. D. Rodgers, "Pareto Optimal Redistribution," *American Economic Review*, September 1969, pp. 542–557.

"realism" of its assumptions or its internal logic. Such theories are only proved if the conditional predictions generated by the theory are confirmed (or, more accurately, fail to be disconfirmed) by the evidence.

The theory developed here generates many conditional predictions about the behavior of bureaus and their review groups. And these predictions are, for the most part, confirmed by my personal experience and casual empiricism.[2] I have not presented a set of critical tests of these hypotheses, and such tests are likely to prove difficult and time-consuming. However, they are necessary to prove the theory developed here, and the value of the prescriptions offered in the following chapters is thus strongly dependent on the confirmation of the positive theory by critical tests yet to be made. In some cases, actual experiments in public administration may be necessary to provide such critical tests, because the range of conditions presented by current and historical experience may be too narrow to provide a basis for statistical tests.

3. The third step of the conceptual process of evaluating these prescriptions should be a comparison of the probable conditions resulting from a prescription (which must be developed from a positive theory) with the optimal conditions (which must be developed from a normative theory). A finding that a specific institution or set of procedures does not generate conditions identical with the optimal conditions is not a sufficient basis for rejecting the prescription, since it still may be better than any identifiable feasible alternative.

Social scientists should be more careful than others about making this mistake, but I am not impressed by their track record. One of the most frequent errors implicit in many prescriptions for public policy is that of proceeding from a finding that some institution does not generate perfectly optimal conditions to the conclusion that some other institution is better, without developing the probable conditions generated by the other institution.[3]

In the present intellectual climate the more frequent error is to conclude, from a finding that the private sector or local government does not generate perfectly optimal conditions, that the national government should assume a greater responsibility for some function. A part of this error, I believe, is attributable to the lack of a positive theory about the behavior of bureaus and the national government and, thus, to the (usually implicit) assumption

2. This is probably a necessary condition for the sustained pursuit of a theoretical development. As a sometime manager of research, I recognize that there is an optimal amount of acceptable surprise in any study. If there is too little surprise, one wonders why the study was done and why others have not already accepted its conclusions. If there is too much surprise, one usually rejects the study's conclusions. In some sense I worry that this book has developed too few conclusions which are surprising in terms of my own experience. But then, what surprises a person depends, in part, on the positive theory through which one views his own experiences, and what may seem obvious to some is a surprise to others.

3. My favorite example of this type of behavior (suggested by George Stigler) is the judge of an opera competition who awarded the prize to the second singer after hearing only the first singer.

that the behavior of the national government is consistent with the normative theory. But this intellectual climate can change, and the growing despair about the performance of bureaus and the responsiveness of national governments may lead to errors in the other direction. Prior to Adam Smith, the intellectual community probably understood the behavior of government better than they understood the behavior of the economy; this relative understanding probably contributed to the widespread acceptance of Smith's suggestion that government spending be sharply curtailed. After two centuries of the development of economic theory and a possible retrogression in our understanding of political institutions, however, the more frequent error is to prescribe activities for the national government, whose behavior we don't understand very well, because the private economy and local governments are recognized not to work perfectly.

The prescriptions offered in this book should thus be judged by whether one accepts the Pareto criterion as a normative ideal, whether one believes that the positive theory developed in this book is consistent with the evidence, and whether the prescriptions would generate conditions closer to optimal than other prescriptions (including the prescription of no change).

This is not, of course, the only way to achieve an agreement on a specific issue. A part of the canon of successful politicians and labor mediators is to avoid argument over objectives or criteria if there is any prospect of agreement on the action.[4] And on many issues, moreover, there may be some actions which are consistent with quite different objectives and criteria. This type of *ad hoc* approach, however, almost denies the possibility of any general patterns of behavior or any general rules for choice.

The search for such general patterns and general rules, I believe, is more than the particular affliction of intellectuals. An understanding of these general conditions is requisite to the difference between barely acceptable solutions and better solutions—most of what human life is about.

Honest Government and/or Good Government

It has long been observed that legislators, the press, and political scientists appear to be more interested in how honestly our public activities are conducted than in how well they are conducted. Legislators apply stringent controls on the portfolios of senior bureaucrats (but not on their own) to reduce potential conflicts of interest during the bureaucrat's tenure. Corruption in government makes good news copy, but the malaise of bad programs administered by good men is hardly mentioned. Many public

---

4. Charles Schultze, a Director of the Bureau of the Budget under President Johnson, writes, "The first rule of the successful political process is, 'Don't force a specification of goals or ends'" (*The Politics and Economics of Public Spending* [Washington, D.C.: The Brookings Institution, 1969], p. 47).

administration reforms are primarily designed to insulate bureaucrats from outside opportunities for personal gain.

In part this is surely attributable to the dominant role of lawyers in American politics; lawyers have an obvious proficiency in writing law and identifying illegal behavior but no special background for deciding what constitutes good law. In part it may be due to the early training of reporters on the police beat.[5] The focus by both the legislature and the press on dishonest behavior is understandable; it is easier to identify scandalous behavior than bad administration, and the payoff in terms of votes and sales is higher. In part this attitude rests on a prevailing belief that honest government *is* good government, that honest men insulated from political and economic pressure will act in the public interest; this view derives from Confucius and Plato and has dominated the modern literature on public administration since Woodrow Wilson.[6]

I believe this attitude leads to an almost wholly misdirected emphasis on prescriptions for public administration reform. In the first place, these reforms do not work very well in assuring honest behavior. No law yet written prevents a Congressman from being influenced by large campaign contributors, even if they make no direct contribution to his personal income.[7] No law yet written prevents the procurement officer or regulatory commissioner from being influenced by the corporate boardroom and the implied promise of future employment, even if he receives no outside income during his tenure in the bureaucracy. More importantly, however, the confusion of honest government with good government has no basis in either theory or evidence. At best an honest bureaucrat is one who strictly follows all rules and regulations, particularly with regard to outside sources of income during his tenure. There is nothing inherent in honest civil subservience to rules and regulations that would cause a bureaucrat either to know or seek out the public interest or to act in the public interest. My impression is that government employees include a large proportion of the most honest people (in terms of following rules and regulations) and least selfish people (in terms of present pecuniary income) in any society.

The combination of honest government and good government, of course, is twice blessed, but I am convinced that most people prefer good government to honest government when there is a choice. The widespread disregard of some laws and the long-term corruption of some regulatory agencies and local governments often represent a functional accommodation to bad law. Any public administration reforms that will be both

5. This intriguing suggestion is made by Richard Bolling, *House Out of Order*, p. 148.

6. The standard prescription from this tradition is to select good men for public office and give them the knowledge and power to do what they believe is in the public interest. McGeorge Bundy's reflections on *The Strength of Government* (Cambridge: Harvard University Press, 1968) provide a representative and recent defense of this view.

7. Murray Chotiner, a long-time advisor to Nixon, is the source of the insight that "The only honest politicians are those who stay bought."

beneficial and enduring must create conditions such that the activities (legal or otherwise) of bureaucrats and review officers, acting in their personal interests, are more nearly consistent with the public interest. Honesty and unselfishness, like other virtues, are limited resources. Because other social institutions also rely on these virtues, they are precious and should not be squandered by the public sector. This is not to deny the power of these virtues when they are mobilized by government in a time of crisis. As long as these virtues are in short supply, however, the activities of government, except during a system-threatening crisis or war, should not demand too much of man's more noble qualities.

Types of Prescriptions

The following chapters offer three general types of prescriptions. The first set involves changes to or within the present bureaucracy. The second set involves changes in the sources of supply of public goods, primarily involving market alternatives. The third set involves changes in the political institutions and processes. In the aggregate these prescriptions are *not* a package deal. Some of the proposed changes, I believe, would be valuable whatever other changes are made. Some of the changes would be less valuable if specific other changes are made. I believe that the national governments of large nations and the bureaucracies that supply public services through these governments are now serving the citizens of these nations rather badly, and, in these conditions, an experiment with any portion of these prescriptions would significantly improve the performance of national governments.[8]

8. For better or worse, I am probably indebted to Herman Kahn for this device. Kahn's favorite technique for influencing public policy is to offer several dozen prescriptions for any major problem. He is usually not prepared rigorously to defend any specific prescription, but he characteristically claims that the adoption of any half-dozen of the prescriptions would significantly reduce the problem at issue. I usually find his arguments unconvincing in some details but most convincing in the aggregate. I hope to convince the readers of this book, of course, on both the details and the aggregate.

18

Bureaucratic Alternatives

The major changes to the present character of bureaucracy that are suggested by the evaluation in this book involve changes in the *structure* of the bureaucracy and changes in the *incentives* of bureaucrats. The value of the proposed structural changes is independent of the proposed incentive changes but is dependent, in part, on changes in the review process. The value of the proposed incentive changes, however, is largely dependent on the proposed structural changes. This chapter concludes with a discussion of the role of analysis in support of the bureaucracy.

Structural Changes

The most important change in the present structure of bureaucracy would be to increase the competition among bureaus in the supply of the same or similar services. Competition among bureaus is generally regarded as undesirable or, at best, in deference to certain institutional traditions, as tolerable. The major structural changes in the U.S. federal government since World War II have reduced the competition among bureaus supplying similar services. The Key West Agreement of 1947 was, in effect, a cartel agreement among the military services to divide the major military missions along bureau lines. A more general concern about unification of the services led to the creation of the Department of Defense, the Reorganization Act of 1958, and later the centralization of force planning under Secretary McNamara. Similar concerns about the coordination (reduction in competition) of civil programs led to the creation of the Department of Health, Education, and Welfare, the Department of Housing and Urban Development, and the Department of Transportation. More recently, some of the programs initiated by the Office of Economic Opportunity have been reassigned to the traditional welfare departments, and the

Nixon Administration has proposed a large-scale reorganization and consolidation of the domestic agencies.

The avowed purpose of these structural changes has been to improve the coordination and Presidential control of related programs. The coordination of related programs has an intuitive appeal, but the benefits of such coordination have always been a little vague. The *operational* coordination of military forces in the same theater, of flood-control programs in the same river basin, and of economic development programs in the same community has obvious benefits. This type of coordination is valuable because the several related types of programs are complements in the production of a higher-level public service. Such operational coordination can usually be achieved by *ad hoc* regional military commands, river basin authorities, development commissions, etc., without a unification of the related activities at the national level. The case for a monopoly supply of the related activities at the national level must be based on economies of scale above the regional level; such potential economies of scale, however, have seldom been demonstrated, and the monopoly supply of these activities would prevent any potential economies from being realized by the taxpayers. The creation of federal departments by grouping competing bureaus has led to larger budgets for the group of related programs in every case, providing historical confirmation of some of the behavioral bypotheses developed earlier.

The case for stronger Presidential control also has intuitive appeal, as it offers the prospect of substituting an executive review, which is more likely to be responsive to the middle-demand group than review by a legislative committee dominated by representatives of a high-demand group. The primary effect of the creation of the monopoly departments, however, has been to *decentralize* the executive review from the office of the President to the offices of the secretaries of the departments. And, with rare exception, the department secretaries quickly abandon their role as representatives of the President and become advocates of the group of programs for which they are responsible. It has even become traditional to appoint department secretaries with personal and regional backgrounds which would lead them to be advocates of the programs they administer. The creation of strong departments which monopolize the supply of a group of related public services has probably weakened the Presidential control of these programs. It may superficially appear that the strong departments have also weakened the control by the legislative review committees; however, the budget and output proposals of a monopoly bureau and a monopoly review committee, both representatives of the high-demand group, will be substantially similar, however much squabbling there is about who conducts the review.

Competition among bureaus, however, continues to develop, contrary to the canon of public administration, and only interrupted by periodic structural reforms. And even more competition would develop if it were not artificially constrained by public policy. Evaluations presented in Chapter 2 suggest that bureaus have a budget-maximizing incentive to broaden their service line to include services with significantly different demand and cost conditions, even if there is no relation among the services either in use or in production. Bureaus also have a budget-insuring in-incentive to broaden their service line to hedge against uncertainties in the demand and cost conditions, and this incentive leads to the addition of services with significantly different demand and cost conditions.

My observation is that bureaus tend to specialize in services that are more related in production than in use, because of a comparative advantage of institutional knowledge of the production processes and some joint economies of supply. The Navy's submarine-based Polaris missile, for example, represents an application of Navy understanding of the development and operation of submarines and some joint economies of training, manpower rotation, communications, and supply with other types of submarines to the supply of a service that is a close substitute for Air Force strategic bombers and missiles and is essentially unrelated in use to the other Navy forces.

Attempts to monopolize the supply of goods and services that are close substitutes are characteristic of bureaucracy and of any other institutional environment. Such attempts are usually undermined, however, by the expansionist activities of other bureaus, unless the monopolization or cartelization is actively reinforced by the executive. The Key West Agreement rapidly broke down in response to tight budgets, the changing military threat, and rapid changes in military technology; each of the services, the most resourceful of which was the Navy, developed competitive forces in several major missions. The Department of Agriculture has been so successful in driving farm labor and small farmers out of farming that it has developed foreign aid programs, food stamp programs, and school lunch programs to dispose of the surplus stocks and to alleviate the urban problems that the agricultural programs created. Resourceful bureaus will generate such competitive programs both in response to changing conditions, some of which are their own making, and in the absence of a contrary executive policy. The challenge for public policy is to use this natural competition in a bureaucracy to generate a more nearly optimal supply of public services.

Only part of the potential benefits are realized if the bureaus supplying the same or a similar service are reviewed by a department secretary or legislative committee representing a high-demand group. In this case, competition among bureaus is likely to reduce the combined budget for a given combined output of the service but would not assure that the combined output is reduced to a more nearly optimal level. The output of a monopoly bureau may be in the demand-constrained region where production processes are indeterminate and the total budget is larger than the minimum total costs. A review committee will usually have an incentive to try to reduce the budget for the same level of output, but, in the absence of an alternative budget-output proposal, it is dependent on the monopoly bureau for information on what is achievable, and thus has no basis for knowing that the same output could be supplied at a lower budget. Moreover, a monopoly bureau may take advantage of the indeterminancy of production processes in the demand-constrained region to use a large proportion of factors from regions or special interests that are strongly represented in the review committee; the extra payment to strongly represented factors may offset, at least in part, the usual incentive of the review committee to reduce the budget for any given level of output.

Competition among bureaus operates to reduce the inefficiency characteristic of a monopoly bureau in the demand-constrained region in several ways. First, the reduction in the level of demand and the increase in the elasticity of demand for the service supplied by any one bureau makes it likely that any bureau, other than one with a substantially superior production process, will be in the budget-constrained region and will thus have a budget-maximizing incentive to seek out and use efficient production processes. Second, the budget-output proposals from the several bureaus give the review committee a better basis for identifying an inefficient budget-output proposal from a single bureau. And third, bureaus operating in the budget-constrained region have a narrower range of discretion in choosing production processes and factor combinations and are not so likely to use factors that may be strongly represented in the review committee. These conditions increase the probability that the review committee will identify and approve a lower total budget for a given level of output than if the service were supplied by a monopoly bureau. One other effect of the competition among bureaus is likely to be a greater diversity of production processes, and this can be very important for services like national defense to insure against the catastrophic failure of any one process.

Competition among bureaus reviewed by a department secretary or legislative committee representing the high-demand group, however, does not directly reduce the more general problem of the oversupply of the service, because the review committee is likely to choose the same level of output as would be chosen by a monopoly bureau—specifically, the largest output that would be approved by representatives of the middle-demand group. The competition among bureaus, however, increases the probability that one bureau will be strongly dissatisfied by the results of the review process. On occasion a dissatisfied bureau may end-run the department or review committee and force the selection from among the several budget-output proposals to be made at the Presidential level or by the aggregate body of representatives, where the representatives of the middle-demand group have the decisive vote. Competition among bureaus thus tends to reduce the monopoly power of review groups dominated by representatives of the high-demand group by providing a known alternative to the proposal made by the review group and by forcing the selection from some set of alternatives to be made outside the review group.

A department secretary or review committee, of course, has a strong incentive to prevent leaks of information to the President's review agents or to representatives outside the review committee and can exercise strong penalties against a bureau which attempts to force the issue to be decided by the superior bodies. End-running the department secretary or the review committee is thus a risky and sometimes very costly activity by a bureaucrat, and it is more risky and costly the stronger are the department secretary and review committee, but such activities by adventurous bureaucrats can be very beneficial in reducing the monopoly power of other bureaus and the review groups and, as a consequence, reducing the oversupply of the service.

The potential value of competition among bureaus for the supply of a public service will be fully realized only under such conditions that representatives of the middle-demand group exercise the effective selection from among the several budget-output proposals. Changes in the review process and other characteristics of our political institutions that would create these conditions are discussed subsequently. For such conditions, the supply of a public service by competitive bureaus should generate about the same output and total budget as would the supply of these services at a price by competitive profit-seeking firms.

The output and budget solution in this case, of course, may not be identical to the solution when the service is supplied by competitive profit-seeking firms, but this depends somewhat on cultural conditions which affect the relative strengths of the profit-maximizing motivation and the budget-maximizing motivation. In this case, however, the primary remaining problems in the supply of public services would be due to the inherent difficulty of defining, contracting for, and monitoring the output of a public service, and to the inherent problems of political processes in identifying the demands for a public service, selecting the optimal level of supply, and distributing the tax charges. The supply of public services by competitive bureaus in combination with an effective review of the several budget-output proposals by representatives of the middle-demand group, in summary, would substantially reduce the problems of the *bureaucratic* supply of public services but would leave several important, but I believe better understood, problems of the *political* supply of public services.

What would be the characteristics of a competitive bureaucracy? One condition is essential to the creation of a competitive bureaucracy—the absence of an explicit, consistent, and enforced executive policy against competition among bureaus for the supply of the same or substitute services. Several other conditions would be helpful. The creation of new bureaus should be encouraged and other bureaus should be permitted to expire gracefully. Existing bureaus should be encouraged and permitted to supply services now supplied by other bureaus. The public administration analog of antitrust policy should be used to prevent collusion (like the Key West Agreement) to divide services or the output of one service among bureaus and to prevent the dominance of one bureau in the supply of a service. The executive and legislative review officers must be prepared to shift some part of the budget of one bureau to another, based on prior budget and output performance.

The bureaucracy that would result from the developing competition would include a larger number of smaller bureaus than at present, with some bureaus supplying several services for which there may be joint economies in supply but no obvious relation in use. A competitive bureaucracy would look more like the corporate sector of our economy. At present, some national bureaus dwarf the largest firms in the private economy, and there is strong reason to believe that the large size of national bureaus is primarily due to their protected monopoly power rather than to any inherent economies of scale in producing public services.

An evolutionary reduction of the monopoly power of bureaus would generate some specialization on the basis of production processes but would generate a size-distribution of bureaus more nearly reflecting the economies of scale in supplying each public service. By traditional public administration criteria, a competitive bureaucracy would look rather disorderly and chaotic. It could never be adequately reflected by an organization chart. There would be no formal division of responsibilities, roles, and missions. The output, employment, and budget of individual bureaus would be more variable than at present. However, there is strong reason to believe that a competitive bureaucracy in the aggregate would be less variable with respect to changes in the demand and cost conditions than a monopolistic bureaucracy. The employees of bureaus thus would have less job security but more employment security.

Modern bureaucracy is the primary manifestation of the rationalized social institution, and many of its problems are due to the periodic attempts to rationalize its structure and procedures. Any attempt, however, to make the organization and activities of a social institution comprehensible to a single human mind—the characteristic approach of the "social engineers"—can succeed only by the restriction of human activity to that which can be programmed by rules and regulations. Lenin's model of a socialist society, not surprisingly, was the post office. The performance of the post office, at least in the United States, should provide ample evidence of the problems of applying this model of social institutions to a wider range of human activity. A bureaucrat, in a sense, is the prototype conservative. However, a society of people who value individual freedom should judge social institutions pragmatically, not in terms of the perceived rationality of their structure and procedures, but in terms of their performance in creating those conditions which they value. A competitive bureaucracy would appear less orderly than the bureaucracy described by Weber but would also be less oppressive, less political, and less inefficient than the bureaucracy described by von Mises, Tullock, and Parkinson. My choice should be apparent.

Incentive Changes

A second major change, which maintains the bureaucratic supply of public services but changes the incentives of bureaucrats, should be considered. The general feature of this change would be some form of reward to senior bureaucrats to induce them to maximize, not the total budget, but the *difference* between the obtainable budget and the minimum total costs of the service. A change with this general feature would create, in effect, a modified profit system within the bureaucracy. The primary value of changing the incentives of senior bureaucrats in this way is that it reduces both the problem of inefficiency and the problem of oversupply that are characteristic of the conventional monopoly bureau. Such a change in the incentives of bureaucrats would be desirable, however, only in a competitive bureaucracy, because the maximization of the difference between total budget and total cost would lead to the undersupply of a service by a monopoly bureau. So this second bureaucratic alternative should be considered only in the context of the first.

A system of rewarding senior bureaucrats to induce them to maximize the difference between total budget and total cost could take one of three forms. These reward systems are ranked, I would estimate, in order of declining effectiveness but, probably, in order of increasing probability of being acceptable to our political institutions in the near future:

1. The first system would allow the senior bureaucrats in a bureau to appropriate as personal income some proportion of the difference between the approved budget of the bureau and the actual costs of supplying the approved level of output of the service. The "property right" in this income augmentation should probably be limited to those bureaucrats whose appointment is subject to political confirmation. This reward system, of course, would work well only in bureaus supplying services for which the output is relatively easy to measure. It should probably also be limited to bureaus that either do not use long-lived assets or, more realistically, rent the use and maintenance of such assets (like office space, computers, etc.) from private firms or some supply agency (such as the General Services Administration).

This system would work in the following way: A bureau would be given an approved budget based on some expected level of output for each service. At the end of the year the bureau would report the actual output and total costs. The senior bureaucrats would retain a previously agreed proportion of the difference between the approved budget and actual costs and return the rest to the general fund. In a strongly competitive bureaucracy, the senior bureaucrats should probably be permitted to appropriate a substantial proportion of the difference between the approved budget and actual costs, because bureaus would enter or leave the market for a specific service depending on the reported incomes of the senior bureaucrats; high incomes would cause other bureaus to bid down the approved budgets in subsequent cycles, and vice versa.

What happens if actual costs exceed the approved budget or actual output is reduced below the expected output to stay within the approved budget? This reward system would probably have to be asymmetric, because the personal wealth of the senior bureaucrats is unlikely to be sufficient to absorb the full cost overrun. This asymmetry of the reward system shifts much of the risk to the government and suggests a somewhat lower sharing rate for the bureaucrats. The asymmetry of the reward system also suggests that the senior positions that are eligible for the sharing of the bureau's "profits" are likely to have a positive value, even in equilibrium, as the individual bureaucrats have more to gain than to lose. This gives the government some substantial favors to dispense by appointment of men to these positions, and aspiring bureaucrats will "bid" for these positions in various ways, most likely by campaign contributions. Because the reward system, I believe, has to be asymmetric, the government's primary instruments to protect itself against unusually bad performance are to terminate the appointment and, for some forms of behavior, to bring legal action against the senior bureaucrat. A review group, preferably reporting to the executive or to a legislative group representing the middle-demand group, would monitor the quantity and quality of the output of the bureau.

At lower levels in the bureaucracy, a loosening of the civil service regulations and a change in the promotion process could have a similar effect and could be used independently or in combination with the above "profit" system for senior bureaucrats. The promotion process for any lower-level bureaucrat responsible for a separately identifiable budget could be structured in the following way: A savings of 10 percent of the approved budget, for example, would make the bureaucrat eligible for a one-step promotion, a savings of 20 percent would make him eligible for a two-step promotion, etc. In order to prevent an uneconomic erosion in the level and quality of the activity for which he is responsible, there should probably be some charge against the accounting savings that is a function of complaints from users of the service. This system would greatly improve the incentives at lower levels in the bureaucracy, regardless of the disposition of the realized savings. The incentives and constraints on the senior bureaucrat would determine whether the realized savings are returned to the general fund, contribute to the "profits" of the senior bureaucrat, or are used to augment some other allowed activity within the larger bureau.

This reward system, I believe, would both increase the efficiency and reduce the oversupply of public services. It should also attract better managers to the bureaucracy. As a side benefit, it should also provide a source of campaign contributions that is independent of the supply of specific public services or the use of specific factors in the production of these services. One possible consequence may be an erosion of the quality of public services, but the review process and competition from other bureaus provide a check on the tendency of an individual bureau to erode in the quality of its output. Such a system would require more precise measurement and control of output than is now usually the case, but would not require the monetary valuation of the output. I would expect this system to have some of the same problems and work about as well as, for example, the private contract construction industry. My estimate is that this would represent an enormous improvement in the supply of most public services financed by national governments.

For what types of services could this system be used? Several services are obvious candidates: the processing of welfare payments and tax returns, air traffic control, and other services for which the output measures are relatively simple. The possibility of using a reward system of this type for certain military activities should not be quickly dismissed. Louis XIV raised an army of 400,000, the most powerful in Europe for half a century, by a variant of this system. Individual colonels were paid fixed amounts to raise, equip, train, and maintain regiments with specified characteristics. Some weapons were provided from a royal arsenal. The colonels could keep the entire difference between the payment from the royal treasury and the actual costs of the regiment. The system was enforced by a corps of inspectors reporting to the Secretary of State for War. The colonels continued to receive payment from the treasury as long as the regiments passed muster, and the penalties for a consistent failure to pass muster were often severe. The asymmetry of the reward system, however, induced most colonels to purchase their commissions. The colonels were usually members of the nobility and served primarily as entrepreneurs; professional officers were assigned as lieutenant-colonels to provide the tactical leadership. The output standards were frequently refined and tested by actual combat. This system proved both effective and efficient for a long time. I see no reason why it should not be tried for some of the more simple military activities in the present forces.

The primary argument against this type of reward system, I suspect, is the improbability that even small-scale experiments with the system would be tried, given the quite modern attitude that it is, for some reason, bad form to organize the public sector by direct monetary incentives. The United States has had only a few decades of experience with a large national bureaucracy, however, and the growing concern about the performance of this bureaucracy may change the prevailing attitude toward such experiments.

2. The second type of reward system would pay senior bureaucrats in the form of large, deferred "prizes" for unusually efficient management. This system, I believe, would be less effective than the first system but probably more acceptable.

It would work in the following way: Senior bureaucrats would be paid only a salary during their tenure in office. Some period after they left office, say, after five years, they would be eligible to be considered for a set of large monetary prizes. The prize committee would consist of respected citizens, representing the major parties, with long overlapping tenures; new members of the prize committee would be nominated by the current executive and confirmed by the legislature. The prizes would be awarded on the basis of the following criteria: the consistency of the actual output of the bureau during the bureaucrat's tenure with the output that is promised in the budget-output proposals and the amount of funds which the bureau returns to the general fund during this period. Individual prizes may be awarded to single ex-bureaucrats or to a group of senior ex-bureaucrats from a single bureau. The prizes should be quite large relative to the annual salary of a bureaucrat and his possible income after leaving the bureau. An annual prize fund of $20 million, 1/100 of 1 percent of the present U.S. federal budget, for example, would provide for 10 annual prizes of $1 million and 100 annual prizes of $100,000. A somewhat larger prize fund would finance either larger prizes, which are probably unnecessary, or more prizes, which may be valuable.

A deferred prize system probably has one advantage, other than acceptability, over the first system. For some public services it is very difficult to recognize the level and quality of output and the possible deterioration in the capital assets of a bureau during a bureaucrat's tenure. It is far too easy to confuse style with substance, to confuse procedures with performance, in the short run. It is now increasingly recognized, for example, that the U.S. defense research and development program in the 1960's was a near disaster and that there was a substantial deterioration of some defense assets. The long lead time in developing new weapons and the small short-run changes in long-lived assets, however, made it difficult to perceive these conditions during that period. An evaluation of "the McNamara system" at the present time would not be free from bias but would be much better balanced than during McNamara's tenure as Secretary of Defense. A similar problem would be faced in evaluating the performance of the director of a medical research program or a regional economic development program. The human mind, however, has a phenomenal capacity for integrating various perceptions, and there is a better basis for judging performance, particularly after a period of reflection, than can be based on conceptually precise and measurable indicators of output.

What might be the consequences of such a deferred prize system? Some bureaucrats may opt out of competition for the prizes at an early stage in favor of the more conventional bureaucratic rewards of higher budgets; even these bureaucrats may have second thoughts, however, when a former colleague is awarded one of the large prizes. Some bureaucrats may try to game the prize system by overstating the budget required to achieve a given output in the expectation of returning a large amount to the general fund; competition from other bureaus, however, will reduce this kind of behavior, as an overstated budget proposal may lead more to a smaller budget for the bureau than an unbiased estimate. Some bureaucrats, individually or in concert, will consciously pursue the potential prizes and, among this group, some will later be awarded a prize.

I would not expect the deferred prize system to be so effective in motivating efficient behavior as the first system, because of the deferral of the rewards and the lottery element in the awarding of the prize. There is also the problem that the prize committee may apply different criteria than those against which the conscientious bureaucrat had been working, owing either to caprice or corruption. A formal, public prize law should reduce the range for caprice, however, and the appointment of either very respected or anonymous citizens to the prize committee should reduce the possibilities of corruption.

This deferred prize system, I would guess, has a substantially greater probability of being accepted, at least as an experiment, than the first system. In part this is for perfectly good reasons—the problem of evaluating current performance and the lower cost of the experiment. In part, however, our public institutions appear to prefer to reward their employees after the fact, for reasons that I do not fully understand. The U.S. government is not now prepared to pay first-term military manpower enough to recruit a volunteer armed force, but (surviving) veterans receive substantial benefits which were entirely unexpected at the time of their service. Most government employees receive a lower salary but a higher pension than their counterparts in private firms. The government is not willing to pay enough to retain good managers, but it seems to be willing to pay the high indirect cost of losing these managers to government contractors or regulated firms. In any case, the combination of a modest salary and an honored, genteel retirement seems to fit the prevailing image of a bureaucrat. A deferred prize system is consistent with this general image but, I believe, even a small fund of quite large prizes would significantly improve the performance of bureaucrats and the benefits generated by the supply of public services.

3. The third type of reward system would permit bureaucrats to spend some proportion of the difference between the approved budget and the actual cost of approved programs on a restricted set of allowed activities, but would not permit them to appropriate any part of this difference as a

direct augmentation of personal income. This reward system, I believe, would be less effective than either of the first two but is substantially more acceptable. Indeed, a reward system of this general type is implicit in the practice of giving the best bureaucrats somewhat more management discretion and amenities. The Soviet "directors fund" is the largest formal experiment of this type. A formalization of this system should have the same type of consequences as the first system but is unlikely to be so effective, as most bureaucrats would not prefer the allowed activities to the same augmentation to their personal income.

This system would work in the following way: A bureau would receive an approved budget and would be expected to perform a set of approved activities. A larger set of allowed activities would include the approved activities but would also include a restricted set of other activities that may contribute to the morale, long-term viability, and amenities of the bureau. If the bureau is able to perform the approved activities at less than the approved budget, the senior bureaucrats would be allowed to spend some part of the difference on the set of allowed activities. The bureau would be required to report the actual cost of the approved activities. If the sharing rate is less than unity, the bureau would return some part of the difference between the approved budget and the actual cost of the approved activities to the general fund. In a military bureau, for example, the senior bureaucrats would be allowed to spend some part of the difference to augment the approved forces, improve the capital assets of the bureau, augment the research and development program, improve base housing and recreational facilities, add to the travel fund and the headquarters staff, etc., at their own choosing.

A sharing rate somewhat less than unity is probably desirable, at least in the absence of strong competition from other bureaus, to improve the accounting of the actual costs of the approved activities. Bureaus that performed the approved activities at lower cost would thus both have more funds for activities of their own choosing and would return some funds to the general fund. This reward system, like the first two, would create an incentive for individual bureaus to erode the quality of the approved programs. The review system and competition from other bureaus, however, should minimize this type of behavior. An unusually high amount of financial flexibility and the consequent amenities in one bureau should induce other bureaus to bid down the approved budget in subsequent cycles.

This is not the most efficient way of inducing good management in a bureaucracy. The direct cost of supporting a senior general, bureaucrat, or legislator—including their immediate staff, personal amenities, travel and mailing privileges, etc.—is often ten times their salary. The indirect cost, in terms of other allowed activities under their control, is usually much higher.

The Department of Defense annually spends $10 billion or more for military systems, the primary purpose of which is to serve the doctrinal interests of the several services and subordinate groups. The U.S. federal government annually transfers around $30 billion to special interest groups other than the poor, the primary purpose of which is to induce around $100 million in campaign contributions. A general who could claim a small part of the cost of these allowable activities as personal income would find this a preferred alternative to the doctrinal interests of his service and return most of the cost of these activities to the general fund. A legislator who could claim a small part of the transfer payments as personal income could finance his own campaigns and return most of the cost of these transfers to the general fund.

At the present time this system of indirect payments is not very efficient, because the costs of the allowable activities are very high and there is a substantial random element between the performance of the bureaucrat and the size of these amenities and allowable programs. Bureaus will continue to have doctrinal interests, usually associated with some process for supplying a public service. Competition among bureaus (with different doctrinal interests), however, would reduce the approved budgets for a given output and thus reduce the amount of resources available to finance these doctrinal interests. And a more formal system for determining the amount of resources available for the allowable activities would reduce the randomness in the relation between bureaucratic performance and the expenditures for these allowable activities. This third reward system should be the most acceptable, as it represents a formalization of what is now a somewhat unstructured practice. Although it would not be the most efficient way to induce good management, even in a competitive bureaucracy, it should reduce both the inefficiency and the oversupply of public services.

This type of reward system would generate a considerable variance in the amenities and other allowable activities among bureaus, based largely on the performance of the bureaus. In this condition, there is an unfortunate tendency for auditors and the more traditional budget review officers to eliminate the differential amenities and other allowable activities of the more successful bureaus. This type of activity by the "green eyeshade" budget reviewers is most counterproductive and reinforces the worst kind of bureaucratic behavior. The opportunity to free resources for these allowable activities is just what motivates individual bureaus to more efficient behavior and the size of these allowable activities in one bureau is what motivates other bureaus to bid down the approved budget for a service. These allowable activities serve the same general function of organizing a bureaucracy as the function of profits in a private industry. The elimination of the differential amount of allowable activities among bureaus and of differential profits among private firms is a characteristic of a competitive equilibrium in both environments, but the *fiat* elimination of these differentials—a mischief perpetrated by both public auditors and socialists—would prevent the realization of the competitive equilibrium.

Any social institution within which objectives are not completely consistent must permit activities that are valued by subordinate units as the price of inducing activities valued by the larger unit. Social institutions should be evaluated by the total cost of the activities financed by the group, not just by that part of the cost that is not directly related to the desired activities but serves the critical function of inducing the performance of these activities. A large part of the problems of modern bureaucracy are attributable to a failure to recognize that bureaus are social institutions, managed and operated by people with quite personal motivations. Many of these problems, I believe, could be reduced by using any one of these three reward systems, given a competition among bureaus, to induce cost-minimizing behavior rather than budget-maximizing behavior.

Although I believe that reward systems based on current income are more effective than those based on future income and that reward systems based on monetary income are more effective than those based on income in kind, I recognize that von Mises' caricature of the bureaucrat is close to the prevailing image and that it is considered bad form to reward the superior management of public programs by current monetary income. A more general recognition of the costs to the public of the traditional bureaucratic reward system, at some time, may change this attitude.

In the meantime, however, the promise of any one of the three reward systems described in this section, I believe, is sufficient to merit an experiment in various parts of the public sector. An experiment with the current income system would be best tested in some set of competitive bureaus that supply an easily measurable service and rent their capital assets. An experiment with the deferred prize system is probably best tested in some set of competitive bureaus responsible for research and development programs; it may also be valuable to evaluate the historical experience with "king's prize" systems which were used by some European governments prior to the development of the modern French-German model of bureaucracy in the nineteenth century.[1] The allowable activities reward system may be best tested in a set of competitive bureaus supplying military forces.[2] The increasing concern about the performance of bureaucracy and the more general attitude that all of our social institutions should be regarded as

1. The general characteristics of a modern version of a king's prize system for research activities is described in a separate paper. See W. A. Niskanen, "Comments on the Evaluation of Federal Research and Development Programs," N-552, Institute for Defense Analyses, Arlington, Virginia, March 1968

2. The general characteristics of a reward system of this type for U.S. military forces that incorporates most of the features of the present force planning process is also described in a separate paper. See W. A. Niskanen, "Defense Management after McNamara," *Armed Forces Journal* CVI, No. 23 (8 February 1969), 17–21.

experiments should create a more favorable attitude toward trying and evaluating such experiments in the public sector.

Analysis and Information

Systems analysis and program budgets are the most important recent experiments in management techniques for improving the efficiency and responsiveness of the bureaucracy. Are these techniques, used in support of the bureaucracy, in the public interest? Sometimes they are, often they are not.[3] The primary purpose of analysis and better accounts is to identify more efficient combinations of production processes for the same public service. These techniques cannot make much of a contribution to determining the level of output of a public service or to determining the preferred combination of different public services, because these decisions involve an essentially subjective element of value; the most that these techniques can contribute is an estimate of the costs and other objective characteristics of the alternative choices. These techniques, used in support of the bureaucracy, can thus address the efficiency problem but not the more general problem of oversupply in a bureaucracy.

It is most important to recognize that neither businessmen nor bureaucrats have any inherent motivation to be efficient. Most businessmen, however, are induced to be efficient because efficiency is necessary for maximum profits and survival. Some bureaucrats are induced to choose an efficient combination of production processes because efficiency is a characteristic of the budget-maximizing equilibrium in the budget-constrained output region. Even in this region, bureaucrats have no incentive to be efficient, as measured by the present value calculus, in their choice among long-term investments. Other bureaucrats, specifically those who head bureaus operating in the demand-constrained region, have no interest in either efficiency production or investment choices. The effects of better analysis and resources accounts, when used in support of the bureaucracy, thus depend on the specific conditions faced by the bureau and the motivations of the senior bureaucrat.

Three cases should be distinguished (they are ranked in increasing order of the value of analysis):

3. This question may seem strange—and the answer even stranger—from one who has spent his entire professional career in such activities. Indeed, my growing unease about the value of systems analysis and program budgets and my developing perception about their effects were my primary motivations for writing this book.

4. For services for which the value of the benefits can be estimated, cost-benefit analysis can contribute to output-level decisions. Even for these services, however, it is not clear that taxing one group to benefit another is desirable—regardless of the difference between benefits and costs. Moreover, even if the conceptual problems are resolved, doing cost-benefit analysis for the bureaucracy (as distinct from the legislature) is unlikely to reduce the problem of oversupply. The long, and rather sad, history of cost-benefit analysis of water resource projects should be sufficient proof of this assertion.

1. In the demand-constrained region, a bureaucrat has no interest in efficiency on any kind of decision and, as a consequence, would not support analysis or the development of improved accounts for that purpose. If some analysis is required by higher authorities, or even if it is considered currently fashionable to have an analysis staff, the bureau will sponsor some analysis but will assure that the analysis is sufficiently self-serving or obscure to avoid any risk of threatening the bureau's demand-constrained status. If, as sometimes happens, some study sponsored by bureaus in this region turns out to be objective, thorough, penetrating, and lucid, it will usually be classified or otherwise restricted; if the distribution of the few penetrating studies cannot be restricted, the bureau will usually sponsor other studies on the same subject as an excuse for delaying action or to dilute the effects of the former studies. Analysts who do good studies for such bureaus soon find that they need another sponsor. The fact that some bureaus consistently spend large amounts for bad studies indicates only that they prefer bad studies to other possible ways to spend the approved budget. The marginal value of studies for these bureaus is zero, but it is only small consolation to the analyst to recognize that the marginal cost of the studies is also zero because the bureau would find other ways to spend the same budget.

2. In the more general budget-constrained region, a bureaucrat has a budget-maximizing incentive to identify and use more efficient production processes. In this case, a bureaucrat will value good analysis and better accounts for their contribution to efficiency. This bureaucrat will prefer good studies to bad studies and will usually permit distribution of the good studies. For the conscientious analyst, this sounds like an ideal sponsor. The effects of good analysis in this region, or any other way to improve efficiency, however, should be recognized. The direct effect of a reduction in the minimum costs is to increase the output and budget of the bureau. This does increase the total net benefits of this service; the increase in output and budget, however, increases the net benefits only of the high-demand group, still leaves the middle-demand group indifferent, and increases the negative net benefits of the low-demand group. It is easy to understand why the analyst may believe his activities are in the public interest, since he probably has relatively high preferences for the public service under study. When an activity leads to an increase in the net benefits of one group and a reduction in the net benefits of another group, the activity is not unambiguously preferable unless the losing group is compensated for the amount of their loss and the other groups are still better off. Such compensations are seldom made, however, except when the low-demand group for one service is a high-demand group for another service. For the aggregate of public services, most of the low-demand group are relatively poor, and an improvement in the efficiency of general public services will usually reduce the net benefits to this group, unless a sufficient part of the increase

in total net benefits is channeled into tax reductions or programs specific to this group.

Increased competition in the bureaucracy, by moving most bureaus into the budget-constrained region, would increase the demand for good public policy analysis. Unless our political system improbably makes the appropriate compensations, however, good analysis is not unambiguously desirable even if it leads to improved efficiency, just because the analysis cannot reduce the more general problem of the oversupply of public services by the bureaucracy. Again, even in this region, good analysis of the long-term investment choices may not even improve efficiency unless the expected remaining tenure of the bureaucrat is longer than the time period of expenditures for the alternatives. In the budget-constrained region, a bureaucrat should be expected to sponsor and implement good analysis of short-term production processes but to use his own personal calculus on long-term investment decisions.

3. In a few rare cases, a senior bureaucrat may conscientiously serve the interests of the President or some other representative of the middle-demand group, at least until his position is made intolerable by the bureaucracy and the review committees. In this rare condition, improved analysis and better accounts can reduce both the inefficiency and the oversupply of the bureau. My impression is that the Secretary of Defense in the first few years of each new administration, for example, has usually tried to serve the interests of the President, but that this is not the general or continuing case. Analysis is valuable to assist the President's representative in probing the production processes of the bureau to provide credible alternatives to the proposals made by the subordinate bureaus. It is less important, frankly, that these alternatives be the most efficient than that they be *feasible* in a lower budget and output region. As demonstrated in Chapter 15, one feasible alternative to the bureau's proposals can significantly reduce the oversupply of the service and increase the total net benefits. In this condition analysis can lead to increased net benefits to both the low- and middle-demand groups at the cost of reduced net benefits to the high-demand group.

Under such unusual circumstances, public policy analysis for a bureau can be most effective and personally rewarding, as it was during the first few years of the McNamara period in the Department of Defense, but the analysts should expect this condition to be transitory and their activities to be opposed by the high-demand group and their representatives in the review committees, by the bureaucracy itself, and by the owners of specific factors used by the bureau. When such conditions arise, good analysts serve the public interest by serving the senior bureaucrat. Unfortunately, only those analysts who are naïve or thick-skinned will do it a second time.

In summary: better analysis and accounts, in some conditions, can improve the performance of the bureaucracy, but more generally the marginal value of analysis in support of the bureaucracy is either ambiguous or zero. In any case, better analysis and information are not a general solution to the problems of bureaucracy. The superior performance of market institutions is not due to their use of better or more analysis. In fact, most of the formal, "sophisticated" resource allocation analysis in this nation now serves the bureaucracy. The primary differences in the performance of different organizations are due, rather, to differences in their structure and the incentives of their managers. Some part of the analytic resources now serving the bureaucracy would clearly be better invested in further developing the understanding of our political institutions and the organizations which supply public services.

19

Market Alternatives

One obvious question is suggested by the previous chapter. If the structure and incentives in a bureaucracy have to be changed so much to improve its performance, why not rely more on private markets, where this structure and incentive system now exist, for the supply of public services? Indeed, why not? A partial use of private sources of supply of public services from either profit-seeking or nonprofit firms can be very valuable whether or not significant changes are made in the bureaucracy or political institutions. The primary value of a private source of supply for a public service is to reduce the monopoly power of the bureaucracy and the review committees by providing the service at a price known to the representatives of the middle-demand group from a source that is not administratively dependent on the bureaucracy and review committees. A private source of supply can significantly reduce the monopoly power of the bureaucracy and the review committee, even if its costs are higher than the minimum possible costs of bureaucratic supply and even if the private source of supply is not, in fact, used.

Marketable Services

A wide range of services financed by government are also marketed, or are potentially marketable, in the private sector. These services have the characteristic that there are direct private benefits to their consumers and presumed benefits to a more general public from the consumption of these services by, at least, some groups; the available marketing technology must also permit the exclusion of nonpaying potential consumers motivated by the private benefits. Some lower amount of these services would usually be supplied by the private sector in the absence of government financing. The government's interest, in this case, is to augment the total supply of these services on the presumption (seldom precisely defined, and almost never measured) that there are public, nonmarketable marginal benefits of the consumption of these services. Where the government's primary interest is the income of certain groups, of course, a direct unrestricted income transfer or, if this creates adverse effects on work behavior, a wage subsidy, would be the most efficient form of government activity. Where the government's interest is dependent on the consumption of specific services, a direct per-unit subsidy of these services is entirely appropriate and is usually the most efficient form.

If the public benefits are independent of the groups in the population that consume the service, the most efficient form of subsidy is usually an explicit output subsidy to producers of the service, which leads to an expansion of the general consumption of the service by reducing the price to all consumers. The government subsidy goes directly to the producers, but the government makes no prior determination of the distribution of the subsidy among producers and does not intervene in the production process. Such a subsidy could take the form of paying a fixed amount per unit for the entire output (or, more efficiently, the additional output above some base-period output) to farmers, universities, hospitals, etc., for specific goods or services supplied by these organizations. Where the government's interest is to increase the general consumption of some service, it is usually more efficient to subsidize output at a per-unit rate, but only because the administrative costs of dealing with producers are lower than the costs of channeling the subsidy through consumers. The consequences of a general output subsidy and a general consumption subsidy, however, would be the same.

Although there are potential administrative advantages of dealing with producers, the record of most governments in the financing of public services through lower-level governments or private producers is not encouraging. The primary problems of most contemporary procedures for financing the supply of public services through producers are due to the use of lump-sum grants (often based on the financial "needs" of the producers) or subsidies of inputs to the production process rather than the use of per-unit output subsidies. The evaluation of mixed bureaus in Chapter 10 demonstrates that the use of grants to universities, hospitals, etc., is a less efficient way of inducing additional output than a per-unit output subsidy, depending, in part, on whether the sponsor or customer demand or both are dominant and whether the mixed bureau discriminates among customers in the sale of the service.

The subsidy of some inputs to the production of a public service does free resources for other uses, but at the cost, often substantial, of biasing the choice of production processes. The number of faculty positions in U.S. medical schools, for example, has increased around fivefold since 1950, largely in response to government grants for general use or ones that are nominally restricted to specified research activities, but the number of graduating medical doctors has increased only around 20 percent. For all these public funds and the research that they have induced, the relative cost of medical services has substantially increased during this same period. For the same public expenditure, a per-unit subsidy based on the number of newly licensed doctors would clearly induce a larger total number of doctors, reduce the monopoly power of the medical association, and lower the costs of medical service. The federal highway program, which subsidizes the construction but not the maintenance of highways, has uniformly led to the construction of concrete highways that have higher construction costs but lower maintenance costs. In contrast, most highways financed by state governments, which also maintain the highways, are constructed of macadam, which has lower construction costs and higher maintenance costs. A part of the difference in the characteristics of federally financed and state-financed highways may be due to differences in expected traffic loads, but there is a strong presumption that the nature of the financing has distorted the selection of construction methods. The federal financing of college dormitories and other buildings has induced the proliferation and expansion of schools with a massive physical plant and a mediocre faculty.

Sometimes the definition, measurement, and monitoring of the output of public services are recognizably difficult. The financing of public services through an unrestricted grant or by subsidizing one input to the production of these services, however, avoids this problem only by sacrificing efficiency and good public accounting. Government financing of public services through lower levels of government or private institutions, with rare exception, should be in the form of per-unit output subsidies.

If the public benefits of a service are dependent on which group consumes a service, the most efficient form of subsidy is generally a voucher for a specified amount or value of the service granted directly to members of the restricted group or a per-unit subsidy of the output supplied to the restricted group and granted to the producer.[1] Vouchers could take the form of food stamps, rent vouchers, tuition vouchers, travel vouchers, etc., that may be restricted to members of families with low incomes, students, or some other identified group. Restricted output subsidies granted to the producers could take the form of scholarships, lower medical charges, or lower-price tickets available only on identification as a member of the target group. There is not a great deal of difference in the effects of these two approaches if all potential producers are eligible to receive the vouchers or the subsidy.

For reasons that are difficult to explain, however, recipients of the vouchers are usually permitted to exchange them for services at any producing institution, whereas the restricted output subsidies are often limited

---

1. A major contribution to understanding of the economics of voucher systems has recently been made by Edgar Olsen. See Edgar Olsen, "Some Theorems in the Theory of Efficient Transfers," P-4018-1, The RAND Corporation, 1969.

to governmental and nonprofit private institutions. Food stamps and veterans' tuition allowances, for example, can be exchanged at profit-seeking firms, but most output subsidies for education and housing are restricted to nonprofit firms. Where this is the case, a voucher system is preferable if only to give the customer access to a wider market for the subsidized services.

If a voucher system is used, identification of the customer at the point of sale is also usually required, to prevent exchange of vouchers for money between the eligible group and the noneligible groups. Any significant exchange of the vouchers for money would transform a consumption subsidy into a general income transfer to the eligible group and would in this case not be so efficient as a direct income transfer. Where the public benefits are dependent on the consumption of a specific service by a specific group, and the identification of customers with this group is relatively easy, the use of vouchers merits greater attention as the means to accomplish the objectives of the government. The role of the bureaucracy in this case is only to dispense the vouchers to the eligible group.

Nonmarketable Services

Many of the services financed through government, of course, are pure public services for which the same output of the service is supplied to everyone and nonpaying beneficiaries cannot be (efficiently) excluded. The traditional functions of government—the courts and police system, military forces, relations with foreign governments, control of communicable diseases, some research and information services, etc.—are the characteristic examples. In some cases, these services would not be supplied at all in the absence of government financing. And at the present time, most of these services are supplied through bureaus.

Some parts of the inputs to the production of these services, however, are usually supplied under contract to the bureaus by profit-seeking firms. In the United States, for example, most buildings used by bureaus are constructed by private firms; most military weapons, equipment, and supplies are developed and produced by private firms; and the food services in government buildings and military bases are usually supplied by private firms.

For these services, the primary market alternatives to the present distribution of activities between the bureaucracy and private firms involve the use of private firms to organize a higher stage of the production of these services. At the next higher stage than the supply of buildings and equipment, private firms could bid to maintain buildings and even some weapons systems. At a next higher level, private firms could bid to supply certain instrumental services, like many of the training activities now provided by the military services or the operation of computer facilities. At a still higher level, private firms could bid on management contracts to operate the full spectrum of activities necessary to supply some amount of a specific public service.

For example, private firms could bid to manage the postal services, the fire protection services, the terminal air traffic control system, or, possibly, even the police services in a local community. (I understand that a profit-seeking firm now provides fire protection services to some communities in the Southwest on this basis.) Some types of military forces should even be considered eligible for operation by private firms. Some parts of the MINUTEMAN, NIKE HERCULES, and SAFEGUARD forces are obvious candidates; operation of these forces consists primarily of specialized technical functions, requires essentially no tactical skills, and is confined to a fixed location in the continental United States. The operation of these military forces is most comparable to the operation of a space launch facility, and private firms now perform most of the functions of the U.S. space program. A management contract is probably preferable to one which also includes the supply of the major assets in order to retain government ownership of the major assets and to assure the necessary standardization of these assets.

It is unnecessary (and self-defeating) to make a case to contract for all of any one of these activities to private firms. The primary value of the use of private firms to supply some of the activities would be to provide a source of supply that is not administratively dependent on the bureaucracy and review committee at a price known to representatives of the middle-demand group and, thus, to reduce the monopoly power of the bureaucracy and review committee. In the 1930's, the primary case for the creation of public power authorities was to provide a "yardstick" with which to evaluate private electric utility monopolies. Whatever the merit of the case for the supply of electricity in some regions by public authorities, the case for the private supply of some public services in some regions is similar—to provide a yardstick to evaluate the performance of budget-maximizing monopoly bureaus. A lot of snide remarks have been made about the risks of a manned lunar program consisting of the activities of thousands of profit-seeking, low-bidding private firms. Whatever the value of the U.S. lunar program, it has been one of the more spectacularly successful public activities in recent years and was accomplished within the budget estimates and schedule projected at the beginning of the program.

The increasing dissatisfaction with the performance of the bureaucracy in supplying some public services and the demonstrated success of private institutions in supplying some should be a sufficient basis for a greater number of experiments with the supply of public services by private profit-seeking firms and nonprofit institutions. In some cases, the present performance of some bureaus would be vindicated by such experiments, and these bureaus should have no reason to fear or oppose such a test. In others the performance of bureaus would prove to be inferior to that of the private institutions; then the bureaucracy, owners of factors used by the bureaucracy, and, possibly, the review committees should be expected to oppose such experiments, so it may be that the public interest is best served by just those experiments that are most strongly opposed by these groups. Where such experiments are considered, the bureaucracy itself, for obvious reasons, should not be given the responsibility for structuring and evaluating them.

Whatever the preferences of the population for public services, as revealed by the decisions of their elected representatives, the government should encourage such experiments to permit the determination of the combination of institutional arrangements for supplying these services to be made, in the long run, on the basis of demonstrated performance. I am convinced that a large part of the bureaucracy would survive this challenge by improving its own performance to equal or exceed that of other forms of organization.

20

Political Alternatives

This chapter focuses on the major changes in the structure and procedures of the legislature and the executive branch that would improve the performance of national governments in supplying public services. A whole set of problems, caused primarily by the procedures for electing public officials that affect how well public officials know and represent the interests of the population, are excluded from this discussion. I personally believe, for example, that a multi-party system with proportional representation (possibly, within each state) would better represent the diversity of interests of the population than the present two-party system with area constituencies. But an evaluation of the consequences of election processes is much beyond the scope of this book. This discussion deals primarily with changes in the structure of the review process, the size of the vote necessary for approval, and the system of tax charges.

The Review Process

The first set of measures, suggested by the evaluations in Chapter 14, would maintain the specialized review committees and executive departments but would reduce the dominant role of representatives of the high-demand group in the review process. In the legislature this would probably best be accomplished by a *random* assignment and periodic random reassignment of legislators to the various review committees. The randomization of committee assignments would make each committee, with some small sampling error, representative of the distribution of interests in the entire legislature, and the decisive vote in each committee, thus, would be representative of the middle-demand group. I believe that a periodic random reassignment, would be necessary, primarily because review agents tend to become advocates over time. This is not due to any special venality, but to the subtle and almost unavoidable effects on one's own views of

219

having to defend the results of the review process before a larger group. For the same reason, for example, teachers of the prevailing orthodoxy in any field tend to become advocates of the orthodoxy.

An objection has been raised that this proposal would destroy and prevent the regeneration of the specialization by legislators concerning related groups of programs, with the presumed benefits of better knowledge and understanding of the programs and the relevant part of the bureaucracy. If the review process operates as described in Chapter 14, however, the value of specialization by representatives of the high-demand group is dubious at best, because the primary role of the review process is to estimate the largest program that will be approved by a majority of the legislature. If the review committee more nearly reflects the interests of the legislature, a professional specialization of the committee staff should be sufficient to develop a continuous understanding of the related programs and bureaus; advocacy on the part of the committee staff would be more clearly recognized and deterred by a committee on which representatives of the middle-demand group have the decisive vote.

In the executive branch the analogous procedure would be to assign able men to the department secretary positions, essentially independent of their personal and regional backgrounds. Someone who, by present selection criteria, might be assigned to the Department of Agriculture, for example, might be assigned to the Department of State; someone who might be expected to be assigned to the Department of Defense might be assigned to the Department of Housing and Urban Development, etc. And the professional specialization, correspondingly, would be maintained primarily by the staff of the secretary's office. Even this nearly random assignment procedure would not be sufficient to protect the interests of the executive, because department secretaries usually become advocates of the programs of the department, at least after the first or second review cycle. A periodic and nearly random reassignment of the cabinet may thus also be necessary. My impression is that this proposed procedure is more nearly descriptive of the actual procedures in parliamentary governments than it is of the American form of executive government.

A second set of measures would maintain the procedures for selecting the review committees and the cabinet but would reduce the monopoly power of these review groups. In the legislature, this could be done by a random assignment of review responsibilities among committees. At the present time the Parliamentarian of the House of Representatives, a professional employee appointed by the Speaker, has some discretion concerning the assignment of new legislation to committees, but his assignments probably best reflect the Speaker's interests. The committees would thus become nonspecialized review groups, not by the assignment of legislators but by the assignment of review responsibilities. This proposal would not permit a professional specialization of the staff of a specific committee, but this could be maintained by the temporary assignment of a specialized staff to the committee responsible for the review of a specific set of programs in one review cycle.

Several other changes in the legislature could accomplish much the same purpose. One or more "watchdog" committees without a restricted charter to which legislators are randomly assigned could exercise a review in parallel with the review by the specialized committee on either a random basis or in response to the request of the entire legislature. This is an occasional practice in most legislatures, and it should not be surprising that the most critical reviews are usually exercised by the nonspecialized review committees. For these watchdog committees to be effective, however, they must be in a position to pose credible alternatives to those recommended by the traditional review committees for consideration by the entire legislature.

One other device could also be helpful—the creation of a large staff with specialized components that reports to the legislature as a whole. This staff could take the form of a policy research institute which would review current and proposed programs and formulate alternative programs; it could possibly be tasked by a general watchdog committee and report back to the legislature through this committee.[1] Obviously, it would be important that the financing of this review staff or institute not be dependent on either the bureaus or the specialized review committees. This staff or institute would also depend on the subpoena power of the general watchdog committee to protect its access to information about the activities of the bureaus. The efforts of this type of professional review staff, however, would be valuable, regardless of the responsiveness and quality of its analysis, only if the legislature were prepared to recognize their proposals as a credible alternative to that recommended by the specialized review committee—and this probably requires the availability of some source of supply that does not report through the review committee.

In the executive branch, the analogous procedure to the random assignment of review responsibilities would be a competitive, less specialized bureaucracy. Bureaucrats would be expected to be advocates, but would be permitted to offer a wide range of public services. The characteristics of a competitive bureaucracy have been discussed earlier, but several points are worth repeating. There would be no strong departments or strong secretaries. The choice of which bureau or combination of bureaus to supply a specific service would be forced to the level of the executive review. The Office of Management and Budget or some other executive review group

---

1. One such watchdog committee, the Joint Economic Committee, has recently recommended the creation of an Office of Economic Evaluation and Analysis to report through that committee. See "Economic Analysis and Efficiency in Government," Report of the Subcommittee on Economy in Government (Washington, D.C.: U.S. Government Printing Office, 1970).

would be strengthened to perform the task of choosing from among the competing proposals.

In the absence of a competitive bureaucracy, the executive review group would have to be even stronger in order to be able to formulate credible alternatives to the proposals by the monopoly bureaus; I don't have much hope that any review group can pose credible alternatives, unless it can find some bureau or other source of supply to provide the relevant information and to implement these proposals. At the present time, the President of the United States is largely a captive of his own bureaucracy and the Congress is a captive of its own committees. A strengthening of both the President and Congress relative to the coalition of the bureaucracy and the review committees will be requisite for effective majority rule.

The Approval Rule

One other measure should be considered as an alternative to the above changes. This is based on the recognition that the combination of the bureaucratic supply of services, a review process dominated by representatives of the high-demand group, and majority rule leads to the oversupply of public services with consequent losses to the low-demand group, indifference of the middle-demand group, and net benefits accruing only to the high-demand group. This alternative would maintain both the bureaucratic supply and the present review process but would increase the vote of the legislature that is required for approval from a simple majority to some higher proportion. As demonstrated in Chapter 16, a two-thirds approval rule would significantly increase the total net benefits of the services supplied by this government. The net losses to the low-demand group would be reduced, the middle-demand group would be substantially better off, and the high-demand group would still benefit most but generally by less than it does with majority rule. The bureaucratic supply of public services in combination with a two-thirds rule would still generate a government somewhat larger than the optimal size.

A common objection to a two-thirds rule, usually raised by political scientists, is that it would lead to an increasing deadlock on legislation. This objection has merit only if it is assumed that most legislation that would be approved by a majority is desirable. The purpose of such a rule, however, would be to reduce the undesirable oversupply of public services generated by the combination of bureaucratic supply and majority rule. On these grounds, more deadlocks would obviously be desirable.

The Tax System

For those public services for which the differences in demand are primarily dependent on differences in income, a progressive tax system could improve both the allocation of resources to the public sector and the distribution of tax charges. Compared to a proportional tax system, a progressive tax system would substantially lower the tax share of the low-demand group, slightly lower the tax share of the middle-demand group, and increase the tax share of the high-demand group. Given the bureaucratic supply of services, the dominance of the review groups by the high-demand group, and majority rule, a progressive tax system would reduce the size of government and increase the total net benefits only if the review committee solution is lower than that which would just win majority approval; if it is higher, a progressive tax system which slightly reduced the tax share of the middle-demand group would lead to a slightly larger government and a lower total net benefit. In either case, the primary effect of a progressive tax system would be the reduction of the absolute loss of the low-demand group, or possibly, the transformation of this loss into a small net benefit to this group. Given the competitive supply of public services and majority rule, the substitution of a progressive for a proportional tax system would somewhat increase the size of government and lead to a higher net benefit to both the low- and middle-demand groups and a lower net benefit to the high-demand group.

For those public services for which the differences in demand are primarily due to other conditions than differences in income, a progressive tax system can significantly distort both the allocation of resources to the public sector and the distribution of tax charges. Specifically, for those services for which the middle-demand group is a low-income and, therefore, low-tax group, either a proportional or progressive tax system could lead to a significant oversupply of these services and a wide divergence between the net losses and net gains of the low- and high-demand groups, respectively. In our present political system, those services for which there is likely to be the most controversy among different groups are those reviewed by committees dominated by representatives of high-demand, low-income constituencies. One protection against this problem would be to change the nature of selection to committees, possibly by the random assignment procedure described above. Another protection provided by our federal system is to delegate the provision of those services for which the differences in demands are strongly dependent on regional conditions to lower levels of government, maintaining the provision through the national government of only those services for which the population demands are homogeneous except for differences in income. In this latter case, a progressive tax system can be an instrument of both allocative efficiency and distributional equity.

VII

Conclusion

21

A Summary Agenda

Most people, considering only their personal relations with government, would prefer a government that is more efficient, more responsive, that generates larger total net benefits, and for which the distribution of taxes and net benefits is more equitable. All of us who are concerned about the viability of our democratic political institutions and the integrity of our national community would prefer a government with these attributes. The unavoidable conclusion of this book is that a better government would be a smaller government. This conclusion accepts as given the demands for public services as expressed through our political processes and is based on the consequences of the bureaucratic supply of public services, majority rule, and proportional taxation—the dominant characteristics of our present system of government.

My later chapters have described a large number of changes to the bureaucracy, the source of supply of public services, and to our political institutions that, I believe, would contribute to better government. The most important general changes are summarized below.

1. A conceptually simple but somewhat brute-force method to reduce government to a more nearly optimal size would be a uniform rule that all appropriations be approved by at least two-thirds of the legislators. This rule could be implemented by the much more frequent threat and use of the presidential veto. From the President's view, the primary purpose of the veto is to protect the interests of the median voters against the advocates, represented by both the bureaucracy and the legislative committees. Given the bureaucratic supply of public services and a proportional tax system, a two-thirds rule would generate a more nearly optimal level of public services, and, possibly as important, it would reduce the present negative net benefits of government to those who have relatively low demands for public services. A two-thirds rule, by itself, would reduce but not eliminate the differences among groups in their preferences for a smaller or larger

government. A two-thirds rule combined with a progressive tax system, however, would generate both a more nearly optimal level of public services and a more general agreement on the size of government.

A general use of a two-thirds rule would represent a fundamental change in our political institutions, and should not be casually adopted. It would be a manifestation of despair that the bureaucracy can ever be brought under control. It would only partially correct for the problem of oversupply by bureaus and would not correct for the inefficiency of some bureaus. With understanding and effort, I believe, the bureaucracy can be controlled. For this reason, I do not favor a general use of a two-thirds rule, but a somewhat more frequent use of the veto would substantially contribute to the more complex process of asserting control of the bureaucracy in the interests of most of the population.

2. A competitive supply of public services in combination with majority rule would generate a nearly optimal level of public services. The process of creating a competitive supply of public services would be most complex but would not require a change in our fundamental political institutions. This process would probably involve all of the following general changes:

   a) increase the competition among bureaus for the supply of the same or similar public services;
   b) change the incentives in the bureaucracy to induce more efficient behavior by the senior bureaucrats;
   c) increase the competition to the bureaucracy by greater use of private sources of supply of public services; and
   d) reassert control of the review process by the President and the legislative representatives of the median voters.

Many possible ways to implement these general changes have been described. All of the suggested detailed changes may not be feasible or desirable, but only one or a few of the changes of each general type are probably necessary. The process of creating a competitive supply of public services should probably involve small-scale experiments with many of these suggested changes and the evaluation of these experiments by the whole body of our elected officials. These changes would represent a fundamental change in the traditional attitudes toward public administration, but these authoritarian attitudes, I hope, do not yet have constitutional status. These general changes to create a more nearly competitive supply of public services should reduce both the problem of oversupply by bureaus and the problem of inefficiency by some bureaus. For this reason, and also to preserve the general use of majority rule, I prefer this more complex process to the general use of a two-thirds rule.

A competitive supply of public services would also reduce but not eliminate the differences among groups in their preferences for a smaller or larger government. A competitive supply of public services combined with a progressive tax system, however, would generate a nearly optimal level of public services and a nearly general agreement on the size of government.

3. At best, any government financed by general taxes which increase with income can effectively manage only those public services for which the population demands are nearly homogeneous except for differences in income. Those public services for which the demands, at a given level of government, are not related to income, will be grossly oversupplied in any identifiable form of government. This condition is usually due to the financing at a higher level of government of public services for which most of the benefits accrue to people in a lower-income component region (within this region, however, the demands for this service are most likely to be positively related to income). One strong implication of this problem is that the financing of public services should be restricted to the lowest level of government that includes most of the beneficiaries of each service. The national government would thus be restricted to the financing of those public services, including transfer payments to lower-income people, for which the whole nation benefits. As the incomes and demands for public services in a small region are more nearly homogeneous than in a larger region, the tax system in the small regions is appropriately less progressive than at the national level. The national government should thus finance a smaller range of public services than at present at lower, but somewhat more progressive, tax rates. A large part of the problems of our government could be reduced by making better use of our federal system to permit individuals to vote for most public services by their choice of state and local government.

4. Whatever changes are made in the political processes or the source of the supply of public services, a progressive tax system is necessary to achieve distributional equilibrium such that each group in the population is just satisfied with the common level of public services supplied. In the absence of a progressive tax system, individuals with a relatively low demand for public services will want less and individuals with a high demand will want more than the common equilibrium amount supplied. The consequent controversy makes good news copy but, I believe, weakens the integrity of our national community. The tax system at any level of government should be more progressive, the larger is the income elasticity of the demands for the package of public services financed at that level. For demand functions that are proportional to income, the analysis in Chapter 16 suggests that the tax system that would achieve a distributional equilibrium would exempt some of the lowest-income families and would be moderately progressive above that level. At a lower optimal level of government, however, the tax rates on income, even at high incomes, would be lower for every group. A distributional equilibrium at the optimal level of government, in summary, could be achieved by a somewhat more progressive tax structure at lower tax rates.

Bureaucracy and representative government are the creations of men. They should be the instruments of men. The parallel growth of bureaucracy and national government, however, has made these institutions less responsive, to the point of confusion about whether the people or these institutions are effectively sovereign. Patriotism is confused, even in the popular mind, with support of the government. Most of us share the liberal ideals articulated in the eighteenth century, and there is nothing inherent in modern technology, higher incomes, or conditions in other nations that makes them unworkable. The closure of the geographical frontiers makes these ideals even more important. A wider understanding of the effects of bureaucracy and representative government and a recognition of the potential benefits to specific identifiable changes, based on something like the theory developed in this book, is requisite, I believe, to realizing these ideals.

The Peculiar Economics of Bureaucracy

I. Introduction

Economics does not now provide a theory of the maximizing bureaucrat. The currently dominant approach to public administration is to provide the organizational structure, information system, and analysis to bureaucrats who, for whatever reason, want to be efficient. This approach, however, does not develop, or explicitly recognize as relevant, the conditions for which the personal objectives of the bureaucrat are consistent with the efficiency of the bureaucracy.

At present, with a large and increasing proportion of economic activity being conducted in bureaus, economists have made no substantial contribution to answering the following questions: What are the distinguishing characteristics of bureaucracies? What are the critical elements of a theory of bureaucracy? Specifically, what do bureaucrats maximize and under what external conditions? What are the consequences of maximizing behavior under these conditions? For example, what is the equilibrium output and budget of a bureau for given demand and cost conditions? What are the effects of changes in demand and cost conditions? What are the welfare consequences of bureaucratic organization of economic activity? What changes in organization and the structure of rewards would improve the efficiency of a bureaucracy? This paper presents a simple model of the maximizing bureaucrat and, based on this model, a set of tentative qualitative answers to these questions.

II. The Model

The model outlined in this section is based on the following two critical characteristics of bureaus: (1) Bureaucrats maximize the total budget of their bureau, given demand and cost conditions, subject to the constraint that the budget must be equal to or greater than the minimum total costs at the equilibrium output. (2) Bureaus exchange a specific output (or combination of outputs) for a specific

First published 1968.

budget. For this paper, thus, bureaus are defined by these two characteristics.

Among the several variables that may enter the bureaucrat's utility function are the following: salary, perquisites of the office, public reputation, power, patronage, ease of managing the bureau, and ease of making changes. All of these variables, I contend, are a positive monotonic function of the total budget of the bureau.[1] Budget maximization should be an adequate proxy even for those bureaucrats with a relatively low pecuniary motivation and a relatively high motivation for making changes in the public interest. It is an interesting observation that the most distinguished public servants of recent years have substantially increased the budgets of the bureaus for which they are responsible.

The second characteristic—bureaus exchange their output for a total budget rather than at a per unit rate—is generally recognized, but the implications of this characteristic for the behavior of a bureau are not. This characteristic gives the bureau the same type of "market" power as a monopoly that presents the market with an all-or-nothing choice.[2] A bureau, thus, can appropriate all of the consumer surplus. As is shown later, however, this characteristic leads to significantly different output, budget, and welfare conditions for a bureau than for a monopoly.[3]

The equilibrium conditions for a bureau, as defined by these two characteristics, are developed below by considering a bureau faced by linear demand and cost conditions. First, consider a bureau that buys factors in a competitive market and for which

$$V = a - bQ$$

and

$$C = c + 2dQ,[4]$$

where

$V \equiv$ marginal value to consumers
$C \equiv$ minimum marginal cost to bureau

and
$Q \equiv$ output of bureau.
For these conditions, then,

1.   This paper develops only the static model of a bureau and does not explore the time dimension of budget maximization.
2.   I am indebted to Gordon Tullock for this powerful insight.
3.   This characteristic applies strictly to a "pure" bureau, such as the Department of Defense. Many economic institutions such as the Post Office, most colleges and universities, and most hospitals sell part of their output at a per unit rate and a substantial proportion of their output for a budget.
4.   The marginal cost function for a bureau that is not a discriminating monopsonist includes the factor surplus. The average cost function to this bureau and the corresponding marginal cost functions for a monopoly or bureau which is a discriminating monopsonist would be $C=c+dQ$.

$$B = aQ - \frac{b}{2}Q^2$$

and

$$TC = cQ + dQ^2,$$

where

B ≡ total budget of bureau

and

TC ≡ minimum total cost to bureau.

The equilibrium level of Q, for these conditions, is determined as follows: Maximization of B leads to an upper level of $Q = a/b$. The constraint that B must be equal to or greater than TC, under some conditions, leads to a lower level of $Q = 2(a-c)/b+2d$. These two levels of Q are equal where $a=2bc/b-2d$. For a bureau that buys factors in a competitive market, the equilibrium level of Q, thus, is where

$$Q\begin{cases} = \dfrac{2(a-c)}{b+2d} & \text{for } a < \dfrac{2bc}{b-2d}. \\ = \dfrac{a}{b} & \text{for } a \geq \dfrac{2bc}{b-2d}. \end{cases}$$

Figure 1 illustrates these equilibrium levels of output for representative demand and cost conditions.

For the lower demand condition represented by V_1, the equilibrium output of a bureau will be in the budget-constrained region where the area of the polygon $ea_1 hi$ is equal to the area of the rectangle *efgi*. At the equilibrium level of output, there is no "fat" in this bureau; the total budget just covers the minimum total costs and no cost-effectiveness analysis will reveal any wasted resources. The output of this bureau, however, is higher than the Pareto-optimal level. The equilibrium level of output is in a region where the minimum achievable marginal costs *ig* are substantially higher than the marginal value to consumers *ih*, offsetting all of the consumer surplus that would be generated by efficient operation at lower budget levels. If minimum marginal costs increase with output as a consequence of increasing per-unit factor costs (rather than diminishing productivity), this bureau will generate a substantial factor surplus equal to the triangle *cfg*—larger than would be generated at the lower, Pareto-optimal output. Legislatures predominantly representing factor interests understandably prefer the provision of public services through bureaus.

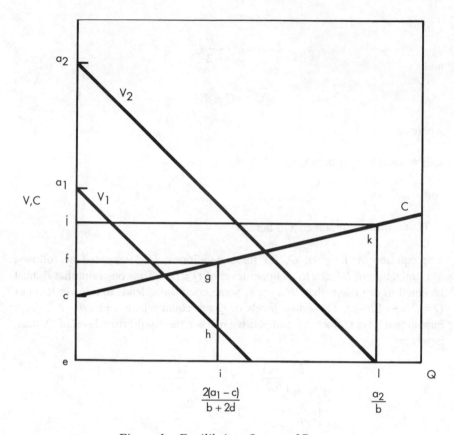

Figure 1   Equilibrium Output of Bureau

For the higher demand conditions represented by V_2, the equilibrium output of a bureau will be in the demand-constrained region where the marginal value of output is zero. In this case the total budget will be equal to the triangle ea_2l and will be larger than the minimum total costs equal to the rectangle $ejkl$. At the equilibrium level of output, there is "fat" in this bureau. A careful analysis would indicate that the same output could be achieved at a lower budget, but the analyst should expect no cooperation from the bureau since it has no incentive to either know or reveal its minimum cost function. In this region, the equilibrium level of output is dependent only on demand conditions. The output of this bureau is also higher than the Pareto-optimal level, operating at an output level where the minimum marginal costs are equal to lk and the marginal value to consumers is zero, again offsetting all of the consumer surplus. The factor surplus generated by this bureau, of course, is also substantially larger than would be generated by a lower, Pareto-optimal output level.

III. Comparison of Organizational Forms

A better understanding of the consequences of bureaucratic organization of economic activity can be gained by comparison with the consequences of other forms of economic organization facing the same demand and cost conditions. Table 1 presents the equilibrium levels of output and related variables for a private monopoly which buys factors on a competitive market, a private monopoly which discriminates among factor suppliers, a competitive industry, a bureau which buys factors on a competitive market, and a bureau that discriminates among factor suppliers. Each form of organization faces the same following demand and cost conditions:

$$V = 200 - 1.00\, Q$$
$$C = 75 + .25\, Q.^{5}$$

Table 1   *Equilibrium conditions for alternative forms of economic organization facing same demand and cost conditions*

Product Market	Monopoly		Competitive	Bureau	
factor market	competitive	monopsony	competitive	competitive	monopsony
Measures					
Output	50	55.6	100	166.7	200
Revenue:					
Total	7,500	8,024.7	10,000	19,444.4	20,000
Average	150	144.4	100	116.7	100.0
Marginal	100	88.9	100	33.3	0
Costs:					
Total	4,375	4,552.5	10,000	19,444.4	20,000
Average	87.5	81.9	100	116.7	100.0
Marginal	100.0	88.9	100	158.3	125.0
Profits	3,125	3,472.2	0	0	0
Consumer surplus	1,250	1,543.3	5,000	0	0
Factor surplus	312.5	0	1,250	3,472.2	0

The traditional concern about private monopolies is that they produce too little output. Operating in an output region where marginal value is greater than marginal cost, they do not generate as much surplus value as would a competitive industry. For the demand and cost conditions shown in Table 1, a private monopoly would generate a sum of profit plus consumer and factor surplus around 75 percent that of a competitive industry.

---

5. This is the average cost function to a monopoly or bureau that is not a discriminating monopolist, the marginal cost function to a discriminating monopsonist, and the supply function to a competitive industry.

For these demand and cost conditions, a bureau that buys factors on a competitive market will have an equilibrium output around two-thirds more than the competitive industry. This bureau will generate no profits or consumer surplus but will generate a factor surplus around 55 percent of the total surplus from a competitive industry. For these conditions, a bureau that discriminates among factor suppliers will have an equilibrium output twice that of a competitive industry and will generate no profits or surplus value.

A comparison of the supply and cost conditions is also helpful. A monopoly has no supply function; it will set an output such that marginal revenue equals marginal cost, with the output sold at a uniform price. A bureau also has no supply function; it will exchange increments of output at the demand price for each increment to an output level such that the budget equals the minimum achievable costs or the marginal value of the increment is zero. In a sense, a bureau also has no separate marginal cost function. The incremental resource withdrawal for a budget-maximizing bureau will be equal to the demand value, as the difference between this value and the minimum incremental cost will be financed from the consumer surplus appropriated at lower output levels. Only if a bureau is efficient at lower output levels, for whatever reason, would the incremental resource withdrawal be equal to the minimum incremental cost. One implication of this condition is that an analyst may not be able to identify a demand-constrained bureau's minimum cost function from budget and output behaviour. All this may yield is the bureau's estimate of its demand function; in the static case, all bureaus will appear to have declining marginal costs and in a sense they do. An estimate of a demand-constrained bureau's minimum marginal cost function must be constructed from detailed estimates of the production function and factor costs—creating an extraordinary demand for analysis.

For different reasons, in summary, both private monopolies and bureaus operate in output regions that are inherently nonoptimal. The substitution of a bureau for a monopoly to provide some product or service, however, solves no problems; this substitution will reduce the aggregate surplus value and serve only the interests of the owners of specific factors.

IV.   Effects of Changes in Demand and Cost Conditions

The model outlined in Section II may also be used to estimate a bureau's response to changes in demand and cost conditions.

Demand Shifts. Figure 2 illustrates the changes in a bureau's equilibrium output and budget, for given cost conditions, in response to shifts in demand.

In the budget-constrained output region, the output of a bureau will grow by more than the amount of a demand shift, even when faced by increasing marginal costs. A bureau producing an output at constant marginal costs will grow at twice the rate of a competitive industry under the same conditions. In this region, the budget per unit output will increase only the amount of the increase in the minimum unit costs.

Figure 2   Effects of Demand Shift

In the demand-constrained output region, the output of a bureau will grow by the same amount as the demand shift, regardless of the slope of the minimum marginal cost function. The slower rate of growth of a bureau in this region is still higher than the rate of growth of a competitive industry facing increasing marginal costs. In this region, the budget per unit output increases rapidly, by an amount proportionate to the demand shift, regardless of the slope of the minimum marginal cost function.

A bureau, like a private monopoly, will often find it rewarding to try to shift its demand function. The incremental budget that would result from a demand shift will be particularly high in the demand-constrained output region. One would expect, therefore, that bureaucrats would spend a significant part of their time on various promotional activities, supported by the owners of specific factors.

Changes in the Demand Slope. Figure 3 illustrates the changes in a bureau's equilibrium output and budget, for given cost conditions, in response to changes in the slope of the demand function. The indicated changes in the intercept and slope are such that the output of a competitive industry, given the same cost con-

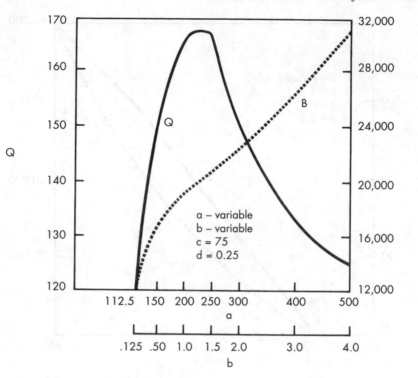

Figure 3   Effects of Changes in the Demand Slope

ditions, would be constant at a level of 100 for each combination.

In the budget-constrained output region, the equilibrium output of a bureau will increase with increasing (negative) demand slopes; in the demand-constrained region, output will decline with increasing demand slopes. A bureau faced by a nearly horizontal demand function will produce an output at a budget per unit output only slightly higher than that of a competitive industry, but the total budget and the budget per unit of output will increase monotonically with higher demand slopes. This suggests that a bureau may find it rewarding to try to increase the slope of the demand function for its output by promotional activities, citing public "need" or military "requirement" to be fulfilled, regardless of cost. A more important suggestion is that a bureau operating in a highly competitive output market would be relatively efficient. However, the present environment of bureaucracy—with severe constraints on the creation of new bureaus or new outputs by existing bureaus, and the passion of reformers to consolidate bureaus with similar output—seems diabolically designed to reduce the competition among bureaus and increase the inefficiency (and, not incidentally, the budget) of the bureaucracy.

Cost Shifts. Figure 4 illustrates the changes in a bureau's equilibrium output and budget, for given demand conditions, in response to shifts in the minimum marginal cost function.

In the budget-constrained output region, a downward shift of the minimum marginal cost function will increase the equilibrium output of a bureau at a rapid rate. A bureau producing an output at constant minimum marginal cost will grow

Figure 4   Effects of Cost Sheets

at twice the rate of a competitive industry for the same downward cost shift. The bureau's budget will grow rapidly with the initial cost reductions and then very slowly as output approaches the demand-constrained output level. In the higher output region, further reductions in cost will not increase either the equilibrium output or budget.

These effects suggest that new bureaus or those facing exogenous increases in costs will be very cost conscious. Such bureaus will have an incentive to determine their minimum marginal cost function and to try to reduce the level of this function. Older bureaus or those facing a rapid increase in demand couldn't care less on either count. Tullock has been intrigued by the observation that bureaus both attempt to reduce costs and manifestly waste huge amounts of resources. This model suggests that, in equilibrium, a single-product bureau will be in one or the other of these conditions. A multiproduct bureau, such as Department of Defense, should be expected to attempt to reduce costs on the budget-constrained outputs and to assure that costs are sufficiently high to exhaust the obtainable budget on the demand-constrained outputs.

Changes in the Slope of the Minimum Unit Cost Function. Figure 5 illustrates the changes in a bureau's equilibrium output and budget, for given demand conditions, in response to changes in the slope of the minimum marginal cost function. The indicated changes in the intercept and slope are such that the output of a competitive industry, given the same demand conditions, would be constant at a level of 100 for each combination.

In the budget constrained output region, the equilibrium output of a bureau that buys factors on a competitive market will increase with a reduction of the slope of the minimum unit cost function to a level, with constant unit costs, that is twice the output of a competitive industry. The bureau's budget will also increase with a reduction in the slope of this function, but relatively slowly. Both output and budget are invariant to changes in the slope of the cost function in the demand-constrained output region.

These effects suggest that bureaus may have an incentive to use production processes with a higher cost at low output levels and a lower cost at high output

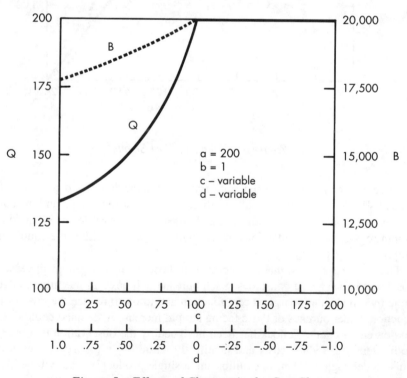

Figure 5   Effects of Changes in the Cost Slope

levels. In the static case, however, this incentive is not very strong and may be offset in part by pressure through the legislature from the owners of specific factors.

V.   Critical Tests of This Model

This model suggests an image of a bureau with a level and rate of growth of output that is up to twice that of a competitive industry facing the same conditions. Demand by consumers may be the basis for establishing a bureau, but the interests of this group in preserving the bureau will diminish or disappear as the bureau creates no consumer surplus, except by negligence. A bureau, however, creates a substantially larger factor surplus than would a competitive industry, and the primary interests in continuing the bureau (or a war) are likely to originate from the bureau itself and the owners of specific factors. In the demand-constrained output region, a bureau's only concern about costs is to assure that they exhaust the obtainable budget. A bureau should be expected to engage in considerable promotion, in cooperation with the owners of specific factors, to augment the demand for its output, and to reduce—through persuasion, restrictions on entry, and consolidation—the elasticity of this demand.

These are serious charges. A set of critical tests of these assertions are difficult to pose. The best tests that I can conceive are to compare the output and costs of a bureau with those of a private firm with the same type of product. A comparison of the Social Security Administration and insurance companies, public and private hospitals, public and private statistics gathering organizations, or public and private police and garbage disposal services may be sufficient. Such tests, however, will be difficult as the existence of potential competition may present the bureau with a highly elastic demand, while some of the private firms producing a similar product have some of the characteristics of bureaus. A test of these assertions about a bureau that is the sole producer of a set of products, such as the Department of Defense, is even more difficult and probably more important. For such bureaus, an internal comparison at different points of time or, possibly, with bureaus producing a similar product in another political jurisdiction could be made.

VI.   Further Implications for Analysis and Policy

Analytic Developments. The static model of a single-product bureau outlined in Section II should be extended in several dimensions. First, the consequences of the time-dimension of budget maximization should be developed. Louis DeAlessi's preliminary analysis suggests that a bureaucrat's concept of his property rights will lead to a preference for capital-intensive production processes. Second, the behavior of a multiproduct bureau that receives a single budget (or several budgets not specific to product type) should be explored. And third, the behavior of "mixed" bureaus, such as the Post Office, educational institutions, and public hospitals should be explored.

Policy Implications. This model of a bureau, if the suggested tests fail to disconfirm its assertions, has important implications for the organization of the production of the large and increasing proportion of our national output now produced by bureaus. What changes could be made to improve the efficiency of the production of these goods and services?

First, and probably most interesting, bureaucratic provision of these goods and services could be maintained, but each bureau would operate in a competitive environment and face a highly elastic demand function. The creation of new bureaus would be encouraged. Existing bureaus would be permitted and encouraged to produce products now provided by other bureaus. "Antitrust" restrictions would prevent collusive behavior to divide products or output among bureaus and to prevent the dominance of one bureau in a single product. The legislature would be willing to shift some part of the output of one agency to another, based on output and budget performance. The resulting bureaucracy would consist of many single and multiproduct bureaus without any obvious relation (in use) to the products offered by any single bureau. (As such, it would look a little like the corporate sector of our economy.)

Second, the incentives of bureaucrats could be changed to encourage them to minimize the budget for a given output or set of outputs. For example, the salaries of the top 5 percent of the personnel of a bureau could be a negative function of the budget of a bureau for a given set of outputs. This would still permit a political determination of the output level for the combination of bureaus providing the same product. Such a system would require more precise measurement of output than now, but would not require the monetary valuation of this output. Such a system may also attract better managers to the bureaucracy.

Third, the type of goods and services now provided by bureaus could be financed through government or foundations as is now the case, but the provision of these services would be contracted to private, profit-seeking economic institutions. The bureaucracy, as such, would disappear, except for the review and contracting agencies. This system would also require better measures of output than now, though of course better measures are necessary for improved efficiency under any organizational form.

Bureaucrats and Politicians

> "The whole hotel has a disease called The Only Game in Town. If you don't like it, too bad. It has a secondary infection called No Ownership. In other words, management has a contract without a piece of the action."
>
> John D. MacDonald[1]

Introduction

Five years ago I completed the manuscript that was published as *Bureaucracy and Representative Government*.[2] This book—an attempt to match a now conventional theory of the demand for government services in a representative government with a new theory of bureaucratic supply—provoked a minor stir, some misunderstanding, and some useful subsequent research. This paper summarizes my reflections on this book and the findings of several empirical studies that bear on some of its conjectures.

These reflections, like the perspectives of the book, are based on a combination of personal experience, the comments and contributions of others, and the available empirical studies.[3] Part I of this paper outlines several suggested

---

1. John D. MacDonald, *The Turquoise Lament* (1973), p. 220.
2. William A. Niskanen, *Bureaucracy and Representative Government* (1971).
3. My personal experience during this period involved two years as an official in the Federal Office of Management and Budget and three years as an academic. The government experience generally reinforced my earlier perspectives, most importantly by improving my understanding of the review process; more on this later. The academy made it possible to read a larger body of academic literature and to conduct several empirical studies.

The most constructive comments on this book, not surprisingly, are also the most critical. The comments that have most affected my views are those by Earl Thompson, "Book Review," *Journal of Economic Literature* 11 (1973), p. 950; Jean-Luc Migué and Gérard Bélanger, "Toward a General Theory of Managerial Discretion," *Public Choice* 17 (Spring 1974), at p. 27; Albert Breton and Ronald Wintrobe. "The Equilibrium Size of a Budget-Maximizing Bureau," *Journal of Political Economy* 83 (1975), p. 195. An important paper by Armen Alchian and Harold Demsetz, "Production, Information Costs, and Economic Organization," *American Economic Review* 62 (1972), p. 777 provided a perspective on how bureaus fit within a general theory of economic organizations.

First published 1975.

modifications to my earlier theory of bureaucracy and representative government. Part II summarizes a set of relevant empirical findings.

I. Modifications of the Theory

My theory represents the relation between an elementary bureau and its government review group as that of a bilateral monopoly. The bureau "sells" its service only to the government, and the government "buys" the service only from the bureau. This market, however, involves the exchange of some output for a budget rather than at a per unit price. In any such bilateral monopoly condition, output is indeterminate within a range, without determining the conditions affecting the bargaining between the two parties. My model of bureaucratic supply determines only the bureau's preferred output based on an assumption that the bureau acts to maximize its budget. The government's preferred output is determined from conventional majority rule models or from my special model of decisions by a "high demand" committee.

The two major criticisms of my theory are (1) that budget maximization by bureaus is not obviously consistent with utility maximizing by bureaucrats and (2) that the theory does not develop the conditions for an equilibrium output between the output preferred by the bureau and the output preferred by the government. Both criticisms are correct and substantial; they have motivated me to suggest the modifications to the theory outlined in this section.

A.   Utility Maximizing Bureaucrats.   My earlier model of bureaucratic supply *starts* with an assumption that bureaucrats act to maximize their budget. Although I made some plausible arguments for this maximand, I did not derive it from a more general utility maximizing framework.[4] Earl Thompson[5] correctly suggested that this leads to the awkward two-region solution where bureaus are perfectly efficient at equilibrium outputs for which the marginal value to the government is positive and are inefficient only at outputs for which marginal value is zero. This conclusion seemed most inconsistent with perceptions about bureaucratic behavior, including mine.

Jean-Luc Migué and Gérard Bélanger[6] suggested an approach that both generalizes and simplifies this model in a way that resolves this inconsistency.[7] They

A coherent set of critical tests of the hypotheses developed in the book has not been performed. Several independent studies that I and others have completed during this period, however, bear on some of the central hypotheses. These studies are identified in the text. I am indebted to Seymour Neustein for assisting me with the statistical work on voting behavior and the effects of bureau consolidations.

4.   In fact, there is good empirical evidence for my early assumption—that a bureaucrat's salary, status, and discretion are a positive function of the bureau's budget. For example, see Robert Staaf, "The Public School System in Transition," in *Budgets and Bureaucrats: The Sources of Government Growth* (Thomas E. Borcherding ed., 1975).

5.   Earl Thompson, *supra* note 3.

6.   Jean-Luc Migué and Gérard Bélanger, *supra* note 3.

7.   They deserve an apology for my failure to recognize the substantial nature of their contribution in my original comment on their article, "Comment," *Public Choice* 17 (Spring 1974) at p. 43.

developed a model of bureaucratic discretion based on an assumption that a bureaucrat maximizes an objective defined in terms of his "discretionary budget" (the difference between his total budget and the minimum cost of producing the expected output) and the bureau's output. This model leads to a general conclusion that a bureau's budget is always too large and that the output is generally too large. At one limit, if bureaucrats do not value output, the output level will be correct, but this output will be produced most inefficiently. At the other limit, if bureaucrats do not value the discretionary budget, the output level will be substantially too high, but will be produced efficiently—the conclusion of my earlier model. Migué and Bélanger have started in the right direction, but they also fail to derive the bureaucrat's maximand from an explicit model of utility maximization in a specific institutional setting. This is the first issue to be resolved.

Consider an individual bureau manager with the following utility function:

$$U = \alpha_1 Y^{\beta_1} P^{\gamma_1} \tag{A.1}$$

Y is the (present value of the) bureaucrat's income from his position, and P is the set of non-monetary perquisites of his position; P includes leisure time, the social and physical amenities of his position, the regard of others, etc. The bureaucrat is not, in this formulation, assumed to have any direct preferences for the budget, output, or efficiency of the bureau. The parameters of this utility function may be different for each bureaucrat, although the common reward structure probably leads the set of bureaucrats to have a relatively high preference for perquisites.

The relations between the conditions valued by the bureaucrat and the performance of the bureau are determined by the reward structure of the institution, as established by the government review group. This reward structure is common to all potential candidates for a specific position, although it may differ among positions. The reward structure is defined by

$$Y = \alpha_2 Q^{\beta_2} (B - C)^{\gamma_2} \tag{A.2}$$

and

$$P = \alpha_3 Q^{\beta_3} (B - C)^{\gamma_3}, \tag{A.3}$$

where Q is the output of the bureau, B is the maximum budget that would be approved by the government review group, C is the minimum cost of producing the output of the bureau, and $(B - C)$, thus, is the "discretionary budget" of the bureau.

The general structure of the three equations A.1 through A.3 could be used to analyze managerial behavior in any form of economic organization. A specific theory of bureaucratic behavior must be based on the characteristics of the reward structure in the bureaucratic environment. The distinguishing feature of the reward structure for managers in a profit-seeking firm, for example, is a relatively high value of the parameter γ_2. In contrast, a bureaucrat's reward structure is characterized by a relatively low value of γ_2. A bureaucrat is not able to appropriate any of the bureau's discretionary budget as personal income, except by promotion to a higher paid position.[8] The parameters β_2, β_3 and γ_3, however, are relatively higher in a bureaucratic environment.

Substituting the equations for Y and P in the utility function and simplifying yields an expression of the utility function in terms of Q and $(B - C)$, as follows:

$$U = \alpha Q^{\beta}(B - C)^{\gamma}, \qquad (A.4)$$

where

$$\alpha = \alpha_1 \alpha_2^{\beta_1} \alpha_3^{\gamma_1}$$
$$\beta = \beta_1 \beta_2 + \gamma_1 \beta_3$$
$$\gamma = \beta_1 \gamma_2 + \gamma_1 \gamma_3.$$

The bureau's discretionary budget $(B - C)$, of course, is also a function of the bureau's output. Using the same form of these relations as in my earlier model,

$$B = aQ - bQ^2, \qquad (A.5)$$

$$C = cQ + dQ^2, \qquad (A.6)$$

and

$$(B - C) = (a - c)Q - (b + d)Q^2. \qquad (A.7)$$

The budget function A.5, of course, is the integral of the demand function facing the bureau over the range of output. At this point, it is worthwhile to digress on the nature of the demand function facing a bureau to clarify an earlier misunderstanding. This demand function, except under special circumstances, is *not* the total demand by the government for the service supplied by the bureau. For any marginal value of the service, the output demanded from the bureau is the

---

8.   The primary limitations on the bureaucratic promotion process in eliciting efficient behavior are the low salaries of bureau managers (relative to those in other economic organizations) and a bureau's monopoly of information on minimum potential costs. A lower-level bureaucrat could inform the review group about these costs to increase his promotion opportunities, but the number of such successful examples is minimal. A senior bureaucrat has an incentive to spread the perquisites among critical lower-level bureaucrats in a way that presents each of them with a prospect of foregoing large perquisites for a small expected pecuniary gain. Such practices involve a distribution of some of the bureau's monopoly power to strengthen the personal monopoly power of the senior bureaucrat in his position. Some other condition is necessary to explain why governments do not strengthen the pecuniary incentives for efficient management or for leaking information to the review group about inefficient practices.

total output demanded *minus* the output that could be supplied from another source or the estimated output that could be supplied from this bureau with a different management team. Thus, if there is any effective competition from other sources of supply or from another management team, the demand function facing a bureau will be both lower and more elastic than the total demand function for the service. A bureau, in turn, cannot appropriate the total "consumer's surplus" for the service, but only that portion that represents the monopoly rent of the bureau or its present management team. In the limit, if the government can procure the service from another service or from the same bureau with another management team at a constant unit cost, the demand function facing a bureau is horizontal at this unit cost, and the bureau's budget is a linear function of output.

Substituting A.7 into A.4 yields a utility function of the bureaucrat defined only in terms of the bureau's output, as follows:

$$U = \alpha Q^{\beta}[(a-c)Q - (b+d)Q^2]^{\gamma}. \tag{A.8}$$

Maximizing A.8 with respect to Q thus leads to a level of bureau output that maximizes the utility of the bureaucrat where

$$Q = \left(\frac{\beta+\gamma}{\beta+2\gamma}\right)\left(\frac{a-c}{b+d}\right). \tag{A.9}$$

If $\beta=0$, which would be the case only if the bureau's output did not contribute to either the income or perquisites of the bureaucrat, then

$$Q = \frac{1}{2}\left(\frac{a-c}{b+d}\right) \tag{A.10}$$

This output level is optimal to the government, but at a high cost of perquisites and inefficiency throughout the bureau. In contrast, if $\gamma=0$, which would be the case only if the bureaucrat could not appropriate any of the discretionary budget as income or perquisites, then

$$Q = \left(\frac{a-c}{b+d}\right) \tag{A.11}$$

This output is twice the optimal output, but is produced at the minimum possible cost. This last case, of course, is the solution for the bureaucrat's preferred output in my earlier model.

An examination of the general output function A.9 indicates that the output will be a positive function of the marginal effect of output on a bureaucrat's rewards and a negative function of the marginal share of the discretionary budget appropriated by the bureaucrat. The directional effects on output of the parameters of the budget and cost functions are the same as in my earlier model, although the magnitude of the partial effects, in each case, are multiplied by the constant factor $\left(\dfrac{\beta+\gamma}{\beta+2\gamma}\right)$.

Substituting the general output function A.9 into the budget function A.5 yields the following general budget function expressed in terms of demand and cost conditions and the parameters of the reward functions:

$$B = a\left(\frac{\beta+\gamma}{\beta+2\gamma}\right)\left(\frac{a-c}{b+d}\right) - b\left(\frac{\beta+\gamma}{\beta+2\gamma}\right)^2\left(\frac{a-c}{b+d}\right)^2. \tag{A.12}$$

An examination of this function indicates that a bureau's budget will also be a positive function of the marginal effect of output on a bureaucrat's income and perquisites and a negative function of the marginal share of the discretionary budget appropriated by the bureaucrat. The directional effects on the budget of changes in the demand and cost conditions are also the same as in my earlier model, though all of the partial effects are weaker the greater the importance of the discretionary budget in a bureaucrat's reward.

Substituting the general output function A.9 into the discretionary budget function A.7 yields the following function for the discretionary budget expressed in terms of the demand and cost conditions and the parameters of the reward functions:

$$B - C = \left(\frac{\beta+\gamma}{\beta+2\gamma}\right)\left[1 - \left(\frac{\beta+\gamma}{\beta+2\gamma}\right)\right]\left[\frac{(a-c)^2}{b+d}\right]. \tag{A.13}$$

The discretionary budget is highest when $\beta=0$, that is, when a bureau's output does not contribute to either the income or perquisites of a bureaucrat. At this limit, the ratio of the discretionary budget to the minimum potential cost is the following:

$$\frac{B-C}{C} = \frac{(a-c)(b+d)}{2c(b+d)+d(a-c)}. \tag{A.14}$$

If the review authorities use the tactic of approving a constant budget per unit of output, as suggested by Earl Thompson, then this expression reduces to

$$\frac{B-C}{C} = \frac{a-c}{a+c}. \tag{A.15}$$

This expression illustrates how the production inefficiency of a bureau is a positive function of the unit cost (a) at which the government can purchase this service from some other source. If ($a-c$) is small, a bureau will be quite efficient even if $\beta=0$.

The above expressions identify the maximum percent of production inefficiency by a bureau when the government can measure the actual budget and output of a specific service. The discretionary budget decreases as β increases relative to γ. At the other limit, when $\gamma=0$, the discretionary budget disappears, and a larger output is produced at a minimum factor cost.

The general output and budget functions are defined for each bureau and for each bureaucrat. They will differ among bureaucrats depending on their preferences for income and the several types of perquisites. There are two processes, however, that probably make these functions more homogeneous among bureaucrats: for a given reward structure, the set of potential bureaucrats probably have higher preferences for perquisites relative to managers of other economic organizations. And the government review group may design a specific reward structure for each bureaucrat, based on their perceptions of his preferences, to elicit more responsive behavior. Nevertheless, some variance in the behavior of different bureaucrats in the same position should be expected.

B. Vote Maximizing Legislators. So far, this analysis has developed only the output and budget preferred by bureaucrats. A theory of government output and budget, however, must also incorporate the behavior of the government officials who establish the demands for government services and monitor the behavior of the bureaus. For this discussion, these functions are assumed to be performed by an elected legislature.[9] The four characteristics of the legislature that are central to this analysis are majority rule decision making, committee review, vote maximizing behavior by legislators, and legislator discretion in the use of his own time and available staff resources.

My earlier model established only the boundaries of the bargaining between a bureau and the legislature. Albert Breton and Ronald Wintrobe[10] have suggested a model of the review process that reduces the range of indeterminacy of the final output and budget. Legislatures can use a variety of control devices—"including direct monitoring, overlapping bureaus, duplication of services, and the purchase and acquisition of information from alternative sources, including sources at lower levels in the bureau itself"[11]—to reduce the misallocation and inefficiency of bureaucratic supply. These control devices are costly, however, and they will be used only to the point where their marginal value equals their marginal cost.

Figure 1 illustrates their simple model of the review process. The triangle OHJ is the difference between the budget preferred by a bureau and that preferred by the legislature, and is equal to the consumer surplus that would be appropriated by the bureau at its preferred output and budget position; the line HJ is thus the marginal value of control devices to the legislature. The line LM is the marginal cost of control devices. Breton and Wintrobe conclude that the legislature will use OK units of control devices. At this point, the bureau's budget is reduced by

9. No assumption is made about how well a legislator knows or represents the interests of his constituency; this is an important issue but is far beyond the scope of this paper.
10. Albert Breton and Ronald Wintrobe, *supra* note 3.
11. *Id.* at 6.

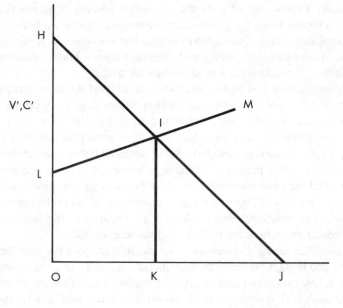

Figure 1   Units of Control Devices

an amount OHIK; the total cost of control devices is OLIK; the increase in consumer surplus from the use of control devices is LHI, and the budget is KIJ. The total loss due to bureaucratic supply—the sum of the costs of control devices and the remaining discretionary budget—is OLIJ. This model is not sufficient to determine the allocation of control devices between correcting the oversupply of output and reducing the costs at a given output, although the authors speculate that it is less costly to control oversupply and, thus, that most of the losses to bureaucratic supply will be in production inefficiency.

The model developed by Breton and Wintrobe provides a starting point for analyzing the review process, but does not incorporate the specific institutions of the review process or the incentives of the legislators. What is known about legislatures that would suggest how many "units of control devices" they use? Is there any reason to believe they would use a quantity of control devices that maximizes the net benefits to the population? This section suggests two modifications to the model developed by Breton and Wintrobe to reflect the specific institutions of the review process and the incentives of legislators.

First, it is important to recognize that a committee, not the whole legislature, conducts the review process for each bureau. More important, at least in the United States, most committees are dominated by legislators who have higher demands for the services reviewed than the median demand in the whole legislature; moreover, the committee decisions are very seldom amended or reversed by the whole legislature. Several recent studies of the committee assignment process—by Rohde and Shepsle,[12] by Shepsle,[13] and by Cohen[14]—have confirmed the casual observations that most legislators receive the committee assignments they request and that these requests are correlated with services that are most important to their regional constituencies.[15] My earlier assertion that review committees prefer a higher output than that preferred by the representative legislator does not require that committee members have a higher absolute demand for the services reviewed, merely that they have a higher demand relative to the tax costs in their constituency.

A high-demand committee will use a different amount and type of control instruments than would a randomly-selected committee. Figure 2 illustrates this condition. In this case, the line HJ represents the marginal value of control devices to the representative or median legislator. If a bureau uses its discretionary budget to increase its output, the marginal value of control devices designed to reduce over-supply will be lower for the representative member of the high-demand committee, here represented by the line NP. A high-demand committee, then, will use only OQ units of control devices to reduce the over-supply of output. At this point, the bureau's budget is reduced by OHSQ; an amount OLRQ is spent for control devices; the gain in consumer surplus from use of the control devices is LHSR, and the remaining discretionary budget of the bureau is QSJ. The total loss due to bureaucratic supply is now OLRSJ, while the loss of consumer surplus due to delegation of the output decision to a high-demand review committee is RSI.

This illustrates my earlier conclusion that the output preferred by a bureau will be much closer to that of a high-demand review committee than to that preferred by the median legislator. A high-demand committee, however, has the same incentives to control production inefficiency as would a randomly-selected committee. Given the costs of control devices to reduce over-supply and to reduce production inefficiency, therefore, a high-demand committee will use relatively

12. David Rohde and Kenneth A. Shepsle, "Democratic Committee Assignments in the House of Representatives: Strategic Aspects of a Social Choice Process," *American Political Science Review* 67 (1973), p. 889.

13. Kenneth Shepsle, "A Model of the Congressional Committee Assignment Process: Constrained Maximization in the Institutional Setting," *Public Choice* (forthcoming).

14. Michael D. Cohen, "The Importance of Member Preferences in Committee Assignment: An Assessment against Optimal Standards and a Simple Process Model" (unpublished paper presented at MSSB Conference on Mathematical Models of Congress, Aspen, Colo., 1974).

15. The following comment by Senator William Proxmire is characteristic of the perceptions of legislators about the assignment process: "In the deliberation of this [assignment] committee, there are enormous pressures to place those Senators whose states benefit from, say, public works appropriations on . . . the Senate Interior Committee. . . . In fact, a Senator who is from a state which benefits from these programs is, at least in the short-run, rather clearly serving his own best interests and those of at least some of his constituents if he obtains a seat on one of these Committees. The net result of all this, however, is that *the Committee structure develops a built-in bias toward higher budgets* [my italics]. Because the people who serve on each committee have an interest in seeing the budget for which they are responsible increase, they often fail to encourage careful evaluation and analysis of expenditures." U.S. Congress Joint Economic Committee, Subcommittee on Economics in Government, "The Analysis and Evaluation of Public Expenditures, The PPB System" (1969).

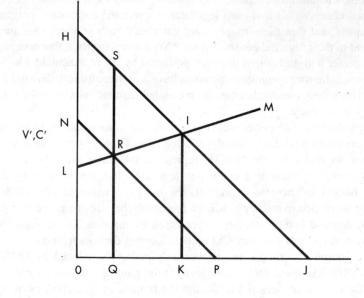

Figure 2   Units of Control Devices

more control devices to reduce production inefficiency. This conclusion would be weakened if the bureau used some of its discretionary budget to purchase higher-cost factors in the constituencies represented in the review committee. In general, a high-demand committee is "in the bureau's pocket" only with respect to the output decision.

A second problem arises from the condition that legislators have substantial discretion in the use of their time and staff resources. Some uses of these resources have benefits that are largely specific to their own constituency and/or campaign contributors. The monitoring function, however, is a public good within the legislature; the benefits of monitoring accrue to the whole population as a function of their tax costs. This creates a substantial "free-rider" problem internal to legislatures and the expectation that monitoring activities will be under-supplied.[16]

Consider a simple world in which the votes for an individual legislator, over some range, are a linear function of the specific services he performs for his con-

16. A recent *Wall Street Journal* column documents the perception of Congressmen about the monitoring, or oversight, function: ". . . oversight has been infrequent and slipshod. It's usually dull, thankless work; there are more reelection brownie points in running errands for the folks back home, and more satisfaction in passing new laws. Tough oversight can make enemies among congressional colleagues or powerful interests groups. Committees supposed to exercise oversight are often the ones that created the programs in the first place, and thus not overly anxious to spotlight flaws.

" 'Everyone recognizes the need for oversight,' says Sen. Edmund Muskie, one of its most effective practitioners, 'but other things come along, and it gets pushed farther and farther down the ladder until it disappears.' " Alan L. Otten, "Oversight," *Wall Street Journal*, 6 March 1975, at 12, col. 3.

stituents and contributors, the level of output of some aggregate government service, and the taxes paid by his constituents, as follows:

$$V = aX + bY - cT, \tag{B.1}$$

where V is the number (or proportion) of votes for the incumbent legislator in the next election, X is the number of hours per day that the legislator spends on activities specific to his constituency, Y is the output of some aggregate government service, and T is the level of taxes in his district.

Taxes, of course, are related to the level of government output in the following way:

$$T = SCY, \tag{B.2}$$

where S is the share of total taxes paid by residents of his district (this will be a function of the number of people, income levels, composition of income, etc. in each district) and C is the actual unit cost of the government service. Substituting B.2 into B.1 yields

$$V = aX + (b - cSC)Y. \tag{B.3}$$

A legislator's time budget constrains the number of hours per day that he devotes to activities specific to his constituency plus the hours spent on monitoring activity to be equal to the total hours that he spends at work. One form of this relation is the following:

$$H = X + e(C - C^*)^{-1}, \tag{B.4}$$

where H is the total hours of work time and C^* is the minimum potential unit cost of the government service. The form of this relation assumes that the actual cost of the government service converges to C^* as more of the legislator's time is devoted to monitoring activities, and that the marginal time costs of reducing C increase as the government service is produced more efficiently.

A legislator, for present purposes, is assumed to allocate his time between activities specific to his district and monitoring activities in order to maximize votes in the next election. Maximizing B.3 subject to B.4 yields the following level of C:

$$C = \left(\frac{ae}{cSY}\right)^{.5} + C^* \tag{B.5}$$

An examination of B.5 indicates that actual unit costs will be a positive function of the vote effect of activities specific to his district and of the time costs of reducing C. Actual unit costs will be a negative function of the vote effects of taxes, the share of total taxes paid by his constituents, and the level of government output.

Substituting B.5 into B.4 and solving for X yields

$$X = H - \left(\frac{ceSY}{a}\right)^{.5}.$$

(B.6)

This relation indicates that the time a legislator will spend on activities specific to his constituents and contributors is a negative function of the vote effect of taxes, the time costs of reducing C, the share of taxes paid by his constituents, and the level of government output; the time spent on district activities, of course, is a positive function of his total hours of work and the vote effect of these activities. The most important observation is that a legislator from a district that pays a small share of the total taxes will spend most of his time on activities specific to his district.

The magnitude of the losses in production efficiency due to the "publicness" of monitoring activities is indicated by the ratio $(C - C^*)$ for a specific value of S over the level for a value of $S = 1$. This ratio is equal to S^{-5}. For the U.S. Congress, for example, the average district pays around 1/435 of the total taxes, so $(C - C^*)$ may be as high as 20.9 times the level if all of the savings due to better monitoring accrued to the district of the representative who conducts the monitoring. These losses would be even higher for services monitored by representatives of low population and/or low income districts because their tax share is lower. The actual losses due to insufficient monitoring are not likely to be as high as this simple model suggests, because the party leadership maintains some internal rewards and sanctions to induce more monitoring by individual legislators and directly controls some of the staff resources. The basic free-rider problem, however, is substantial in any political system, such as the United States, in which the party leadership cannot deny membership in the legislature as a sanction to enforce activities in the interests of the group. Individual citizens, of course, face a similar but much more massive free-rider problem in monitoring the performance of their representatives.

This discussion suggests the value of some new instrument to induce legislators and individual citizens to increase their monitoring activity. Maybe public financing of campaigns could be limited to a set of prizes that would be awarded by some independent body to those legislators with the highest perceived monitoring effectiveness. Maybe legislators should be subject to tax rates that are, say, double those on other people with the same income. Maybe class action suits against the government for demonstrably inefficient performance should be authorized. Such ideas are superficially appealing, but an analysis of these and other alternatives is beyond the scope of this paper.

II.   Some Relevant Empirical Studies

My book developed a large set of hypotheses concerning the level of government budgets, the production efficiency of bureaus, the level of output of government services, the combination of factor inputs, and the effects of the structure of the bureaucracy and review process. It is important to recognize that these
hypotheses are derived from a theory of bureaucracy *and* representative government. A bureau does not operate in a vacuum, nor does it (usually) sell its output
at a price in a competitive market. *All* of the monopoly power of a bureau derives
from the monopoly power of the government that finances its services. A government that has no discretion will be well served by any form of organization
used to supply government services. *Some* of the monopoly power of the government will be appropriated by a bureau, depending on the structure of the
bureaucracy and the review process. The data on which any tests of these
hypotheses must be based, therefore, reflect conditions that are *jointly* determined by bureaucracy and representative government. As a rule, we do not have
an opportunity to observe bureaus that sell their services at a price in a competitive market. Similarly, we do not have an opportunity to observe governments
that purchase their services from competitive profit-seeking firms. The historical
reasons why government, at least since the 19th century, has chosen bureaus as
the dominant form of organization for the supply of government services are
somewhat vague, but the contemporary combination of monopoly bureaus and
monopoly governments is a fact that cannot be dismissed. As a consequence,
most of the empirical studies summarized in this section do not provide satisfactory estimates of the partial effects of specific characteristics of the structure of
the bureaucracy and of the government. Some new empirical approach, and
probably the use of less aggregated data, will be necessary to provide satisfactory estimates of the partial effects of specific characteristics of the structure of
the bureaucracy and of the government. Some new empirical approaches, and
probably, the use of less aggregated data, will be necessary to provide satisfactory tests of these partial effects. For the most part, at the present time, all we can
do is to estimate the joint effects of these two dominant institutions.

A.   *The Overspending Hypotheses*   The most important hypothesis derived
from this theory is that government budgets are too large. That is, they will be
larger than that preferred by the median legislator and, in a representative government, larger than that preferred by the median voter. Moreover, the amount of
overspending will be larger, the larger is the monopoly power of both the government and the bureaus that supply government services.

The most dramatic test of the overspending hypothesis is provided by voting
data. The general relation between the popular votes for the candidate of the
incumbent party and the level of government spending and revenues is illustrated by Figure 3. If government spending is too low, the observed partial effect of
increases in government spending on the votes for a candidate of the incumbent
party should be positive. At the vote-maximizing level of spending X^0, the

Figure 3   Government Spending and Revenues

observed partial effect should be zero. If government spending is too high, the observed partial effect of increases in government spending on the popular vote for a candidate of the incumbent party should be negative.

A sample consisting of the popular vote for the President of the United States in the 20 elections from 1896 through 1972 is used to test this hypothesis.[17] The tests equation is summarized below:

$$\ln\left(\frac{I}{1-I}\right)_t = \alpha + \beta_1(\ln NP_t - \ln NP_{t-4}) + \beta_2(\ln FX_t - \ln FX_{t-4})$$

$$+ \beta_3 ID + \beta_4 WD + U,$$

where

I = fraction of major party popular vote for candidate of incumbent party,
NP = real per capita net national product,
FX = real per capita total federal expenditures,
ID = 1 if incumbent is candidate, 0 otherwise, and
WD = 1 if election is war year, 0 otherwise.

17. An earlier version of this test is described in detail in William A. Niskanen, "Economic and Fiscal Effects on the Popular Vote for the President" (unpublished paper presented at the International Society for Public Economics Conference on Measurement of the Demand for Public Services, Siena, Italy, 1973).

An alternate form of this test equation substitutes the percent change in real per capita total federal revenues for the federal spending variable. For this formulation, the partial effect on I of each of the independent variables is equal to $I(1 - I)$ times the β coefficient; in close elections, this effect is approximately equal to .25 times the coefficient.

Estimates of these two test equations, based on ordinary least squares procedures, are presented in Table 1 below. For our purposes, the most important of these results are the estimated coefficients on DFX and on DFR. A 10 percent

Table 1   Economic and fiscal effects on the popular vote for President

Variables						Test Statistics		
C	DNP	DFX	DFR	ID	WD	R^2	S.E.	D.W.
.020	1.511	−.313		.143	−.190	.732	.176	1.885
(.075)	(.306)	(.077)		(.090)	(.133)			
.077	2.220		−.572	.077	−.351	.864	.126	2.0774
(.055)	(.273)		(.084)	(.066)	(.091)			

Numbers in parentheses are standard errors of the coefficients.

increase in real per capita federal expenditures over the four years between elections appears to reduce the popular vote for the candidate of the incumbent party by around .8 percent. A 10 percent increase in real per capita federal revenues appears to reduce the popular vote for the candidate of the incumbent party by around 1.4 percent. Both coefficients are highly significant. (The difference in these coefficients suggests that there is considerable "tax illusion"; voters appear to be substantially more affected by changes in taxes than by changes in the total resource costs of federal services.) These results, by my reading, strongly confirm the overspending hypothesis. Moreover, the general set of these results are surprisingly consistent over equal subsamples of the elections from 1896–1932 and from 1936–1972, and over equal subsamples of elections in which a Republican was the incumbent President and elections in which a Democrat was the incumbent President.[18]

An estimate of the *amount* of overspending can be derived by using both the DNP coefficient and the DFX (or DFR) coefficient. From the first test equation, at the margin of 1974 conditions, a $8.86 billion increase in real net national product would be necessary to offset the votes lost by a $10 billion increase in real federal expenditures. This suggests that voters are only willing to forego $1.14 billion of other uses of national output for the services financed by an additional $10 billion of federal expenditures. From the second equation, a $11.3 billion increase in real net national product would be necessary to offset votes lost by a $10 billion increase in real federal revenues. This suggests a negative value of $1.3 billion of the services financed by an additional $10 billion of federal tax

18.   The whole set of results are available from the author.

revenues. Voters appear to be roughly indifferent to an increase in federal spending or revenues only if there is no reduction in the resources available for other uses, and the marginal value of federal services appears to be nearly zero. This result is most disturbing but should not be considered conclusive, without support from other forms of evidence.

Other tests of the overspending hypothesis are provided as secondary results from a set of studies of state and local expenditures. The most advanced of these studies are by Tom Borcherding and Robert Deacon and by Ted Bergstrom and Robert Goodman.[19] These two studies independently developed an ingenious technique for estimating demand functions for government services without using output data. This technique, in addition to providing estimates of the price and income elasticities of demand for government services, also provides an estimate of a parameter measuring the degree of "publicness" of a government service; this parameter, if estimated correctly, would be 0 for a purely public service and 1 for a purely private service. The most interesting result from these studies is that the estimated publicness parameter is 1 or greater for most state and local services. (The Borcherding and Deacon estimates indicate some degree of publicness only for higher education, highways, and some sewer and sanitation services; the estimated parameters on these services are around .9.) These results lead Bergstrom and Goodman to ask "why, if there are not increasing returns in the municipal provision of the goods and services we study, is their provision in the public domain?"[20]

Borcherding, in a subsequent paper with Winston Bush and Robert Spann,[21] suggests an explanation of this result: the monopoly power of governments and bureaus is a positive function of the population served. The original model, which assumed a government that is perfectly responsive to the median voter and a competitive supply of services at a constant unit cost, is thus misspecified. As Downs and Tullock earlier suggested[22], voters have less incentive to monitor government, the larger the number of voters. The discussion in Part I, Section B of this paper suggests that legislators have less incentive to monitor bureaus, the larger the number of legislative districts. And the costs of monitoring a bureau is larger, as Tullock[23] suggested, the larger the absolute size of a bureau. Finally, if legislators and/or bureaus prefer larger budgets, they will use some of their monopoly power to supply private services for which expenditures increase with population; this effect was also suggested earlier by Stigler.[24] We are left with the somewhat ambiguous conclusion that the services supplied by state and local governments are either (1) public, but that the economies of collective supply are

19. Thomas E. Borcherding and Robert T. Deacon, "The Demand for the Services of Non-Federal Governments: An Econometric Approach to Collective Choice," *American Economic Review* 62 (1972), p. 891; T. C. Bergstrom and R. P. Goodman, "Private Demand for Public Goods," *American Economic Review* 63 (1973), p. 280.

20. T. C. Bergstrom and R. P. Goodman, *supra* note 19, at 293.

21. Thomas E. Borcherding, Winston C. Bush and Robert Spann, "The Effects of Public Spending on the Divisibility of Public Outputs in Consumption, Bureaucratic Power, and the Size of the Tax-Sharing Group" in *Budgets and Bureaucrats: The Sources of Government Growth* (Thomas E. Borcherding ed. 1975).

22. Anthony Downs, *An Economic Theory of Democracy* (1957); Gordon Tullock, *Towards a Mathematics of Politics* (1967).

23. Gordon Tullock, *The Politics of Bureaucracy* (1965).

24. George J. Stigler, "Director's Law of Public Income Distribution," *Journal of Law and Economics* 13 (1970), p. 1.

appropriated by monopoly governments and bureaus in the form of overspending, and/or (2) private and divisible at the margin of the existing scale of governmental jurisdictions, in which case there is no obvious reason for governmental supply. In either case, the observed results do not appear consistent with simple models of responsive governments and efficient production.

Both of the above studies report, but do not discuss, another similar result: expenditures for many state and local services increase as a function of the *area* of the jurisdiction. For highway services, this probably reflects production costs, but this explanation seems unsatisfactory for general municipal expenditures, local education, and higher education. An alternate explanation is that the monopoly power of a government increases with the area of its jurisdiction due to the higher costs of moving and finding comparable private opportunities. The monopoly power of a government that derives from the area of its jurisdiction apparently also leads to increased government expenditures. As Richard Wagner[25] has suggested, this strengthens the case against the formation of regional governments for our major metropolitan areas.

Four other studies provide estimates of the expenditure effects of more detailed characteristics of the conditions facing state and local governments. Richard Wagner and Warren Weber[26] demonstrate that the monopoly power of a government derived from the opportunity for "full-line forcing" will be a function of the number of different services it provides. They estimate, based on a sample of large counties in the South, that total public expenditures in counties with a subordinate school system are 10.5 percent higher than in counties with independent school systems. A study performed by the (California) Governor's Local Government Reform Task Force[27] reports a similar conclusion: total taxes in each tax reporting area appear to be a negative function of the number of different taxing authorities in that area. Any substantial reduction in the overlapping of local governments in a common area would apparently increase local expenditures.

Sharon Oster has recently completed a study of municipal water pollution abatement expenditures.[28] Although the variance of these expenditures is strongly constrained by federal regulation, she finds that the per capita expenditures in fifty cities and towns in the Merrimack River basin in New England vary roughly in proportion to the plurality of the elected official in the prior election. Again, an increase of the monopoly power of elected officials appears to be translated into higher expenditures rather than, if their preferences were neutral, merely into a higher variance of expenditures.

25. Richard Wagner, "Supply-Side Aspects of the Theory of Local Government: Owners, Managers, and Take-Over Bids," *Journal of Political Economy* (forthcoming).

26. Richard Wagner and Warren Weber, "Governmental Overlapping and Full-Line Forcing", *Journal of Law & Economics* 18 (1975).

27. Report of the California Local Government Reform Task Force, "Public Benefits from Public Choice" (1974).

28. Sharon Oster, "Municipal Expenditures for Water Pollution Abatement," *Journal of Political Economy* (forthcoming).

The Borcherding, Bush, and Spann study,[29] using the model and data developed earlier by Borcherding and Deacon, provides an estimate of the effect of civil service systems on state and local expenditures. One would expect a civil service system to increase government expenditures, through both a change in incentives internal to the bureaucracy and by increasing the returns to collective political activity by civil servants. For five of the six state and local services studies (other than highways), they estimate that expenditures range from 8 to 35 percent higher in states with a civil service system prior to 1940 than in the other states. Moreover, for the states with a civil service system prior to 1940, state and . local expenditures appear to have increased by around one-third of one percent for each year that the civil service system had been effective. (One might ask: Effective for whom?) This study does not provide a basis for separating the bureaucratic and political effects of a civil service system, but the combination of these effects appears to have increased over time.[30]

None of the studies summarized in this section, of course, is conclusive, but they all suggest a similar conclusion: conditions that increase the monopoly power of governments and bureaus lead to an increase in government expenditures.

B. The Production Inefficiency Hypothesis. Overspending by government bureaus may take the form of inefficiency in producing a given set of outputs and/or a higher level of some output. The theory summarized in Part I suggests that we should study both inefficiency and higher output, with the relative amounts dependent on the bureaucrat's preferences, the reward structure, and the characteristics of the review process. This section summarizes a set of studies of the production efficiency of bureaus.

Contemporary governmental conditions unfortunately provide only a few cases that permit a comparison of bureaus and private firms supplying the same final output. The number of studies of these cases is even smaller. The evidence from these few studies, however, is roughly consistent: bureaus are significantly less efficient than profit-seeking firms in supplying the same output.[31] Roger Ahlbrandt's study of public and private fire services[32] concludes that the unit cost is 88 percent higher in public fire departments. David Davies' study of two airlines in Australia[33] with nearly identical routes, schedules and equipment concludes that the private airline carried 104 percent more freight and mail per man-hour and 22 percent more passengers per man-hour than did its bureaucratic twin. Lou De Alessi[34] summarizes several studies of private and public production of

29.   *Supra* note 21.
30.   A dynamic model of government expenditures, based only on the political effects of voting by civil servants, has recently been developed by Gordon Tullock, "Dynamic Hypothesis on Bureaucracy," *Public Choice*, 19 (Fall 1974), p. 127.
31.   This conclusion holds even though there is other evidence that bureaus supplying services for which there is an alternative private source are more efficient than other bureaus.
32.   Roger S. Ahlbrandt, Jr., *Municipal Fire Protection Services: Comparison of Alternative Organizational Forms* (1973).
33.   David G. Davies, "The Efficiency of Public versus Private Firms: The Case of Australia's Two Airlines," *Journal of Law & Economics* 14 (1971), p. 149.

electricity which conclude that both the capital and operating costs per kilowatt hour are higher in the public firms. Robert Spann's study[35] of refuse collection concludes that the unit cost in public firms is 43 percent higher than in private firms.

Two available studies which compare the performance of private stock companies and mutual companies reach a similar conclusion. David Barton and Ted Frech[36] estimate that the unit cost of processing insurance claims is 15 percent higher in the mutual companies and the time is around 60 percent higher. Alfred Nichols[37] estimates that the unit cost of processing new loans is over 60 percent higher in mutual savings and loan banks than in stock banks. Since mutual and non-profit firms are essentially similar to bureaus in their reward structure, these studies illustrate the inefficiency that is due to the general bureaucratic form even when the output is sold at a price.

Several other studies bear on the comparative efficiency among bureaus providing a similar output. The efficiency of bureaus should be a negative function of the size of both the government and the bureau. A larger government has more monopoly power, and the incentives of both voters and legislators to monitor the bureaus are smaller. The costs of monitoring a larger bureau are larger—both to the legislature and to the senior bureaucrat—because "control loss" is a function of the number of managerial levels. Two studies illustrate these effects. My own study of student performance in California public schools[38] indicates that median scores on standard reading and mathematics tests at both the 6th and 12th grade are a significant negative function of school district size for districts larger than 2,000 students. Other studies of the school district size issue reach a similar conclusion.[39] These studies control for family and community characteristics and school expenditures per student, but not for other possible outputs of the school system. A study by Carr-Hill and Stern[40] examines the performance of police among police districts in England. This study reports that the "clear-up" rate is a significant negative function of the size of the police district. A similar study by Ehrlich[41] reaches the same conclusion with respect to the population of

34. Louis De Alessi, "An Economic Analysis of Government Ownership and Regulation: Theory and the Evidence from the Electric Power Industry," *Public Choice* 19 (Fall 1974) at p. 1.

35. Robert M. Spann, "Public versus Private Provision of Government Services," in *Budgets and Bureaucrats: The Sources of Government Growth* (Thomas E. Borcherding ed. 1975).

36. David M. Barton and H. E. Frech III, "The Property Rights Theory of the Firm: Empirical Results from a Natural Experiment" (Working Paper 28, University of California at Santa Barbara, May, 1974).

37. Alfred Nicols, "Stock versus Mutual Savings and Loan Associations: Some Evidence of Differences in Behavior," *American Economic Review* 57 (2), at p. 337 (Papers and Proceedings, May 1967).

38. William A. Niskanen, "Cities and Schools: A Case for Community Government in California" (Working Paper 14, University of California at Berkeley, Graduate School of Public Policy, 1974).

39. H. Thomas James and Henry M. Levin, "Financing Community Schools," in *Community Control of Schools* (Brookings, Conference on the Community School, 1971).

40. R. A. Carr-Hill and N. H. Stern, "An Econometrical Model of the Supply and Control of Recorded Offences in England and Wales," *Journal of Public Economy* 2 (1973), p. 1240.

41. Isaac Ehrlich, "Participation in Illegitimate Activities: A Theoretical and Empirical Investigation," *Journal of Political Economy* 81 (1973), p. 521.

states in the U.S. Both overspending and production inefficiency appear to be a function of the scale of bureaus at the margin of their present size.

The efficiency of a bureau should also be a function of the potential competition for the supply of the same or a similar service. Such competition—even if only latent—reduces the cost of monitoring a bureau, increases the credibility of a threat to transfer funding away from one bureau, and increases the incentive for each bureau to compete on an efficiency basis. Some sense of the effects of competition can be derived from a recent study of output per man-year in the federal government.[42] This study estimated the output and man-years for 114 elements of 17 agencies constituting 55 percent of the federal workforce for five years from fiscal 1967 through 1971. The estimated annual percent changes in output per man-year from this study are presented in Table 2.

These estimates of the rate of increase of output per federal employee are almost perfectly correlated with the extent of existing competition with private firms and among bureaus. The federal government does not contract for any final

Table 2   *Increase in federal output per man-year*

Service Activity	Annual Percentage Increase
Final Services	1.25%
Operating	.84%
Processing	3.62
Support Services	3.24
Management	1.32
Procurement and Supply	1.11
Maintenance	6.32
Industrial Services	5.38
Overhead and Repair	5.05
Manufacturing	6.53

services whose output is difficult to compare across bureaus. The government contracts for some support services and most industrial services. Among activities, the rate of increase of productivity is correlated with both the extent of contracting and the ease of comparing output across bureaus. The output measures are necessarily crude and the productivity estimates do not control for changes in other factors, but this pattern is too strong to dismiss. (One might plausibly conjecture that the rate of increase of productivity is lower among the services and activities for which no output measure could be identified.) Bureaucrats, like most of us, appear to shirk when they can get away with it and are efficient when they have to be. These estimates suggest the value of developing satisfactory output measures to permit contracting for final services and non-comparable activities with private firms or other bureaus.

42.   U.S. Congress Joint Economic Committee, "Measuring and Enhancing Productivity in the Federal Sector" (Joint Committee print, 1972).

In summary, these studies suggest that inefficiency is not a necessary characteristic of the supply of government services. For a given output, these studies suggest that costs can be reduced by contracting with private firms, by reducing the size of bureaus, and by increasing competition among bureaus. Some improvement in output measurement and contracting techniques is probably necessary to make better use of these efficiency-inducing instruments.

C. *The Oversupply Hypothesis.* No available study, to my knowledge, directly addresses the oversupply hypothesis, and I have not been clever enough to formulate a critical test. In its general form, the hypothesis is that a bureau will supply more of some dimension of output valued by the legislature than would be approved by the whole legislature if monitoring were costless. The primary problem of testing this hypothesis is the determination of which dimensions of output are valued by the legislature and what output they would select if the minimum costs of producing that output were known. The Postal Service illustrates this problem. As Earl Thompson observed, first-class mail service in urban areas is obviously not oversupplied. On the other hand, the amount and quality of second-class service (to magazines and newspapers), rural delivery services, and the number of post offices are probably larger, given the demands of postal users, than would be approved by the whole legislature. A formal test of the oversupply hypothesis, however, requires a base case that is not directly observable.

Several studies of the behavior of non-profit and government firms illuminate this issue but do not provide a critical test. Ken Clarkson's comparison of non-profit and proprietary hospitals[43] concludes that non-profit hospitals tend to be larger, to produce more research and teaching, to provide a broader set of services, and to provide more philanthropic care. The study does not identify, however, whether the additional output in these dimensions is a result of the non-profit form or is an efficient reflection of the preferences of the trustees of these hospitals. The Barton and Frech study of stock and non-profit insurance companies, discussed in II B above, reports that the non-profit companies have a 55 percent lower error rate in processing claims and that the marginal cost of reducing the error rate appears to be much higher than its value. The De Alessi study of private and government electric utilities, also discussed above, reports that government utilities are larger, offering a smaller range of services at a lower price. These conclusions are similar to those of the Clarkson study, except with respect to the range of services, but neither separates the effects of the bureaucratic form from the preferences of governmental sponsors. Non-profit firms and government bureaus appear to supply more output in some dimensions than do proprietary firms serving the same general market; this is consistent with the oversupply hypothesis, but is not yet a conclusive test. Some innovation in test procedures and more detailed data are probably necessary to improve the tests of this hypothesis.

---

43. Kenneth W. Clarkson, "Some Implications of Property Rights in Hospital Management," *Journal of Law and Economics* 15 (1972), p. 363.

Table 3   Capital per employee in the public and private sectors

Sector	Book value per Employee	Year
Federal[a]		
Defense	$59,164	1963
Civil	28,252	1963
Public Schools[b]	26,456	1965
Private[c]		
Industry	12,030	1960
Services	4,380	1960

[a]Book value of fixed assets other than public domain; excludes inventories, accounts and loans receivable, cash, etc.
[b]Book value of fixed assets: Virginia Public School System.
[c]Book value of all assets: Victor Fuchs, *The Service Economy* (National Bureau of Economic Research, 1963).

D.   The Overcapitalization Hypothesis.   My book, developed on a model suggested earlier by De Alessi,[44] also conjectures that a bureau will use more capital-intensive production techniques than would a private firm producing the same service. The primary reason for this is that a bureaucrat's rewards are specific to his tenure in that position; this leads him to prefer present spending to future spending, and thus to prefer production processes with higher capital costs and lower operating costs. This is not necessarily inconsistent with an hypothesis suggested earlier by William Baumol[45] that the production of government services, like private services, are inherently labor-intensive and "non-progressive."

Two recent studies bear on both the De Alessi and Baumol hypotheses. De Alessi's study of electric utilities, discussed above, reports that government utilities are more capital intensive than private utilities—a conclusion that is consistent with his own hypothesis. William Orzechowski has recently provided some estimates of the aggregate capital intensity of the public sector that permit a rough comparison with the private sector.[46] His results are presented in Table 3. These results are not strictly comparable because of different aggregations of capital assets, different accounting conventions, and different observation years. Nonetheless, the pattern is dramatic: government civil activities appear to use more than twice as much capital per employee as private industry and over five times as much capital per worker as the private service sector. (Moreover, the addition of inventories and other excluded assets to the government capital aggregates would increase this difference.) If the production function of public civil activities is similar to that in the private service sector, as Baumol suggests, these results confirm the De Alessi hypothesis that bureaus will choose production processes that use too much capital. In any case, these results are strongly

44.   Louis De Alessi, "Implications of Property Rights for Government Investment Choices," *American Economic Review* 59 (1969), p. 13.
45.   William Baumol, "Macroeconomics of Unbalanced Growth: The Anatomy of Urban Crises," *American Economic Review* 57 (1967), p. 415.
46.   William Paul Orzechowski, "Labor Intensity, Productivity, and the Growth of the Federal Sector," *Public Choice* 19 (Fall 1974), at p. 123.

inconsistent with the Baumol hypothesis of low relative capital intensity in the public sector, and one must look for another explanation of the relatively low rate of growth of public sector productivity. In the face of this evidence, it is difficult to understand how the Baumol hypothesis came to be accepted as conventional wisdom.

E. *The Bureaucratic Structure Hypothesis.* Conventional public administration theory and my theory of bureaucracy share one common perspective: the structure of the bureaucracy makes a difference. Almost every President in recent decades has established a commission on government organization. These commissions, reflecting the views of conventional public administration theory, consistently recommend the consolidation of bureaus and departments supplying related services. These consolidations are expected to increase governmental efficiency by reducing the President's span of control, by improving the coordination of related services, and by reducing administrative overheads. An implicit objective of these consolidations is to reduce the direct ties between bureaus and Congress. As a rule, the proposed consolidations are opposed by Congress.

My theory of bureaucracy, in contrast, suggests that the consolidation of bureaus supplying competitive services would increase the monopoly power of the remaining bureaus, primarily by increasing the costs to Congress (and to the President) of identifying the actual and potential costs of a service and by changing the incentives of bureaucrats from competing on an efficiency basis to promoting total demand for the service. One might also expect that the additional organizational level would increase the "control loss" and thus production efficiency within a department. These effects suggest that a consolidation of bureaus supplying competitive services would increase the budget for these services.

The major structural changes in the federal bureaucracy that have been approved since World War II provide a potential test of these two competing theories. Four new departments have been established by consolidation of bureaus supplying related services: the Department of Defense in 1949; the Department of Health, Education, and Welfare in 1953; the Department of Housing and Urban Development in 1965, and the Department of Transportation in 1966. My theory suggests that spending by these departments would be higher than the total spending for each set of services prior to consolidation (controlling for other conditions that affect the total spending for these services).

The following equation is used to test this hypothesis:

$$O = \alpha(ETO)^{\beta_1}\left(\frac{O_{-\hat{1}}}{TO_{-1}}\right)^{\beta_2}(X)^{\beta_3}e^{\beta_4 D + u},$$

where O is the outlay for a specific service by fiscal year, ETO is the estimated total federal outlay in that year, O_{-1} is the outlay for that service in the prior fiscal year, TO_{-1} is the total federal outlay in the prior fiscal year, X is some other variable that affects outlays for that service and D is a dummy variable that reflects the establishment of a department that includes the service. All outlay variables are in current dollars. The *ETO* variable is calculated from another equation that estimates total federal outlays in current dollars from another set of variables including the implicit price index on federal services, the implicit price index on private consumption, real GNP, and the number of armed forces overseas. The economic variables in this equation are specific to the calendar year that includes the first six months of the fiscal year. The departmental dummy is 1 for all years subsequent to the year in which the department was established and 0 in earlier years.

A positive coefficient on the departmental dummy would be consistent with the hypothesis that the establishment of a department that includes competing bureaus increases spending. I also expect that the coefficient on the lagged budget share will be between 0 and 1; this would indicate that the percentage increase in outlays for a component of the budget is a negative function of its budget share.

This test equation is estimated for six services: national defense, education and manpower, health, income maintenance, transportation, and community development and housing. The sample period for the first four services is FY48 through FY73. The sample period for the last two services is FY60 through FY73, as estimates of outlays for these services in earlier years are not available.

Each of these services, other than education and manpower, is now dominated by one department. Conceptually, education outlays should be separated from manpower outlays to test the effect of the HEW dummy, but the requisite data are not available for years prior to FY60. In addition, education outlays serve a different constituency than that for health and income maintenance outlays, so education is probably not an effective substitute for the other functions of HEW. For these reasons, the effect of the establishment of HEW on education outlays is expected to be weak.

Several of the test equations include another variable to reflect conditions that may change the demand or cost for the specific service. The national defense equation includes the number of armed forces overseas. The health and income maintenance equations include the relative price of medical services, while the community development and housing equation includes the corporate bond rate. It is not obvious, of course, that these conditions are fully exogenous, so several of the equations exclude these variables.

Table 4 below presents ordinary least squares estimates of the logarithmic form of each of the test equations.

The pattern of these results is generally consistent with the hypothesis that the establishment of these four departments increased spending. The coefficients on the departmental dummy are generally positive, highly significant for the two largest services (defense and income maintenance), and nowhere both negative and significant. The magnitudes of the outlay increases associated with the establishment of DoD and HEW are substantial—around 34 per cent for defense, maybe as high as 25 percent for health, and around 25 percent for income maintenance. Coefficients on the other departmental dummies are not significant.

Table 4 Federal outlays by function

	Constant	Total Outlays	Lagged Share	Departmental Dummy	Other Variable	R^2
Defense	2.040	.759	.548	.428		.982
	(.418)	(.044)	(.099)	(.084)		
				[53.4]		
	.564	.757	.488	.293	.235	.992
	(.411)	(.030)	(.069)	(.064)	(.047)	
				[34.0]		
Education and	−2.985	1.185	.797	.090		.984
Manpower	(4.008)	(.280)	(.187)	(.117)		
				[9.4]		
Health	1.907	.848	1.047	.224		.986
	(3.587)	(.276)	(.117)	(.153)		
				[25.1]		
	5.982	.504	.795	−.063	3.792	.988
	(3.992)	(.316)	(.171)	(.207)	(1.969)	
				[−6.1]		
Income	−1.962	1.107	.654	.182		.987
Maintenance	(1.173)	(.082)	(.147)	(.099)		
				[20.0]		
	2.621	.722	.460	.222	1.961	.991
	(2.091)	(.169)	(.152)	(.090)	(.774)	
				[24.9]		
Transportation	−23.152	2.384	−1.221	−1.235		.886
	(13.364)	(1.321)	(.787)	(1.016)		
				[−70.9]		
Community	−20.888	1.613	−.905	.739	.675	.928
Development and	(11.993)	(1.162)	(.497)	(1.358)	(.393)	
Housing				[109.4]		

Notes: Figures in parentheses are standard errors of the coefficients. Figures in brackets are the estimated percentage change.

These results are not consistent with the public administration hypothesis that the establishment of these departments contributed to efficiency and economy.

These results, however, are consistent with one other hypothesis—that the increased spending and the establishment of these departments are *joint* results of an increased demand for these services that is not reflected in the other variables. This hypothesis is consistent with the rhetoric of these reforms and is quite plausible. The above tests, unfortunately, do not distinguish between the monopoly bureau hypothesis and the demand shift hypothesis if there are any important excluded variables that are correlated with the departmental dummies. For the moment, the burden of proof should rest with those who claim that these results really reflect some important excluded condition. Again, the available tests on the several hypotheses derived from my theory of bureaucracy and representative government seem to be roughly consistent, interesting, and suggestive—but not yet conclusive.

A Reassessment

"This book represents a new approach to the study of bureaus; only time and testing will prove whether the theory developed is valuable and merits further development and whether the conclusions merit some practical experiments."

More than two decades have passed since I wrote these words in the preface to my 1971 book on *Bureaucracy and Representative Government*. Since that time, to my pleasant surprise, this book has spawned a growing body of comment, criticism, theoretical development and testing by economists, political scientists and public administration scholars.[1] My only substantial contribution to this subsequent literature was my 1975 article on "Bureaucrats and Politicians," which is republished in the last section of this volume. Moreover, the policy implications of this literature have encouraged many "practical experiments" in privatizing the supply of government services, primarily by American state and local governments and by the British government under Prime Minister Margaret Thatcher.

I have been honored by both the academic and practical developments thus stimulated and now value this opportunity to reassess the general theoretical approach developed both in my book and in the subsequent literature.

The general framework developed in *Bureaucracy and Representative Government* was clearly incomplete. In an important sense, it was also wrong! That may seem like a damning self-indictment, but perhaps not so. Most accepted theories have developed by fits and starts, progressively refining a seminal core idea. My initial framework was the *first* formal economic theory of the behavior of bureaus, not a synthesis of a long theoretical development.[2] The appropriate test of the initial framework is whether subsequent developments have led to a theory with predictive power and useful policy implications. My

---

1. See Blais and Dion (1991) for a collection of recent articles on this general topic.
2. The only significant prior analyses of bureaus by economists were by Mises (1944), Tullock (1965), and Downs (1967), but these did not develop the outcomes of the interaction between bureaus and their political sponsors. It is interesting to note that each of the early economic analyses of bureaus, including my book, were written by economists working outside the academy.

own judgment is that there has been substantial progress in this direction.

Let me develop these issues in four steps:

- a summary of the initial framework,
- developments bearing on the objectives of bureaucrats,
- developments affecting the interaction between bureaus and their political sponsors, and
- a summary of the empirical evidence.

This should provide readers of this re-publication of my 1971 book with a better understanding of the strengths and weaknesses of both my initial framework and of subsequent developments.

A Summary of the Initial Framework

The central insight of conventional economics is that the provision of private goods and services is an *incidental* effect of the incentives and constraints of consumers, entrepreneurs, and employees. In other words, the provision of private goods and services is an effect, but is not the direct purpose, of any participant in the private economy. Similarly, the central insight of the literature now described as public choice is that the provision of government services is an incidental effect of the incentives and constraints of voters, politicians, and bureaucrats. Although this perspective on government services is now more broadly shared, one should recognize how radical this perspective was first regarded and how radical it still seems among some groups.

First, some definitions are in order. A bureau is defined as an organization with the following two characteristics:

- the owners and employees do not appropriate any part of the difference between revenues and costs as personal income, and
- some part of the recurring revenues of the organization derive from sources other than the sale of output at a per unit rate.

In a simple sentence: bureaus are nonprofit organizations that are financed, at least in part, by a periodic appropriation or grant. The focus of most of my analysis (and that of others) has been on government bureaus, but this definition would also apply to most private nonprofit organizations. The word "bureaucrat," in turn, is used to describe a senior officer of a bureau and has no inherent normative implication.

Any theory of the behaviour of bureaus must be based on the relationship between bureaucrats and politicians. My own incentive to explore this was based on a recognition that there is a significant "agency problem" in this relationship; in other words, the incentives of bureaucrats do not lead to behaviour that is fully consistent with the interests of politicians. My judgment is that there is a much more substantial agency problem between politicians and voters, but that must be another story for another day. Such agency problems, of course, are not unique to the public sector. My own experience in a very large private firm led me to conclude that there is also a significant agency problem between private managers and shareholders. In a private economy with extensive property rights, competitive firms, and an efficient outside labor market, however, the interests of both consumers and employees are quite well served.

The first insight that led to my theory of the behavior of bureaus was the observation that some of my best friends are government officials. Like most of my other friends, these officials are characteristically intelligent, industrious, and genuinely committed to their organization. They do not, moreover, fit the polar stereotypes of government officials. They are neither the selfless mandarins portrayed by the public administration literature from Confucius to Woodrow Wilson, nor are they the dumb, lazy, or corrupt bureaucrats portrayed by populist fiction and editorial cartoons. Most government officials, from my experience, seem much like their counterparts in business and the professions. Secondly, I was also disturbed to recognize that some of the major policy failures of our time were initiated by "the best and the brightest" of these officials.

This observation was the seed that led me to question the prevailing theories that explain the behavior of bureaus in terms of the presumed distinctive attributes of bureaucrats, and then to develop a new theory based instead on their distinctive incentives and constraints. My reflections, based on my own subsequent experience and the contribution of other scholars, have led me to modify my perspective with respect to some details, but my basic approach to the study of bureaucracy has survived this reassessment.

The seven core elements of my theory of the behavior of bureaus that have survived this reflection are summarized below.

1. The first element of this theory is that bureaucrats are much like officials in other organizations. Their behavior will differ, not because of different personal characteristics, but because of the incentives and constraints that are specific to bureaus.

A footnote: this assumption does not deny that bureaucrats may have different characteristics, nor would the theory be refuted by observing such differences. People will choose to work in organizations whose rewards are most consistent with their own preferences. In effect, people "choose their own pond," and different ponds will attract people with different preferences and characteristics (Frank 1985). The conventional theory explained the behavior of bureaus in terms of the distinctive characteristics of bureaucrats, but this confused cause and effect. My theory is consistent with the observation that those who choose to work in the distinctive environment of a bureau may have distinctive personal characteristics. An assumption that bureaucrats have different characteristics may thus be correct but is redundant. It is crucial, however, to recognize that bureaus are very different from private firms, most importantly in terms of the characteristics summarized in the following paragraphs.

2. Most bureaus have a monopoly buyer for their service, usually some group of political officials. Effective demand for the output of a bureau comes from this political sponsor, rather than from the ultimate consumers of the service.

3. Most bureaus are monopoly suppliers of their service. More specifically, most bureaus face a downward-sloping effective demand function, even if alternative actual or potential suppliers of the same or a similar service exist.

4. The bilateral monopoly relation between a bureau and its sponsor involves the exchange of a promised output for a budget, rather than the sale of its output at a per-unit price.

5. As in any bilateral monopoly, there is no unique budget-output equilibrium between the preferences of the sponsor and those of the bureau. The sponsor's primary advantages in this bargaining are its authority to monitor the bureau, to approve the bureau's budget, and to replace its management team. The bureau's primary advantage is that it has much better information about the costs of supplying the service than does the sponsor.

6. The sponsor's role in this bilateral bargaining over budget-output combinations is weakened or modified by another condition. The sponsor does not have sufficient incentive to monitor the bureau because it shares only a small part of any benefits accruing from a more efficient performance by the bureau (Niskanen 1975); in other words, efficiency monitoring is a public good among legislators and voters. This leads the sponsor to use its authority primarily to capture part of the bureau's surplus in ways that serve the specific interests of the sponsor group, rather than the interests of the broader group of legislators and voters.

7. Finally, neither the members of the sponsor group nor the senior bureaucrats has a pecuniary share in any surplus generated by the bureau. The effect is that the surplus will be spent in ways that indirectly serve the interests of the sponsor and the bureau, though not as direct compensation.

The above characteristics, I suggest, should be the core elements of a theory of the behavior of bureaus; in other words, these are the elements of my earlier theory that have survived my own reflections on these issues.

My initial framework, in addition, included three assumptions about the behavior of bureaucrats and their political sponsors. Specifically, bureaucrats were assumed to act to maximize the expected budget of their bureau. Second, the sponsors were assumed to be "passive" in accepting or rejecting the bureau's budget-output proposal without any careful monitoring or evaluation of alternatives. A third implicit assumption that I did not recognize at the time was that bureaucrats and their sponsors bargain over the full range of possible combinations of budget and output.

The implications of this framework were first summarized in my 1968 article

on "The Peculiar Economics of Bureaucracy," which is re-published in this volume, and were developed more extensively in the 1971 book. The general implication is that both the budget and output of a bureau are larger than optimal; more
precisely, the marginal value of the bureau's output to the constituents of the
median voter in the legislature is lower than the marginal cost, appropriating the
potential surplus to this group by expanding output beyond the optimal level.
This outcome also generates a larger surplus to any labor or capital resources that
are specific to the production of the bureau's output.

This framework (or model) also led to an awkward two-region solution to budget-output outcomes. In the "budget-constrained" region, the budget is equal to
the minimum total cost of producing the output promised to the sponsor; here the
output of the bureau is produced efficiently, with any waste due to the bureaucratic supply of government services being limited to the effects of a larger-than-
optimal level of output. At a sufficiently high level of demand, however, the
resulting budget-output outcome is in a "demand-constrained" region. In this
region, the marginal value of output is zero, and the budget is larger than the minimum total cost of producing the promised output. In this region, the waste due
to bureaucratic supply is some combination of both allocative and productive
inefficiency.

At the time that I developed this framework, I recognized that it was incomplete. Specifically, the framework did not develop the other side of this market—
the behavior of political sponsors in monitoring the bureau and bargaining over
the budget.

Over time, I have also come to recognize that the three behavioral assumptions
in my initial framework lead to conclusions that are both theoretically inelegant
and inconsistent with the available evidence.

The following sections of this reassessment develop the reasons for these conclusions and put forward some suggestions about how to address each of these
issues.

The Objectives of Bureaucrats

What assumption about the behavior of senior bureaucrats best corresponds
with the assumption that business executives act to maximize the profits of their
firm? Specifically what, if anything, do bureaucrats maximize? My views on this
question, which I will develop, have changed over time. The specific model of
the behavior of bureaus developed in my 1971 book assumes that bureaucrats act
to maximize the budget of their bureau. This seemed to be a plausible assumption and was consistent with the observation that the opportunities for promotion
within each bureau increase with the level of that bureau's budget. Given the distinctive characteristics of bureaus and the political markets in which they operate, this assumption led to the conclusion that bureaus supply a larger-than-opti-
mal output (in terms of the demand identified by the political authorities), but
that this output, except in certain special cases, is produced efficiently.

For various reasons, I now believe that this is not the best assumption on which to build a theory of the behavior of bureaus. Even as I wrote my book, I was uncomfortable with this assumption, because my personal observation was that inefficiency in production was more general—not a special case in the demand-constrained region of output. At that time, my perspective was probably also biased by my long experience as a defense analyst. In the military, opportunities for promotion are exclusively limited to one's own service, which possibly strengthens the incentives for budget-maximization. This incentive, however, is likely to be much weaker for bureaucrats who have a more general opportunity for promotion in other bureaus (Breton and Wintrobe 1975). Subsequent empirical evidence also indicates that the salaries of bureaucrats are only weakly related to the level and growth of their bureau's budget (Johnson and Libecap 1989).

In an early comment on my book, Jean-Luc Migué and Gérard Bélanger (1974) suggest an approach that both generalizes and simplifies my model in a way that resolves this inconsistency. They suggest an assumption, more consistent with that of a profit-maximizing firm, that bureaucrats act to maximize their bureau's discretionary budget, defined as the difference between the total budget and the minimum cost of producing the output expected by the political authorities. Since neither the bureaucrats nor the political authorities can claim this discretionary budget as personal income, however, this surplus is spent in other ways that serve their interests. Some part of this discretionary budget will be allocated to serve the bureau, such as with additional staff, capital, and perquisites. The remainder will be spent in ways that serve the interests of the political review authorities. The distribution of this surplus between spending that serves the interests of the bureaus and that which serves the interests of the review authorities will depend, as in any bilateral bargaining, on the relevant information, alternatives, and bargaining strategies available to the two parties. This assumption leads to somewhat different conclusions: the budget of a bureau is too large, the output (again in terms of the demand revealed by the political authorities) may be too low, and the production of this output is uniformly inefficient.

An interesting aspect of the bargaining between a bureau and its political sponsor concerns the distribution of this surplus (the discretionary budget) between spending that serves the interests of the bureaucrats as opposed to the interests of the political review agents. The distribution of this surplus (as in any bilateral monopoly) is not determinate. The political review agents exercise their authority by threatening more thorough monitoring as a means to capture some part of the discretionary budget to serve their own special interests (such as the relative use of factor inputs and the geographic distribution of employment and contracts). The bureaus, in turn, share some part of the discretionary budget with the review agents as the price for spending the remainder as they wish. The distinctive conclusion of this modified model is that inefficiency in production is the normal condition. Bureaucrats and politicians will differ on how to distribute the bureau's surplus, but neither group has sufficient incentive to reduce excess spending.

My prior model of bureaucratic behavior should now be recognized as a special case. Bureaucrats committed to the output of their bureau—the "zealots," to use the term suggested by Anthony Downs (1967) have an incentive to discipline inefficiency in order to expand output beyond the level that maximizes the discretionary budget. The behavior of zealots could be described as output maximizing; thus any assumption about budget-maximizing behavior (along with its negative connotations) can be dropped entirely. The zealots, however, should expect to be opposed by those bureaucrats and political officials whose interests are served by spending the discretionary budget in other ways. (For a model of bureaucratic behavior in which the utility of a bureaucrat is a function of both the discretionary budget and the output of the bureau, see my 1975 article that is republished in this volume). As a rule, I suggest, the zealots are likely to be frustrated. My own long career as a policy analyst (a zealot for efficiency) has led me to conclude that efficiency in government cannot be much improved without changing the basic institutions and processes that affect the demand for and supply of government-financed services.

The Objectives and Behavior of Sponsors

Most of the analysis in my 1971 book was based on an assumption that a bureau's sponsor is an unbiased subset of the legislature, but is passive in its review of the bureau's proposal. In other words, the effective demand represented by the review committee was assumed to approximate that of the median voter in the legislature, but the sponsor's activities were assumed to be limited to approving or rejecting the bureau's proposals without any bargaining to achieve an outcome superior for the legislature. Some of the analysis also explored the implications of a self-selection process that would lead the review committee to represent those legislators with the highest relative demand for the service provided by the bureau but, again, one that was passive in its review activities.

Of course, congressional committees and other budget review authorities are not passive. (My own experience in several federal positions, for example, was as a quite active budget and regulatory review agent of the president.) The budget review process involves substantial effort to elicit additional information, considerable bargaining between the sponsor and the bureau, and almost always leads to outcomes somewhat different from the bureau's opening proposal. As pointed out in the first review of my book (Thompson 1973), these review committees have ample authority and several possible bargaining techniques to achieve a wide range of budget-output outcomes. The important contribution by Gary Miller and Terry Moe (1983), for example, explores the effects of a range of sponsor bargaining techniques for conditions that assume an unbiased sponsor and a budget-maximizing bureau. The important issue is how the review committees use their authority and bargaining techniques, to what effect, and to whose benefit.

What, if anything, do review committees maximize? These sponsors are not passive, but neither are they neutral agents of the whole legislature, voters, or the public interest. As mentioned earlier, efficiency monitoring is a public good within the review committee, the legislature, and among voters. My current judgment is that the behavior of the review committee is best evaluated by assuming that it maximizes the interests of its members, subject to the approval of the committee proposal by the whole legislature. I have not worked out the full implications of this assumption for the budget-output outcomes of the bargaining process with a surplus-maximizing bureau and, to my knowledge, neither has any other scholar. My current judgment, however, is that most of this bargaining involves the distribution of the bureau's surplus between spending that serves the interest of the sponsor and that which serves the interest of the bureau. In that case, as in both my initial and revised models, only part of the net benefits of the bureaucratic supply of government services accrues to the general population. This issue, however, is not yet resolved and should be the highest priority for subsequent research.

The theory developed in my book also assumed that bureaus bargain with the political review authorities over the full range from a zero budget to the proposed budget. As a former budget official, I knew better; this implicit assumption was an oversight but one with important implications. In fact, budget bargaining is usually restricted to a range from some base budget to the proposed budget, the base budget often being the most recent budget. If Congress fails to pass an appropriation before the end of the fiscal year, for example, the base budget is the prior year's appropriation or the level approved by the House or the Senate if that level is lower. The implications of this smaller range of bargaining were first developed in an important series of articles by Thomas Romer and Howard Rosenthal (1979 and 1987). The most important conclusion of their model is that the level of the approved budget increases with the *difference* between the base budget (what Romer and Rosenthal term the *reversion level*) and the budget preferred by the decisive voter. The magnitude of the expected overspending in this model will be less than that in my initial model if the base budget is larger than zero.

The cross-sectional studies by Romer and Rosenthal of spending per student in Oregon and New York school districts indicate that spending is generally higher than that preferred by the median voter. For districts in which the base budget is higher than the preferred budget, average spending per student is about equal to the base budget. For districts in which the base budget would be insufficient to keep the schools open, average spending per student is about 15 percent higher than in districts in which the base budget would be just sufficient. In addition, spending per student increases with the size of the school district, a reflection (in part) of the stronger monopoly power of larger districts. These careful empirical studies are probably the strongest evidence to date for my general theory of the behavior of bureaus.

The modified model developed by Romer and Rosenthal also suggests several interesting implications for the rate of change in government spending. In general, an increase in the preferred budget relative to the base budget will increase the approved budget by an even larger amount. If the base budget is defined in nominal dollars, for example, the approved budget will increase faster than the rate of inflation even if there is no increase in the real preferred budget. And even if the base budget is indexed to the price level, the real approved budget will increase at a higher rate than the increase in demand for that service. In any political system in which those that determine the proposed budget have a higher relative preference for either the discretionary budget or the output of some service, the approved budgets will be higher than that preferred by the decisive voter, whether inside the legislature or among the general voters. As a consequence, both the time-series and cross-section data on government spending reflect a complex interaction of popular demands for government services and the personal preferences of those politicians and bureaucrats who have the authority to set the budget agenda.

The next issue that should be addressed is the extent to which bureaus or the legislature are most responsible for the budget-output outcomes. I do not know how to resolve this issue; it may be like asking which blade of a pair of scissors does the cutting. Several leading scholars—most notably Morris Fiorina, Roger Noll and Barry Weingast—attribute these outcomes primarily to the structure and decision rules of the legislature. All budget measures must be approved by the legislature (except for those rare issues subject to a popular referendum), but the important issue is who controls the agenda of the proposals submitted to the legislature.

In the United States, budget proposals are subject to a multiple-step approval process, with each party to this process having distinctive interests and advantages. Bureaus make the initial budget proposals, have the best information on production and cost functions, and control the production process. Bureau proposals are reviewed by budget review offices reporting to the chief executive, who then makes a comprehensive budget proposal to the legislature. The interests of this executive are likely to be close to that of the majority of the electorate; its primary advantage is the authority to make a comprehensive budget proposal and to veto measures approved by the legislature. The executive budget is then reviewed by specialized committees of the legislature which design specific proposals to be approved by the body of the legislature; the primary advantage of these committees is that most of their proposals are reported under a "closed rule" and are not subject to amendment. (For this discussion, I abstract from the effects of a two-house legislature and the new institutions of comprehensive legislative budget committees.) The interests of a majority of the legislature are likely to be close to a somewhat different majority of the electorate than is represented by the chief executive, whose power derives from the authority to approve the final budget. (The media and political intellectuals also have important roles in defining the range of acceptable alternatives, but the effects of these roles are not yet very well understood.)

In summary, in terms of the language of this framework, the bureaus, the executive, and the legislative committees are each agenda setters. And the executive, the legislative committees, and the legislature are each sponsors. How should one evaluate this system of overlapping responsibilities?

My judgment is that it is best to regard the bureaus and the legislative committees as the dominant agenda setters. Their interests are substantially in common, and each serves as the agent of the other: the committees modify the bureau's proposals to assure approval by the legislature, and the bureau implements the program preferred by the committee. The bargaining between a bureau and its committee is limited primarily to the division of the net surplus of the bureau.

Similarly, the executive and the legislature are best regarded as sponsors, both of which must approve the proposed budget. Their interests differ primarily to the extent that they represent different majorities. The bargaining between the executive and the legislature is limited primarily to the division of issues for which one or the other majority is best served, given the proposals approved by the legislative committees.

The final issues that should be addressed bear on the structure of government. Why do legislatures, for example, delegate the formulation of budget proposals to functionally specialized committees, probably with full knowledge that they will propose a budget that does not best serve the interests of the majority? The most obvious answer is the benefit from a division of labor, since no large body can have sufficient information to formulate a budget proposal on all issues. The more cynical answer is that this delegation of the agenda-setting role gives most members a share in the spoils of some program. And these spoils, not the general benefits of government services, are the currency that rewards their supporters and finances their re-election.

And why do governments choose bureaus to supply most of the services that they finance? I once thought that this was due to the difficulty of contracting with private suppliers and of monitoring their performance. This may be so, but it is not apparently less difficult to contract with a bureau and monitor what it does. The most obvious answer is that the supply of government services by bureaus generates a net surplus that is shared with members of the government. There is strong evidence that privatization of many government services is feasible and would benefit the general population, but this is not likely to be approved in the absence of conditions that would lead to a mutual relinquishment of the spoils by members of the legislature.

In summary, bureaus are inefficient suppliers of government services as measured by the interests of the general population, though not in terms of the interests of members of the legislature. In that sense, Fiorina, Noll, Weingast, and others are correct: most of the problems often attributed to bureaus are more fundamentally caused by the structure and decision rules of the legislature, for which bureaus are merely their preferred agents. My 1971 book was correctly titled *Bureaucracy and Representative Government*. The behavior of bureaus must be evaluated in the context of the specific political market to which they supply services.

Some Suggestive Evidence

Even a cursory examination of the recent performance of the public sector provides some evidence consistent with two implications of my revised theory of the behavior of bureaus: (1) the increase of real government expenditures is likely to exceed the increase in the popular demand for government services; and (2) much of the increase in real government expenditures is likely to be waste—that is, expenditures that may serve the interests of the suppliers of the services and the political officials, but that do not increase the output of these services. A more comprehensive theory of the political system and more precise empirical methods would of course be necessary to estimate the specific effects of the popular demand for government services, supply conditions specific to each service, the role of politicians, and the supply of these services by bureaus. For these reasons, the following evidence is only suggestive, and further work is necessary to identify the effects of these several conditions. An article by D. Roderick Kiewiet (1991) provides the most comprehensive summary of this evidence.

A broad range of evidence is consistent with the overspending and inefficiency hypotheses of my revised model (1975). None of these tests, unfortunately, is sufficient to distinguish between a political and bureaucratic explanation of these conditions.

The most general evidence for the overspending hypothesis is the difference between cross-sectional and time-series patterns of government spending. The best studies of cross-sectional data, such as those by Borcherding and Deacon (1972), conclude that the income elasticity of demand for most services provided by state and local governments is less than unity. Over time, however, expenditures for these services have increased relative to income. In a later study, Borcherding (1977) concludes that cross-sectional evidence on the popular demand for government services explains only about half of the increase in government spending in the United States. One possible explanation of this difference is that the cross-sectional studies of government expenditures may underestimate the income elasticity of demand; this seems unlikely, because the cross-sectional studies of the demand for private goods and services generally yield higher demand elasticities than do the time-series studies. The more plausible explanation is that the combination of political and bureaucratic conditions leads government expenditures to increase relative to the popular demand for government services.

Several other types of evidence are also consistent with the overspending hypothesis. Government grants to other governments lead to an increase in spending by the recipient governments that is far higher than the effect of an equal increase in personal income in the recipient jurisdiction (Courant, Gramlich, and Rubinfield 1979). My own study of the popular vote for the president confirms the common perception that a tax or spending increase reduces the popular vote for the candidate of the incumbent party (1979). A similar study by Sam Peltzman (1987) finds that the popular vote for the gubernatorial candidate of the incumbent party is a negative function of the increase in real per capita state spending since the prior election. These findings indicate that government spending is higher than would be the case if politicians and bureaucrats were unbiased, albeit imperfect, agents of the median voter.

One implicit hypothesis of my bureaucracy model (in either its original or revised form), as first recognized by Thomas McGuire (1981), is that the revealed (absolute) price elasticity of demand for government services should be higher than unity, whatever the elasticity of the underlying popular demand. In other words, an increase in the unit cost of government services should reduce spending for these services. The evidence for this hypothesis is generally supportive but mixed. The revealed price elasticity for most state and local services, according to the Borcherding and Deacon study, appears consistent with this hypothesis. These studies suggest that conditions, including waste, that increase the unit cost of government services reduce the output of such services. These results are contrary to the common perception that the demand for government services is price inelastic. However, they are not a sufficient test of my bureaucracy model because the elasticity of the underlying population demand is not (cannot be?) known.

A large and growing body of evidence has documented the inefficiency inherent in the production of government services, at least in terms of those outputs of value to the general electorate. The aggregate evidence is more disturbing (but less widely known) than is the selective evidence of high prices for defense equipment and scandals in the housing program. During the 1980s in the United States, for example,

- total real expenditures for defense increased 60 percent without a significant increase in the level, readiness, or sustainability of the military forces (Niskanen 1988);
- real expenditures per student in the public primary and secondary schools increased 40 percent without any increase in high school graduation rates or student test scores; and
- real expenditures per person on medical care increased 60 percent without a significant effect on average health status.

For the general population, most of the increase in real spending for these services must be considered to be waste.

There is an inherent difficulty in attributing the shares of the total waste in government services to the separate effects of politics and the bureaucracy. Where waste has been apparent for some years without provoking a political response, one must assume that this waste serves some other political objective; in that sense, revealed waste is there for the same reason that the programs are there—because it meets some political demand. Waste that has not yet been revealed, however, is more likely to be a consequence of the bureaucratic supply of government services. By its nature, the unrevealed waste is not (cannot be?)

known. At this time, I must confess that I do not know how to pose a testable hypothesis about the shares of the total waste (the discretionary budget of a bureau) that is attributable to these two effects. I am prepared to conclude that the public sector does not serve most of us very well.

Conclusion

In retrospect, I suggest, I and other scholars have made a major start toward understanding the behavior of bureaus. Moreover, I am encouraged that bureaus and regulatory agencies have become a recognized field of study in university departments of both economics and political science, and that we seem to be learning from each other. My own reflections on this subject lead me to several general conclusions:

1. The basic structure of the theory outlined in my 1971 book will continue to be the most useful approach to understanding the behavior of bureaus. Specifically, it will continue to be more useful to focus on the distinctive characteristics of bureaus and the political institutions and processes in which they operate than to explain the behavior of bureaus in terms of the distinctive attributes of bureaucrats.

2. My prior assumption that bureaucrats act to maximize their budget should now be dropped entirely in favor of an assumption that they act to maximize their discretionary budget.

3. A great deal of useful research remains to be done. Most of the subsequent research, I suggest, should focus on the characteristics of the political environment in which bureaus operate. Who reviews a bureau's proposed budget? What are its incentives and constraints? What are the effects of different rules (the "effective constitution") which govern the cabinet, legislative committees, legislatures, and the popular vote? What are the effects of different rules for determining the base budget and the long-term effects of a sequence of votes? What determines the distribution of the discretionary budget between spending that serves the interests of the review authorities and that which serves the interests of the bureaucrats? To what extent are the problems that may be attributed to bureaucratic supply really due to incentives and processes in the cabinet and legislature?

   More work on the structure of the bureaucracy will also be valuable. What are the effects of actual or potential competition from private firms or other bureaus? What are the effects of potential future employment in other bureaus or in private organizations on the behavior of bureaucrats? What are the effects of changes in the compensation structure or the rules for promotion and termination? On examination, some of these effects will prove to be interrelated; the availability of private alternatives to a government service, for example, may lead to multiple-peaked preferences for the government service, exacerbating the problems of achieving political decisions and increasing the variance of outcomes.

Over the past twenty years, we have learned that private firms and markets are more complex than the prior simple models suggested. During this same period, we have only started to converge on a simple model of bureaus and political markets. That is an important start, but only a start. I will read with interest and some pride how research on this issue develops.

References

Blais, André and Stéphan Dion (eds) (1991), *The Budget-Maximizing Bureaucrat*, Pittsburgh: University of Pittsburgh Press.

Borcherding, Thomas (ed.) (1977), *Budgets and Bureaucrats: The Sources of Government Growth*, Durham, N.C.: Duke University Press.

Borcherding, Thomas E. and Robert T. Deacon (1972), "The Demand for the Services of Non-Federal Governments," *American Economic Review*, 62, 891–900.

Breton, Albert and Ronald Wintrobe (1975), "The Equilibrium Size of a Budget-maximizing Bureau: A Note on Niskanen's Theory of Bureaucracy," *Journal of Political Economy*, 83, 195–207.

Courant, Paul, Edward Gramlich and Daniel Rubinfield (1979), "The Stimulative Effects of Intergovernmental Grants: Or Why Government Money Sticks where it Lands," in *Fiscal Federalism and Grants in Aid*, edited by Peter Miezkowski and William Oakland, Washington, D.C.: Urban Institute,

Downs, Anthony (1967), *Inside Bureaucracy*, Boston: Little, Brown.

Fiorina, Morris and Roger Noll (1978), "Voters, Legislators, and Bureaucrats: Institutional Design in the Public Sector," *American Economic Review*, 68, 256–260.

Frank, Robert (1985), *Choosing the Right Pond*, New York: Oxford University Press.

Johnson, Ronald and Gary Libecap (1989), "Agency Growth, Salaries, and the Protected Bureaucrat," *Economic Inquiry*, 27, 431–451.

Kiewiet, D. Roderick (1991), "Bureaucrats and Budgetary Outcomes: Quantitative Analyses" in Blais and Dion (1991).

McCubbins, Matthew D., Noll, Roger and Weingast, Barry R. (1989), "Structure and Process; Politics and Policy: Administrative Arrangements and the Political Control of Agencies," Working Papers in Political Science P–89–4, Stanford: The Hoover Institution.

McGuire, Thomas (1981), "Budget-maximizing Governmental Agencies: An Empirical Test," *Public Choice*, 36, 313–322.

Migué, Jean-Luc and Gérard Bélanger (1974), "Towards a General Theory of Managerial Discretion," *Public Choice*, 17.

Miller, Gary J. and Terry M. Moe (1983), "Bureaucrats, Legislators, and the Size of Government," *American Political Science Review*, 77.

Mises, Ludwig von (1944), *Bureaucracy*, New Haven, Conn.: Yale University Press.

Niskanen, William A. (1968), "The Peculiar Economics of Bureaucracy," *American Economic Review*, LVIII (2), 293–305. Reprinted in this volume.

Niskanen, William A. (1975), "Bureaucrats and Politicians," *Journal of Law and Economics*, 18, 617–643. Reprinted in this volume.

Niskanen, William A. (1979), "Economic and Fiscal Effects on the Popular Vote for the President," in *Public Policy and Public Choice*, edited by Douglas W. Rae and Theodore J. Eismeier, Beverly Hills, Calif.: Sage.

Niskanen, William A. (1988), "More Defense Spending for Smaller Forces: What hath DOD Wrought?" *Policy Analysis* 110, Washington, D.C.: Cato Institute.

Peltzman, Sam (1987), "Economic Conditions and Gubernatorial Elections," *American Economic Review*, 77, 292–297.

Romer, Thomas and Howard Rosenthal (1979), "Bureaucrats vs. Voters: On the Political Economy of Resource Allocation by Direct Democracy." *Quarterly Journal of Economics*, 93, 563–587.

Romer, Thomas, Howard Rosenthal and Vincent Munley (1987), "Economic Incentives and Political Institutions: Spending and Voting in School District Referenda," Pittsburgh, Pa.: Carnegie Mellon University.

Thompson, Earl (1973), Bureaucracy and Representative Government review, *Journal of Economic Literature*, XI (3), 950–953.

Tullock, Gordon (1965), *The Politics of Bureaucracy*, Washington, D.C.: Public Affairs Press.

Weingast, B. R. and Moran, M. J. (1983), "Bureaucratic Discretion or Congressional Control: Regulatory Policy Making by the Federal Trade Commission," *Journal of Political Economy*, 91, 765–800.

Index